W9-ACC-507

DISCARDED

The Russian Novel

Books by F. D. Reeve

Aleksandr Blok: Between Image and Idea
Robert Frost in Russia
The Stone Island
Six Poems
The Russian Novel

The
Russian
Novel

by
F. D. Reeve

McGraw-Hill Book Company
New York   Toronto   London

THE RUSSIAN NOVEL

Copyright © 1966 by F. D. Reeve. All rights reserved. Printed in the United States of America. This book, or parts thereof, may not be reproduced in any form without permission of the publisher.

Library of Congress Catalog Card Number: 65-24895

FIRST EDITION

51697

To Julian Oksman
and
the memory of Richard Blackmur

Parea ciascuna rubinetto, in cui
raggio di sole ardesse si acceso,
che nei miei occhi rifrangesse lui.

Paradiso, XIX

Acknowledgments

Grateful acknowledgment is made to the following for permission to include material which originally appeared in their publications, in some instances in a different form:

To Random House for lines quoted from W. H. Auden's poem "The Novelist" in *The Collected Poetry of W. H. Auden* © W. H. Auden 1945, and for lines quoted from Griboedov's play *The Trouble With Reason* in *Anthology of Russian Plays*, vol. 1 © F. D. Reeve 1961; To The Bodley Head for a paragraph from Charles Chaplin's *My Autiobiography* © Charles Chaplin and the Bodley Head, Ltd. 1964; To L. N. Stilman for having pointed out Gogol's letter from Lübeck cited on pp. 99–100; To *Symposium* for "Through Hell on a Hobby-horse," XIII, 1 (1959), 73–87; To *The Slavic Review* for "Oblomovism Revisited," XV, 1 (1956), 112–118; To Bantam Books for material from the introduction to *Five Short Novels by Turgenev*, 1961 © Bantam Books 1961; To *The Slavic and East European Journal* for "In the Stinking City," IV (XVIII), 2 (1960), 127–136, and "Tension in Prose," XVI, 2 (1958), 99–108; To Dell Books for material from the introduction to *Six Short Masterpieces by Tolstoy*, 1962 © Dell Books 1962; To *Modern Fiction Studies* for "Art as Solution," III, 2 (1957), 110–118; To *The Kenyon Review* for "Doctor Zhivago: From Prose to Verse," XXII, 1 (1960), 123–136, "A Geometry of Prose," XXV, 1 (1963), 9–25, and "The House of the Living," XXV, 2 (1963), 356–360 © The Kenyon Review 1960, 1963; And to those authors, scholars and critics in Russia whose material, whether or not used in the text, helped shape this book.

Contents

By Way of Introduction

In the Russian intellectual world of the nineteenth century, the literary work of Alexander Pushkin caused changes the extent of which we are still trying to assess. Russian literature was reshaped and redirected by Pushkin's verse and prose, especially by *Eugene Onegin* (published 1825–33). Two themes which had been literary topics in the eighteenth century became the socially acknowledged responsibilities of literary work: concern with style and language itself, and understanding of the sources of the values of social existence and their relation to any individual.

Extensive sociopolitical protests and late eighteenth-century inquiries into the nature of language expressed the aptness of both topics, but their inevitability as themes followed from the way Pushkin combined them to reveal the highest awareness of life. In "The Art of Fiction," Henry James said that, "As people feel life so they will feel the art that is most closely related to it." Conversely, an obligation of art is to make people feel it and, through that feeling, to feel life. Responsiveness to art and consciousness of one's own vitality go together. For Pushkin concern with the manners of language was inseparable from definition of the meaning of the social manners of the age. This would not distinguish him from any other serious artist were it not that he had the talent to express subtleties which no previous Russian writer had expressed. Unexpressed, the subtleties had been nonexistent,

1

for, as Baudelaire put it, what cannot be said does not exist. In language of high skill and resourceful imagery, Pushkin expressed the fundamental contrariety of social life: that the actuality of the things of this world, assumed to be physical and final, is denied by assertion of faith in potential human freedom, the enactment of which, no matter how impossible, is the basic motive behind all human activity. The denigration of established reality is ultimate freedom and is contained, Herbert Marcuse has said, in all genuine artistic images.

It is not difficult to identify aspects of Pushkin's influence on the poets and novelists around him and after him. Pushkin had the fortune to be born in an age when talented and leisured gentlemen of good education were becoming socially conscious and when literature was taking on social responsibilities.

There are a number of reasons for the preeminence of literature at this time. Censorship and autocracy are only two —that is, men were driven to write fictionalized and poetic analyses of what they could not reform by political action. More nearly basic was the formation of a social attitude very much under the influence of late eighteenth- and early nine-teenth-century European social philosophy, according to which the worth of a man was not definable by status. We see reflections of this in fiction. For example, gradually there developed, over a period of some thirty years, the idea that the central figure in a narrative need not occupy an "accept-able" social position. In the late eighteenth century, in, say, Karamzin's story "Poor Liza" (1792), the hero is a young nobleman who naturally, even properly, forsakes a peasant girl's devotion, after he has won it, for a marriage that gives him status. We readers are supposed to feel sympathy for the abandoned girl—once upon a time people went and shed tears by the pond outside Moscow where in the story she drowned herself—but we are also supposed to support the "naturalness" of the existing social system. Our social position like our emotional pose, Karamzin seems to say, is a proper aspect of us, though it inevitably conflicts with other people's poses and positions and at times even with our own surprising desires. The social significance of the story lies in the impossibility of the hero and the girl living happily ever after. But the hero is no villain, and the author sums up with a moral to sensitive young things, not with an incentive to social reform.

Other stories of about the same time propose solutions to "problems" by resolving the emotional conflict supposedly aroused in the reader. In Emin's novel *The Play of Fate* (1789) an old count, having learned that his young wife is in love with a young man, helps them out and wishes them his best. In Lvov's *A Russian Pamela, or the Story of Maria, a Virtuous Peasant Girl* (1789), hair-shirt-poor Maria is abandoned by the young nobleman who has married her; he says that his relatives insist on it, but later he relents, returns, and they are joyfully reunited. "I called my tale *A Russian Pamela*," said Lvov, "because in our country the lower classes have such tender hearts."

Karamzin began his literary career writing for the journals of social and political satire edited by N. I. Novikov. So did Alexander Radishchev, who in 1785–89 wrote *A Journey from St. Petersburg to Moscow*, privately published in 1790. Only a few dozen copies escaped burning by Radishchev himself before his own arrest after the arrest of the bookseller who handled it. Radishchev was as radical and reformist as Karamzin was conservative and monarchist. Radishchev was affected by experiences of suffering and deprivation around him; he was moved to pity and, out of pity, to reform. His emotional involvement—his sense of deep commitment to working people and peasants—compelled him to argue for changing the institutions which enforced deprivation. "Radishchev's *Journey*," Pushkin commented, "is an appeal through satire to insurrection." Karamzin, who later became court historian, adopted the style of literary sentimentalism as being equivalent to social manner: he invents a story, such as "Poor Liza," to exaggerate his readers' emotions; actually, he extenuates them. The pose of sympathy subverts the capacity for pity. Karamzin knew Jean François Marmontel's *Contes moraux*, vignettes of French society life written in a "refined" style, one of which tells of a nobleman who retires and lives with a peasant girl to preserve her honor. Conditions in Russia were different, said Karamzin, and he made his nobleman abandon the peasant girl, titillating his emotion-filled readers.

M. D. Chulkov's novel *The Fair Cook, or the Adventures of a Debauched Woman*, which appeared in 1770, like much of the eighteenth-century literature in Russia—like the formal music and the art, too—was extensively imitative of western European work. On the other hand, Novikov's sketches in his magazine *The Drone* (1769–70) were the first presentation in a hard, colloquial tone of analytical descriptions of peasant life. I. A. Krylov, best known for his fables, published a series of letters which are supposedly about a fantastic world, but are in fact trenchant comments on intolerable social inequality. The language of the letters is simple and strong. Published in part serially in 1789 under the title *The Spirits' Mail, or the Scholarly, Moral, and Critical Correspondence of the Arabian Philosopher Malikulmulk with Aquatic, Ethereal, and Subterranean Spirits*, they were not published as a complete book until 1802 after a relaxation in censorship. Naturalistic scenes are combined with sociophilosophic analyses—for a long time critics believed it the work of both Krylov and Radishchev— proposing reform in the very expression of the perversities of

human society which the author has perceived. The gnome
Buriston writes to Malikulmulk about his visit to a nearby
island:

*. . . I was walking along one of the most celebrated streets
of the city and suddenly I saw before me a magnificent house,
in front of which there was a large crowd of people seeking
entrance. A great number of mutilated old men were trying
to catch up with the healthy, and the lame, hopping along
on their crutches, envied the armless, who were running on
ahead of them. At the same time a half-dozen strong horses
drove up pulling a small box which contained, so I thought,
a human figure made of multicolored marble. . . .*

"What statue are you talking about?" my host asked. . . .
"This herd of horses has driven up with a very lean man. . . ."

*"Sir," I said to my host, "please explain this strange custom
to me: why does a great number of horses here pull a single
man who, as I see, can very well walk by himself, and, on the
other hand, a stone is hauled by a huge crowd of people, a
stone so heavy that even the same number of horses could
hardly pull it?"*

Sterne's A *Sentimental Journey* played an important role
in late eighteenth-century Russian literature for its innovations
in attitude. (In the nineteenth century, especially for Pushkin
and Tolstoy, it was important for its innovations in style.) A
means had been discovered for combining in literary presentation the gaiety of peasant life, the pathos of its suffering, and
the philosophic basis for supporting reform. Most eighteenth-
century satire assumes that institutions falter because of human weaknesses; Radishchev's satire, in A *Journey from St.
Petersburg to Moscow*, assumes that human beings falter
because institutions oppress them. Inspired by Rousseau, he
believed, very much like Dostoevsky later, that institutions

were the source of human evil, that "man is wholly free from birth." Furthermore, he believed that the freedom of art depends on expanding old traditions, and that the freedom of social life depends on the work of the writer, on the meaning of language in life. The source of understanding of men is identification with humanity. Radishchev presents his journey in three literal, but also politically allegorical, stages: from the capital to Novgorod, he questions what he observes, decides that "the old system has gone to hell." During the second stage, to the town of Mednoe, he tries to imagine a way out by instituting reform from above. In the last stage, he concludes (though he states his conclusion indirectly) that reform can be meaningful only if it is complete, that is, only peasant rebellion and elimination of existing institutions can be socially significant. The center of the journey is the ode "Freedom," a poem which the narrator–traveler Radishchev supposedly hears from a "modern poet" on the trip (but which Radishchev wrote himself). The poem is not only a very sharp attack on empery, Catherine herself, and her abandoned, countermanded *ukaz* of 1766 (in which she declared, citing Montesquieu's *Esprit des lois*, that "Liberty is the right of doing whatever the law permits") but also an important step in the elaboration of a satisfactory syllabo-tonic verse scheme. Radishchev's poetry was even better than his prose, Pushkin said, who regarded Radishchev's use of blank verse as exemplary.

The political center of the book is the chapter on Klin. The second paragraph constructs the façade of style through which the social analyst works. It is "straightforward" sentimentalism:

. . . *my tears were as sweet for me as those from the heart by Werther*. . . . *Oh, my friend, my friend! why didn't you, too, see these scenes? You would have shed tears with me, and the sweetness of mutual sensation would have been far more delighting.*

The traveler gives a blind beggar a ruble, not just the usual five kopecks, but the blind man points out that the money is useless to him now: he could have used it once to feed his neighbors' children; if he weren't blind, he could use it to help some one in need; but with that much money in his pocket (indeed, where has he a pocket to put it?) he can now only turn another man into a thief. This is the corruption in fact against which charity is pointless. Earlier, the old man had asked for a neckerchief to keep his sore throat warm. The traveler had given it to him:

On my way back through Klin, I didn't find the blind singer. He had died three days before I arrived. But I learned from the woman who brought him the meat pie on holidays that he had put my neckerchief on his neck, having fallen sick, and wore it into his grave. Oh! anyone who is aware of the value of this neckerchief also senses what was going on inside me when I heard that.

Some writers maintain that freedom and thinking freely became valued or desired in Russia only after the Napoleonic invasion and the introduction of freemasonry. A. A. Bestuzhev, the early nineteenth-century novelist, said that "when Napoleon invaded Russia the Russian people felt its own strength for the first time. That was the beginning of free thinking in Russia." Actually, an intelligentsia had begun to develop in the last half of the eighteenth century. The change, among aristocratic intellectuals and educated persons, from social activity designed to "preserve the purity of the past" to social reform intended to acknowledge the central role of the individual in political and historical events, had begun under Catherine, although, to be sure, it became definitively significant only in the early nineteenth century. The founding of the several academies and universities in the middle of the eighteenth century was the beginning of institutionalization of a means for programing social change. The academies were not only to represent the cultural excellence of the Enlightenment but also actively to promote it and to nationalize it.

Institutions tend to be conservative, and the Russian academies quickly became establishments where "cultured," "educated," "civilized" people worked and were trained—people who differed sharply from the "intelligentsia." The universities, much as did Catherine's *Instructions to the Commissioners* (1765–67), brought closely together western European values and Russian social questions. The universities and academies were cultural banking houses. The dichotomies between the values which these banks declared they supported and the experiences of real people provoked the work of men who formed the first Russian intelligentsia. Their work was journalistic, reformist, philosophic, and educational, above all directed not to supporting the aims of any class but to reorganizing the entire society in the name of the good of the individuals who constituted it. The letters, satires, poems, plays, and prose of such men as Novikov, Fonvizin, and Radishchev in the period 1769–92 put an end to literature's being an agreeable handmaiden to a nobleman's life. They made it serious intellectual labor, and they showed that literary goals, often incompatible with prevailing social patterns, were superior to those existing patterns and could be pursued independently. In 1769, Catherine, in her own journal *All Sorts of Things*, argued, for example, that weakness was a common human failing and must be understood. Novikov, in his reply in *The Drone*, said that weakness often led directly to vice: "In short, in both weakness and vice I see neither any good nor any difference. Weakness and vice, to my mind, are one and the same thing, but lawlessness is something quite different." He was prepared to defend not a class structure which enriched the strong at the expense of the weak but only the values which, wise men asserted, made life meaningful. He was the first successful literary "philosopher" to put allegiance to ethical values above allegiance to class and by his own life to show that the effort to support these values was socially useful work.

For the first characteristic of the intelligentsia is that it is a body of intellectual persons highly trained and educated who are bound together by disinterested commitment to what they define as universally legislatable values. The intelligentsia is "liberal," "advanced." Its members, drawn largely from the middle classes, are non-class, ethically oriented. The intelligentsia behaves like a class in that it tends to perpetuate itself, but it is not a class because of the nature of its faith as producers of ideas and because of the fact that its membership is based on ability and performance, not on birth or fortune. The members are experimenters and innovators, energetically introducing both new ideas and new forms of expression. Their basic concern is the physical, moral, and philosophic good of the individuals who constitute the society in which they live. In Russia, the history of the intelligentsia is almost the story of the development of literature.

It is not the entire story, for the story of literature is equally the story of style. And in Russia we find that a writer like Karamzin, who began his career in association with Novikov and who was as "sentimental," in a literary way, as Radishchev, ended his career in allegiance to monarchy. But his prose fiction and his letters remain to remind us that the innovations in style which Karamzin canonized by his literary success became identified with him and with the development of a national literature. What Fonvizin had inaugurated in his *Letters* (an informal, socially responsive tone, reflecting educated Russian speech) Karamzin established as formal canon. One may disagree with Karamzin's politics, but one cannot deny that his successful work was one of the chief models for the "realism" of Pushkin's great writing. For the development of Russian realism in general, Pestel's secret society, even Stankevich's circle and the articles by Belinsky, are, in this sense, of secondary importance. Without a precedent, art is handicapped, for art proceeds from art, always responding to and reshaping in consciousness the prevailing social values. Sumarokov's drama, like Molière's or Dryden's before it, not only reflected the language and the ideas of the court but also influenced them. All reform in art, as in politics, is always made in the name of enacting the abandoned or unfulfilled legacy of the past. All modern art, all art of the last fifty years, like all the great novels of nineteenth-century Russia, is the endeavor to define the relationship between the one and the many, between the self-conscious, lonely individual and the society which depends on his labor.

Realism in art is, of course, a concept broader than that of any "school," extends beyond the work of any one artist. It involves both esthetics and politics, both principle and practice. Essentially, as Boris Reizov has said, it is based on a concept of veracity: "The *only* specification of the 'realists' is that their works reflect actuality and reflect it more or less veraciously—more or less, since no work alone can reflect actuality with complete accuracy."

Classicism, or at least the neoclassicism of the eighteenth century, may easily be considered an artistic method and a style, as G. A. Gukovsky said. The romanticism that followed, V. V. Vinogradov has pointed out, is a method but not a style.

Realism is not definable as either one or the other. From one point of view, it represents a continuation of "sentimentalism," that adjustment in literature of classical method to individual style which closed the eighteenth century and opened the nineteenth. Fonvizin, Novikov, and Radishchev would have agreed with Karamzin that they wished to extend language to include the general reader, to bring about one language "for literature as for social life," so that "people may write as they speak and speak as they write." From another point of view, as in the work of Luganskoy or, better, Melnikov-Pechersky and the French naturalists of the 1840's, "realism" is an effort at photographic reproduction of the ordinary —a point of view against which both Gogol and Dostoevsky sharply reacted and which they successfully transformed by the method of parody and by the idiosyncrasies of refined style.

From a third, essential point of view, realism in literature is, though not a style, a method: it assumes that the things of this world are verifiable, but that their veracity lies in understanding of their *possible* relationships. What we consider the finest works of realism are strikingly *ethical*. Whatever the style—the puns in *Eugene Onegin*, the digressions in *Dead Souls*, the mock self-denigration in *Notes from the Cellar*, the conflict of political philosophies in *Rudin*, the antihistoricism in *War and Peace*—the author's concern is always through expression of actual practices to define human nature. Unlike the classicist or the romanticist, the realist has been forced by prevailing social conditions to assume that what men do or think they can do, though it suggests the grandeur of human nature, is always at individual expense, that men are therefore suffering, and that the institutions available to men can be made to effect their freedom only if men will understand the necessary reinterpretation of freedom which the realist presents.

These three criteria for literary realism must be applied simultaneously. Only these criteria taken together seem to me adequately to explain such seemingly "unrealistic" facts in nineteenth-century Russian prose fiction—the greatest body of realism we have—as the absence of description of sexual acts and the insistence on the instrumentality of art for effecting social change.

The realist presumes that the substance of his work deals with human relationships and that these relationships can be meaningfully circumscribed only in ethical terms, that human activity of any sort is significant only in terms (even if negative) of human good, moral duty, and social obligation.

The realist asserts the inexorability of the experience of suffering. He does not necessarily assume that change (and the attendant experience of loss) must lead to a notion of a transcendent world (although, conspicuously, Dostoevsky did so after his return from exile) or that the pain of living—the fact that we all suffer ourselves to death—is equilibrated 'in the harmony of some eternity (though at the end of his life Gogol insisted on this). He asserts that change—want, repression, loss, suffering—is a fact, that as such it holds for all observers, and that, though it is actually experienced individually, the reality of it is communicable only by acts of creative imagination.

The realist affirms that the limits of art are absolute freedom. In one sense, of course, all art is realistic. The prose realism of nineteenth-century Russia, the methods and import of which are still very close to us, seems to assume that the ideal condition which it (like the characters whose lives it dramatizes) would enact is a condition specifically contrary to what obtains, regardless of what in fact obtains. The freedom it posits is not definitive of some thing, some place. It is absolute in that it is a denigration of fundamental, actual experience. In that sense, it is as concrete as it is abstract. For example, however absurd the arbitrariness of Bazarov's death, we sense that the idealism which patterned his life is directed to the same ideal as that of the author who killed him off in the name of human nature.

Once the writer loses touch with his reader—as soon as his personal ethical concern becomes incredible in his society —he becomes a figure isolated from his public and from his characters. He must use nonrealistic devices to communicate an understanding incompatible with the values behind existing social institutions. Such a writer is our contemporary. We are talking about him when we try to analyze the mystery and the incommunicable sadness in, say, Chekhov's work, the work of a man who stood almost literally on the threshold between the realism that asserted faith in the goodness and efficacy of social consciousness and the modernism that moves by irony to make us at least aware of the dignity of our isolated selves.

In eighteenth-century Russia, culture was an upper-class activity. In the nineteenth century, it was a general social program. Now it has been dumped on the individual artist's hands. Problems of working out an individual style are now magnified by the pressing need to establish a fresh and socially significant artistic method.

Eugene
Onegin

1

Pushkin's *Eugene Onegin* divides the improbable novel from the probable, speaking both historically and artistically. The eighteenth century is more remote from us than the sixteenth or the twelfth or, for that matter, the Athenian fifth. The "real life" of an eighteenth-century hero is invariably presented as illustrative of class behavior, as an expression of some general (and generally accepted) essence, not as an end in itself. The eighteenth-century protagonist, like a bird dog, always points to morality, which is interpreted as being the permanent substance of actual experience. The actuality of experience is tolerated only within restricted codes or conventions. In the seventeenth century, for example, Archpriest Avvakum, in his polemical *Autobiography* (1672), could use words like *crap* and *son of a bitch*, but in the eighteenth century Sumarokov felt called upon (like Nahum Tate) so to redo *Hamlet* that Ophelia and Hamlet married. The impossible was rationalized. For us now it is improbable. We cannot tolerate Sumarokov's artificial marriage between the implausible lovers, if only because we have the more recent and entirely probable experience of Tatyana and Onegin's failure. The success of their failure, in their "novel in verse," is represented by Pushkin's courtship of the Muse and by our acknowledgment of the book as not merely an eighteenth-century-like description of class behavior but as a new and essential statement about man's nature. Pushkin at first called

14

his work a long poem, but by November, 1823 he had termed it a special sort of novel: "I'm now working on not a novel but a novel in verse—one hell of a difference."

Even in the first chapter and, clearly, later on, Onegin, the "London dandy," the poet's "friend," "bright," and "an adorable fanatic," becomes disillusioned with the poses and "sacred" terms of the new romanticism. Friendship palls, he ceases to flirt, "the lips and glances of the lovely things" become for him "deceptive, like their dainty feet." Pushkin the author separates himself from the Pushkin who is Onegin's friend; as friend, he separates himself from Onegin. Onegin, embodiment of a social pattern, withdraws from his society. He is driven out. He becomes bored. In his boredom he finds his distinctiveness.

As Pushkin finds his language beyond the vocabulary of the Academy dictionary (the 1789 edition, which excluded "all foreign words unnecessarily introduced into Russian"), the epigrams of salons, and the new romanticism, so Onegin finds his language beyond the drawing-room talk and the fashions of love. Pushkin and Onegin are distinctly different figures in this novel, but they strikingly resemble each other in this: they both "grow," Onegin as protagonist, Pushkin as poet. The habits of romanticism are made the instruments of realism, as we see in the "Travels" section, in stanzas 12–14 of Chapter VIII, or in the reference (VIII,50) to the "free novel," by which Pushkin meant, as B. V. Tomashevsky pointed out, that he was working on a book which unlike the neoclassical and sentimental romanticism of his time, would be part of a new literature, which would introduce new forms, new style, a fresh language, which (way beyond the conventions of Byronism) would be impelled by life itself.

In eighteenth-century Russian literature, ideas, like everyday experiences, were presented as reflections of social patterns or as parts of a definitive, quasi-metaphysical scheme. Few writers took up radical positions as openly and powerfully democratic as did the scientist and philosopher Yakov Kozelsky in his *Philosophic Propositions* (1768). Some writers, such as Chulkov, tried to avoid ideas, appealing not to standards of "good" and "bad" but to the reader's imagined sensuality, assuming without expressing approval or rejection a fixed social order. Matrona, the central figure and narrator of *The Fair Cook*, says:

Whether I could have then had any love for mankind is, I'm sure, something the reader wonders about, so in order speedily to remove all doubt from his mind I hasten to say that even depraved women are not wholly without rational principles, and if they were not vanquished by inconstancy and fickle luxury they would naturally be more virtuous than the usurer or the miser. To calm my old man I disdained annoyance and danger and decided to go confess my guilt to him, all the while relying on my own artfulness, in case he was stern, at easily deceiving him.

Fedor Emin's novel *The Letters of Ernest and Doravra* (1766), a hopelessly nationalistic, bourgeois imitation of *La Nouvelle Héloïse* (1761), blatantly defends the prevailing system:

Come, dear friend. . . . Here everyone is satisfied with what he has. . . . No place else and never before in my life have I ever been so much at peace as here; never has my heart felt such gaiety as that with which it is now filled, and I dwell in the house of your adored Doravra and her spouse as if in my own.

By the end of the century the best writers were more inquiring than that. A short while later, the romantics disengaged idea from status quo. Bestuzhev's *Ammalat Bek* (1832), with its famous "Songs of Death," is an adventure tale exemplifying a deliberately, now seemingly artificially, exalted idea of romance. Dostoevsky's antiromantic story "A Romance in Nine Letters" (1847) is a bright parody on the pretentiousness of both ignoble and ennobled sentiment. Pushkin's own understanding of romanticism may be assumed from his attitudes toward several aspects of it. Of French romanticism contemporary to him, he wrote to Vyazemsky in 1824 that "All the volumes of the new, supposedly romantic, poetry are the disgrace of French literature." After 1824, he became progressively dissatisfied with Byron, whom he had highly praised previously. And he left among his notes the comment that "Delvig used to say that 'the closer to Heaven, the colder it is.' "

For Pushkin the most important difference was not between verse and prose (under the impact of powerful emotion beautifully arranged, the difference disappears), between classicism and romanticism, between the poet and the mob, between cultural tradition and social problems. It was between the real and the artificial, between the original and the imitation, between the poet as hero and the banalities of everyday life. The romantic novel of his time, Pushkin thought, failed because it mimicked the triviality of a superficial understanding of the moment although it pretended to adore the greatness of the cultural tradition:

In our time, by the word novel *one means an historical period presented through fictitious narration. Walter Scott has drawn along behind him a whole crowd of imitators. But how far they all are from the Scottish enchanter! Like Agrippa's apprentice, they have evoked the demon of antiquity but do not know how to handle him and have made themselves the victims of their own impudence. In a period in which they*

want to sweep the reader off his feet, they themselves are trans-
ported along with all the heavy baggage of domestic habits,
prejudices, and daily impressions. . . . Through the silk frieze
à la Henri IV peeks the starched cravat of a modern dandy.
Gothic heroines are taught by Madame Campan, and six-
teenth-century government officials read The Times and the
Journal des Débats. What absurdities, how many useless tri-
fles, what important omissions . . . but above all, how little
life. These pale productions, however, are read all over Europe.
. . . Is it because the portrayal of times gone by, even a feeble
and inaccurate portrayal, has an inexplicable charm for the
imagination drowned in the monotonous hodgepodge of the
present, of the everyday?

The history of the nation, Pushkin said, belongs to the poet.

The romantics accomplished two extremely important
changes: by focusing on the issue of what makes culture vital
and morality true, they turned blind nationalism into a concept of nationality, and they made the problem novel over
into a fictional analysis of the relationship between public
culture and individual morality. These same romantic themes
occur in the first works of Pushkin, Turgenev, Dostoevsky,
Tolstoy, but soon in subsequent work they are overcome, that
is, transformed. Just as we cannot recognize the Turgenev of
Fathers and Children (1862) in the long poem *Parasha*
(1843) or the Dostoevsky of *The Karamazov Brothers* (1880)
in *Poor People* (1845), so we are hard put to recognize the
Pushkin of *Eugene Onegin* in the conventionally romantic
narrative poem "The Prisoner of the Caucasus" (1822). From
biography we know that the author is the same man. From
reading the works, we see how a poet's talent, developing, has
not only reordered his accomplishments but has also altered
the requirements and the possibilities for writers who come
after him.

In *Eugene Onegin* a double-plot love-story of failure
(Tatyana/Onegin and Olga/Lensky) becomes a realistic account of success through an unexpected central figure, the
author, who unites the two stories and transcends them both
in his own "affair" with art and society. The novel is based
on the stories of the two couples, but it clearly goes beyond
them, if only in the literal sense that it continues without interruption after Lensky's death. The death is incidental. The
plot of the book is not delimited by the events, but is, in an
Aristotelian sense, that imitation of central social action which
is the substance of drama:

> *One cannot bear to see ahead*
> *A series of mere evenings out,*
> *To think of life as rituals,*
> *To follow up the stately crowd*
> *Without participating in*
> *Its general notions, loves, or whims.*
>
> (VIII,11)

G. A. Gukovsky defined the romantic novel as "a narrative based on a single hero intimately connected with the
author himself, carrying the burden of the author's lyricism, a
hero whose essence somehow defines the nature and content
of the rest of the world delineated by the author, including
our understanding of the other characters." *Eugene Onegin*,
Gukovsky adds, is not a romantic but a realistic novel ("based
not so much on central characters as on a unity of events").
Whether we are dealing with Scott and Balzac or with
Bestuzhev and Pushkin, the feature that distinguishes romanticism from realism depends, I think, on the author's complex
attitude to prevailing social actuality. In *Ammalat Bek*, Bestuzhev extols the so-called noble and free life of the semicivilized
local native, alien to the culture whose language and con-

ventions the author is using. In *Eugene Onegin*, Pushkin extols the values which celebrate the artist's talent and his tradition, despite both the successes and failures possible in existing society. In short, even though the realistic novel is, to a large degree, an art form developed in post-Renaissance bourgeois society and although most realistic novels are antirevolutionary, all successful realistic novels focus on the despair that follows from the intrinsic impossibility of the individual ever realizing himself in existing society. Onegin, a typical man of his generation, as typical in his time as Raskolnikov is typical in his, does not fit into society. Like Rudin in Turgenev's *Rudin*, he is connected with but not closely tied to his author. Indeed, Pushkin, like Turgenev, uses the form and devices of narrative itself to get free of his hero. The immutability of actuality, a fact which the novel asserts, is contradicted and transcended by the idea of freedom, the central political, social, and philosophical idea in the book.

Victor Shklovsky was the first to point up the crossed plot of *Eugene Onegin*. But closer to our notion of the development of plot (in this book, not the romantic love story, which is only part of it, but the story of the incompatibility between man and society) are the definitions of Onegin offered by the lists of the books he read. The first list is given in the first chapter; the other, in the last. They frame Onegin's literal, or social, development, and they frame the novel itself, at the same time showing how Pushkin has moved from the romantic tradition of the first list to a position beyond even the consequences of reading, which are given as part of the second list. In Chapter I, stanzas 3–27 present a light-toned survey of Onegin's education, costume, habits, and literary vocabulary, conspicuously representative of the "society man" of early nineteenth-century Russia:

> Not having any noble passion
> To spare for living and its sounds,
> No matter how we tried to teach him
> He confused the trochee and the iamb.
> He swore at Homer, Theocritus,
> On the other hand knew Adam Smith,
> And was a great economist,
> That is to say could give opinions
> On how the state was getting rich. . . .
>
> (I,7)

Onegin's life over (romance for him ruined), he turns wildly to reading. Tatyana has made no reply to his letters, he feels forgotten:

> He started reading things at random.
> He went through Gibbon and Rousseau,
> Manzoni, Herder, and Chamfort,
> Madame de Staël, Bichat, Tissot,
> Read the skeptical Pierre Bayle,
> Read the works of Fontenelle,
> Read some of our own native sons
> Without rejecting anything. . . .
>
> (VIII,35)

With the consequences that:

> His eyes continued reading,
> But all his thoughts were far afield;
> Vague dreams, desires, sadnesses,
> Were crowded deep down in his soul.
>
> (VIII,36)

The literature that had been example for his life has yielded to a literature inadequate to life. Life has transcended its habitual, easy, quasi-metaphysical definitions. Or, we might say, the story of Onegin's life has become demonstrably more true than the literature from which it sprang, just as Onegin's life itself is said by the poet to have become definitively, because hopelessly, real.

The notion that the world of a realistic novel is a surrogate for reality is wrong. In an essay on Byronic elements in *Eugene Onegin*, one critic, following an academic method of classification, has written that "The realistic method . . . precludes anything that might remind the reader that he is dealing with a poetic invention. . . . Realism presumes an agreement between author and reader as to what will be accepted as actuality, and this agreement, once established, is observed to the end." In fact, this is not so. We find quick agreement among readers that *Don Quixote, The Karamazov Brothers,* and *War and Peace* are realistic novels. Poems and stories frequently interrupt Cervantes' narrative; one section of Dostoevsky's novel is called a poem, the literary nature of which is emphasized by Ivan's insistence on a foreword; and Tolstoy constantly stops the activity in his book to argue the meaning of history. *Moby Dick,* supposedly a first-person narrative, contains many digressions and even footnotes on the techniques of whaling (for example, Chapter XXXII); Chapters XXXVII–XL, but especially XL, are formally presented as one-act plays. One cannot maintain that because "Pushkin constantly reminds the reader of his presence . . . and discusses the creative process itself . . . [*Eugene Onegin*] does not satisfy the basic requirements of realism." The basic requirements are not formally delimited by any notions of illusion or its violation. The "actuality" of the world of a realistic novel always seems pressing in so far as the author insists that the activity of either the protagonist or himself relates always to other coeval humans in ethical terms, assumes that suffer-

ing or consciousness of loss is the basic experience of human life, and asserts that the limits of art, as of actual life, are absolute freedom. These conditions are satisfied in *Eugene Onegin*. They are not satisfied in the Greek romance of *Daphnis and Chloe*, as we sense by the substitution of the convention of matrimony for the ethics of love. They are so satisfied in *The Devils* that most readers do not in fact notice that two-thirds of the way through the novel the putative narrator, Mr. G—v, drops out for some time and Dostoevsky interposes himself as an omniscient author. Devices which are believed to draw attention to the artificial nature of literary composition—epigraphs, asides, chapter divisions, and so on —may actually very powerfully assert the reality of the world which they help compose. We know this from Sterne's writings, of course; we see it here in Pushkin's.

The distinction between realistic novels and historical novels is not one of detail, for *Ivanhoe* and *The Captain's Daughter* are full of "realistic," family-life details. Both novels, however, designedly avoid satisfying the criteria which characterize realistic fiction. In so far as the details are actual, they are also remote. In so far as the relationships are true, they are also conventional. And in so far as the heroes' actions celebrate freedom they also acknowledge the propriety of existing institutions. How, then, can the books be real?

The shift from neoclassicism to sentimentalism to romanticism to realism is nowhere else so clear as in nineteenth-century Russia, and well illustrates the point that the realistic novel is as closely connected with (as Pushkin puns on "romantic ravings") "prosaic ravings" as with intellectually political reform (the discussion circles of the 1830's, especially the groups around Stankevich and Granovsky). Furthermore, the realistic novel is grounded in the present. It asserts, ideally, that what it describes is always actually happening.

Boris Godunov is dramatized history; the unevenness of the play follows from the fact that for Godunov, an historic figure remote from us, the author has devised motivation, that Pimen, the monkish scribe, is a romantic exemplification of pressing, always contemporary motivation: how to express the meaning of history by proper recording of events. The play (which Pushkin called "a truly romantic tragedy") resembles an historical novel, although moments of it are, in a literary sense, real. *War and Peace* assumes not that it puts an end to war but that it describes all wars to come. It describes "this war" forever. I am reminded that Gogol, Tolstoy, and Dostoevsky proposed enormous prose trilogies, encompassing all aspects of human life, of which *Dead Souls*, *War and Peace*, and *The Karamazov Brothers* are, each, the first and only parts. Dante could properly assert that the real world was not actual and that the plausibility of the first part of his trilogy depended on the actuality of the third. The Russian realists could not, for by their time actuality had come to be understood as the substance of the here-and-now.

In Griboedov's play *The Trouble with Reason* (1825), Chatsky loses Sofia, the girl he loves, by being excessively idealistic. Her father's house, family, and way of life is a closed, unified society. What Chatsky believes in, this society claims it honors, but Chatsky urges reform, and the morally indolent, somewhat sybaritic group cannot tolerate it. The class prevails; what *is* goes on. Chatsky is right, but alienated. The hero's support of society's values requires the "sacrifice" of the hero:

The scales have fallen from my eyes, the dreams are gone!
　It would not be a bad thing now
　　To vent my spleen and all
　My spite on both the daughter
And the father, the stupid lover and the world together!
　　. . . he will pass through fire unharmed

> *Who manages a day with you,*
> *Who breathes the same air that you breathe*
> *And whose intelligence stays whole.*
> *Away from Moscow! I will not come back again.*

Pushkin read Griboedov's play in 1825 and cuttingly commented on it in a letter to Bestuzhev. Chatsky was an unsuccessful hero, Pushkin said, because he was only a mouthpiece, an alter ego for Griboedov himself, and because he addressed his witty remarks not so much to the thick-headed louts around him in Famusov's house on stage but directly to the audience, thereby behaving atypically. Mere social opposition, characteristic of romantic heroes, seemed to Pushkin inappropriate and untrue. Pushkin asserted that his own Eugene Onegin was typical (that is, both common and independent of the author) and that the plot of events and the development of scenes proceeded from everyday life.

In *Eugene Onegin* the everyday, comic, "real-life" figure of eighteenth-century satire and early nineteenth-century adventures (which Pushkin discusses in the novel itself, in letters about the novel, and in his preface to it—"the first chapter is reminiscent of *Beppo*, the comic work of the somber Byron") is combined with the outspoken, noble-minded protagonist of early nineteenth-century romanticism into a figure often called the first of the superfluous men but for which we have, really, no adequate label. Pushkin's manuscript carries the notation: "The first chapter of *Eugene Onegin* is something complete in itself. It is a satiric description of the life of a young Russian nobleman in Petersburg toward the end of 1819."

The young nobleman puts his socially acceptable upbringing to the test of actuality. Because he is sensitive, he finds the life of society empty. Because he is compassionate, because in the emptiness of his life he has become aware of his similarity to other people, he becomes conscious of his

aloneness, of how the life for which he was trained and which he at first tried to lead has prevented his accomplishing what originally was that life's goal:

> *Onegin with a look of pity*
> *Glances at the swirls of smoke*
> *And thinks, his mind befogged by sorrow:*
> *Why haven't I been shot and wounded?*
>
> .   .   .   .
>
>   *Oh, Lord in Heaven!*
> *I'm young, there's much more life in me;*
> *But what's ahead? ennui, ennui!* . . .
> (Travels)

At the end of the novel, after Tatyana has rejected him and said in mournful triumph that she will be faithful to her husband forever,

> *She left. Eugene was standing there*
> *As if he had been struck by lightning.*
> *His heart was heavy with the air*
> *Of thunderstorms of tones and feelings.*
> *There came the sudden sound of spurs:*
> *Tatyana's husband had appeared,*
> *And at this point, reader of mine,*
> *We'll leave my hero at a time*
> *Disastrous for him, for very long,*
> *Indeed, forever. We've chased along*
> *Enough, the wide world over, down*
> *One path. Congratulations on*
> *Our making shore together. Hurrah!*
> *It long has (hasn't it?) been time.*
> (VIII,48)

Whatever the protagonist be defined as, the author here dis-associates himself from him, referring us back to the metrical and metaphoric organization of the novel as a unit. The author's new friend after Onegin (and seemingly more con-sciously a friend than the Muse) is the reader, to whom the author says:

> *Whoever you may be, my reader,*
> *A friend or foe, I want to leave*
> *You now the way a dear friend would.*
> (VIII,49)

The upper-class concept of friendship which was mocked in the beginning of the novel as a spuriously social value:

> *He was fed up with friends and friendship*

(although honored as part of romantic tradition in the preface to the novel) becomes entirely different at the end. It is friend-ship based not on assumptions of class or assumed community but on common intellectual experience. The "friends" with whom the poet has had the "sweet conversation" referred to in stanza 50 of Chapter VIII are his readers. The restricted, upper-class, cultured society for whom the poem seems de-signed and to whom it was first read (VIII,51) is only a partial audience. The typicality of the hero's experiences requires that they be interpreted and applied as universal; the author even finally asks us to do this:

> *Blessed is he . . .*
> *Who didn't finish the novel of life*
> *And suddenly could let it go,*
> *As I let go of my Onegin.*
> (VIII,51)

B. V. Tomashevsky has cautioned us not to think of Gogol and Pushkin as contraries, except with regard to certain aspects of style. I would add that Turgenev, Goncharov, Dostoevsky, Tolstoy, Leskov, Grigorovich, Saltykov-Shchedrin, all the important nineteenth-century novelists whatever the idiosyncrasies of their talents, followed Pushkin in intentionally creating adequately representative protagonists. Before Pushkin, the central character in a work of fiction had only to be conventionally plausible; the "meaning" of the story lay in the merit with which human relationships were described and social values affirmed. After Chekhov, a central character was understood as necessarily only a partial representation of an age or of an attitude, a figure more dependent on the world around him than that world is dependent on him. Pushkin's Onegin, however, is typical for his faults as well as for his excellences. He *is* his society. The stupidities of a badly assimilated, imitation-French culture encourage him to play the dandy; the worth of classical literature and of Russian cultural tradition prevent him from taking society's habits as final values and make him seem a *pedant*, a man in the upper-classes who, as Brodsky defines the meaning of the word in the 1820's, by inclination and convictions cannot fit in. However superficial Onegin seems to us, we understand that he understands. In the beginning of the novel, he understands possibilities; at the end, he understands actualities. The failure of his life is defined by the success of his understanding, even as the frivolity of society life is given meaning by being encompassed by an esthetic scheme classical in structure, strict in form, and consistent in its autobiographical–intellectual aim. Onegin, as the man of his time, knows he has failed, but he is never conscious of the extent of his failure. Like many of us, he is never without hope even in a hopeless situation. A manuscript passage asks:

But sometimes such strange sounds would burst
Forth from his lips, from inside himself,
So deep, so astonishing a groan,
That to Lensky he still seemed
A figure of unfading pain. . . .
. . . What sorts of feelings did not surge
Through his tormented breast? Had they
Died down so long ago? For good?

Hope of consciousness is the highest hope. Onegin keeps it to the end. The author skitters away from him at the point of climactic failure, when Onegin's consciousness is no longer efficacious. The boredom which drives Onegin to his *Travels* puts the travels finally outside the novel. They illuminate Onegin's character, but they are background to the book, the world of which is defined not so much by the geography of Russia as by Onegin's consciousness of the manners of a society, not so much by reminiscences of the glory of the past (to which Chatsky appeals in *The Trouble with Reason*) as by the dramatization of the past in the present, by the aptness of Pushkin's style itself, of which the striking characteristic is its contemporaneity. It encompasses peasant speech, salon conversation, lovers' talk, gossip, literary analysis, dream sequences, traditional, patriotic, and "lofty" sentiments, irony, landscape descriptions, philosophic reflections, political opinions and judgments—and so on. The novel's success lies in the plasticity of its words. As Tatyana, for all her traditional charm, is transcended by the Muse, so Onegin is "overcome" by the author. The author separates himself from Onegin and from society by his novel, as if by a translucent wall. The instrument of social judgment, which the novel is, is also the instrument of personal liberation. The realistic novelist (Pushkin) delimits the romantic poser (Onegin).

The function of style is to assert the immediacy of consciousness. The more varied the style, within limits of credibility, the wider the scope of a work. This accounts for the size of Shakespeare (*Macbeth*) over Marlowe (*Tamburlaine*), of Dante (*Vita Nuova*) over Cavalcanti (*Canzone d'Amore*), of Pushkin (*Eugene Onegin*) over Izmailov (*Eugene*) and Narezhny (*A Russian Gil Blas*). Onegin may not be able to tell an iamb from a trochee, but Pushkin did; the scope of his technique and the aptness of his judgments make him the most skillful Russian poet.

2

Rhythm is measure in motion. Aristotle's "plot" is accessible to our understanding only in the motion of formal measure. Whether a pattern be the hourglass (to borrow a figure from E. M. Forster) of *Eugene Onegin* or the grand chain of *Dead Souls*, it is esthetically pleasing but less important than rhythm. A pattern is a design, an expression of pleasure in invention. Rhythm is the movement of the rational imagination.

The romantic terminology which in the prologue to *Eugene Onegin* Pushkin announces is his equipment, his measure, set in motion by the style, marks the moments of a tragic rhythm: the aims and boundaries of a man's life in the age into which he has been born, the passionate suffering of losses in that life, and the final perception (partially by the protagonist and wholly by the poet and the reader) of an equilibrium between the losses and the forces of life.

The eighteenth-century neoclassicists and sentimentalists handed down to the early nineteenth-century romantics the concept that verse was lofty and prose base. The romantics added the notion that only the inner life of the struggling hero was fit subject for serious narrative or drama (*Faust*; Pushkin in the mid-1820's said that one aspect of Byron's inadequacy was his incapacity to reckon successfully with Goethe). From Byron, Pushkin borrowed the new form of long lyric-narrative poem and, within that form, a series of motifs and themes. Unlike earlier romantic poems, Byron's celebrated a novelistic subject.

Eugene Onegin is as consciously chronological in its way as Dante's *Comedy*. Written in 1823–1831/32, it covers a time from the late winter of 1819 to the spring of 1825, the period of greatest intellectual ferment and social optimism after the Napoleonic invasion and before the Decembrist uprising. In the context of this literalness, Pushkin uses the romantic "device" of focusing on the hero's personality. The engine which drives the plot is the history of Onegin's inner life, the problems of love. (In this sense, also, Pushkin is surprisingly close to Dostoevsky, whose first literary work was a translation of *Eugénie Grandet*.)

One may talk of Byron's "eastern poems" and of Pushkin's "southern poems," as one may list a set of devices common to them both: the lyric openings, the abrupt or sudden action, the dramatic skits and monologues, the incomplete narrations within the story, the lyric repetitions, the innovations in rhyme, pauses, diction, the frequently prevailing tone of light irony, and so forth. "By a lyric style of narration," V. M. Zhirmunsky has written,

I understand a system of devices which gives a story heightened emotional coloring, creating the impression of the poet's interestedness, of his emotional participation in the fate of his heroes, of his intimate, even private, relation to what they say

and do, frequently even an emotional identification on the part of the poet with the personality and the fate of one or another of the dramatis personae.

Story, here, means fictional narrative, what I should call a consequential arrangement of incidents elaborating motive. But just as Tolstoy, in his Caucasian stories ("The Cossacks," "The Raid") wished to make a greater than traditional use of the Caucasus (Marlinsky's "Mulla-Nur"), so Pushkin wished to go beyond the restrictions of a lyric pose. In *Eugene Onegin* the lyric digressions from the lyric narrative give scope. They suggest partiality to Homer's side in what Pushkin called the classic–romantic debate between Homer and Byron. They introduce into the poem the classical attitude of man as an object in nature, contrary to the romantic concept of man the subject of nature. In the Byronic tale (*Childe Harold*) the hero is central. After the first chapter in *Eugene Onegin* there is little description of the "central character," there is increasing insistence on nature and natural elements, on the independence of events. The hero, although central *in* the narrative, is not central *to* it. The conditions are those of a novel.

The first suggestion of this comes in the epigraph, which, though "from a personal letter," was most likely written by Pushkin himself: ". . . suite d'un sentiment de supériorité, peut-être imaginaire." How is a man to resolve that *perhaps* without applying to himself the facts of social judgment of him? Pushkin announces that he is not praising individuality; he is measuring it. The first tools he uses are those he has at hand, the romantic vocabulary including *die schöne Seele*, as given in the brief prologue that follows. The epigraph to the first chapter, one line from a poem by Vyazemsky, is fitted to the protagonist. N. L. Brodsky, author of the most extensive, reliable, and scholarly commentary on the novel, points out that readers "who remembered Vyazemsky's poem connected the end of it with the final stanzas of the first chapter [of *Onegin*], which treat of the cooled passions of Eugene, who 'has no more illusions,' " with characterizations of the "attitude typical of young people of that time." *Eugene Onegin* was intended· from the start as a serious critique of an age. As such it has encouraged modern poems like Blok's *Retribution* (1921).

There were at hand for Pushkin models such as Voltaire's *Le Mondain* or, better, Ya. Tolstoy's 1821 "Epistle to an Inhabitant of St. Petersburg" or Kantemir's 1730 Satire II, "Filaret and Eugene. On the Envy and Pride of Ignoble Nobility," a typically eighteenth-century study of morality, in which Eugene, the "well-born," the "noble," asks in his first speech:

> *Think for yourself how easy it is for me to perceive*
> *That, despite such noble forebears, I am forgot,*
> *That wherever I may be I am, of all men, least.*

But Pushkin (and he was therefor accused of immorality) separates his poem and his hero from these antecedents by punning on another example. Krylov's fable about "The Ass and the Peasant" (1819) begins:

> *The Ass was of the highest scruples . . .*

which Pushkin turns into:

> *My uncle of the highest scruples . . .*

The author is ironic. He is committed to his time as Eliot is in "The Love Song of J. Alfred Prufrock" with its

> *Let us go then, you and I . . .*

The "you and I" and "my uncle" propose the circumference of the poem–story; nobody else is to enter. As readers we must find out how many are "in," how many the "you and I" includes. In Eliot's poem, the narrative proceeds by examination and dissection, as of the evening or of the patient etherized on the table. The "I" unbecomes the poet; the "you" unbecomes the reader. In Pushkin's poem "my," which initially refers to the poet, to everyday life and its relations, comes to refer to the protagonist. The poet is eliminated as persona, remains as audience, as author, as observer, as commentator. The poet : reader = I : you equation alters the poet : hero = I : you equation. In "Prufrock" or in *The Age of Anxiety* we have dramatization by masks, a morality, the masks of emotion. In *Eugene Onegin* we have dramatization by social gesture, a novel, the gestures of emotion. Onegin writes to Tatyana, after intimacy or even friendship between them has become impossible:

> *I know: my time is circumscribed,*
> *But if my life keep on at least*
> *I must be certain in the morning*
> *That in the afternoon we'll meet.*
>
> (VIII, Letter)

Eugene Onegin has been given many sorts of readings, has been called a study of the tranquil life of early nineteenth-century Russian gentry and an autobiography, a purely lyric poem. Indeed, the novel admits both extremes, and one is encouraged in such a reading by the legendary aspects which the figure of Pushkin has taken on. Never mind the statues of him all over the world or the continual editions of his works; speeches like Dostoevsky's at the 1880 celebration (in which Dostoevsky said that Pushkin was a prophecy and a revelation), or the special 1899 Imperial edition for the army to mark the centennial of his birth, suggest the myth of a man greater than the writer, of a writer who became greater than anything he wrote about. The myth is partly substantiated by Pushkin's dynamism, by his keen and even scholarly interest in Russian history, to which he felt closely tied. Unlike Dostoevsky, a professional man of letters, he was an aristocrat, a liberal, at times the "gay blade" he called Onegin (and as he called himself in some of his short lyrics). He was also a literary man, an editor, who in 1836 founded *The Contemporary*, the most important literary journal in Russia in the nineteenth century. His discovery of the world of literary realism, quite unlike the worlds of *Adolphe* and of *Beppo* from which he partially and very obviously derived (or, as Dostoevsky would have said, came out from under), was built around understanding of the isolated individual as a social force, a cognitive agent determined by and in turn determining his environment. The environment becomes significant only to the degree that it is realized in the individual's performance.

A common view of *Eugene Onegin* is that it remains an encyclopedia of Russian life. Belinsky shared this view, emphasizing, in the spirit of his interpretation of Hegelian philosophy, the exemplification in the book, through opposition between Onegin and society, of the conflict between spirit or consciousness and actuality, of the dichotomy between romantic terms and everyday details. Belinsky, and others, considered Onegin a superior type, typicalness of character being for them the criterion of a book's excellence. Such a criterion is admissible only if the function of literature is to educate; for Belinsky, it was. Though Onegin may successfully represent a type, the type which he represents is not "typically Russian," and—to follow the argument out—the "real hero" of the novel, the typical and genuine Russian, is Tatyana.

On the other hand, for Brodsky and other critics, the novel is a literary monument, its importance guaranteed by its prominent features: its intimacy, its artistic effects, and its contrasting use of the romantic and naturalistic styles of storytelling.

The opening stanza of Chapter III, on Tatyana, set against the first chapter on Onegin, reports the basic pattern and helps establish the rhythm of the novel, even as it rubs against the formality of the pattern. A colloquial conversation is housed in the intricate iambic tetrameter stanzaic scheme rhyming ababccddeffegg. Superficially, and then finally, the hero is characterized by social judgment of his social function:

> "Where, now? I'm tired of these poets."
> "Good-bye, Onegin, I have to go."
> "I'm not keeping you, but tell us
> Where you spend your evenings out."
> "At the Larins." "You really don't!
> For Heaven's sake! It must be hard
> For you to knock off evenings there?"
> "Not at all." "I don't see why.
> I picture how the whole thing is:
> First of all (listen: right?),
> There's a simple Russian family,
> Much cordiality to guests,
> Preserves, and endless conversation
> About the rain, the flax, the barnyard. . . ."
>
> (III,1)

The novel is framed by the lists of Onegin's reading; the characters are defined by identification with literary tradition. Tatyana's bovarysm brings to life the romantic mode which Pushkin is transforming:

> Fancying the heroine
> Of her beloved books was she—

Clarissa, Julie, or Delphine—
Tatyana wandered in the woods
Alone, the dangerous book in hand. . . .

(III,10)

The eleventh stanza outlines the moralistic novel of the eighteenth century; the twelfth stanza, the "new novel" of Lord Byron's "despondent romanticism"; the thirteenth, in a tone of light irony and with cultural pride, Pushkin's program. The three novels which are listed as defining Tatyana—*Clarissa Harlowe* (1748), *La Nouvelle Héloïse* (1760), *Delphine* (1802)—encompass both the sentimental and the romantic moralities and, all three, tell of unhappy, unsuccessful loves. The crossed plot of Rousseau's novel, Julie's faithfulness to her unloved husband when her beloved St.-Preux has returned, is close to the Tatyana–Onegin plot, but only as idea. Julie's father compels her obedience, prevents her marriage to her beloved; Tatyana fails to attract Onegin. In *Eugene Onegin* the plot is not manipulated by opposition between social conformity and the "free emotions of the heart" but depends on the dramatic decisions of two independent actors, who are not ruled by their time but who embody their time. By the end of the novel, Onegin's position is hopeless; Tatyana's, strong. Psychology has replaced conventional morality. Motivation has replaced machination. And the study of Onegin's and Tatyana's motivation is itself part of the study of cultural tradition, which the novel also is.

That Tatyana with her bovarysm and Onegin with his adaptation of the romantic mode are three-dimensional figures (and not psychological instances, like some characters in Tolstoy novels, for example) is pointed up by the flatness of Olga and of Lensky. Again, the sharpest definition of the frame within which the characters move is made by literary reference. Mocking the misquotes of half-educated literary pretenders, Pushkin has Lensky ineptly say over General Larin's grave:

> Poor Yorick! *he said despondently* . . .
> (II,37)

and adds a footnote to refer the reader not to Shakespeare but to the four chapters in Sterne's A *Sentimental Journey* in which the parson gets the name of Yorick and in which the count says of the parson's talk, "Voilà un persiflage!" Olga does not imagine herself a literary heroine come to life; on the contrary, she is described as being the model for any heroine in literature:

> *As gentle as a lovers' kiss,*
> *Her eyes as azure as the sky,*
> *Her smile, her flaxen locks of hair,*
> *Her movements, voice, her slender waist—*
> *All that was Olga . . . but just you take*
> *Any novel and you'll find*
> *Her portrait: it is very sweet;*
> *I used to like it much myself,*
> *But now it bores me beyond belief.*
> *Reader, if you please, allow*
> *Me to describe the older sister now.*
> (II,23)

That Olga is a flat character assists the construction of "plot," of course, and helps overcome the romantic–sentimental story. The advantage of a stock character is recognizability. Within limits, the stock character is easily maneuvered. Or the author can, if he pleases, easily move around it. Pushkin uses figures of conventionality and uses Tatyana as a conventional figure, at the name-day party in Chapter V, as excuses for Onegin's "perhaps imaginary" sense of superiority. Onegin's

condescending caricaturization of the guests, including Tatyana next to him, his own "composing," unlike Pushkin's
sympathetic irony, only exposes his improper supercilious-
ness:

> *Now, triumphing ahead of time,*
> *He started drawing in his mind*
> *Caricatures of all the guests.*
> (V,31)

Lensky is a modish and, therefore, false poet. Olga is
a conventional and, therefore, unreal girl. Onegin is an ego-
tistic and, therefore, inconstant friend. Literature and literary
sources define them, define Tatyana, shape the novel. The
stanza form of the verse is one source of pattern. The literary
form, which in turn is held against its sources—

> *The frost's already stinging noses*
> *And blanketing the fields with white . . .*
> *(The reader wants the rhyme of* roses:
> *Here, damn it, hurry up and take it!)*
> (IV,42)

—is one source of rhythm. All together, we have the pattern
and the rhythm of an ordering of the conversation which
proceeds from the language of the court, the talk of the town,
the examples of intellectual tradition. As a lyric narrative,
Eugene Onegin is equally a reformation of a literary genre. It
is also an effort to create a literary genre, the socially apt realistic novel in the nineteenth century. It is an attempt to give
a novel (a fictional narrative of a certain extent, to chop
Chevalley's definition down further) a social function so that
it may as much illuminate the possibilities of the future as
illustrate the failures in the past.

An outline of the "plot" says little that is relevant to

understanding the book. There is here no succession of events such as that by which Macbeth or Don Quixote or Tom Jones measured their progress. In that sense, there is no progress, no motion here at all (as there is none in any of Dostoevsky's novels). What shapes the book, finally, is our awareness of the movement in coincidence of natural and human events—for example, of the occurrence in winter of the nameday party, the meaning of which is revealed only in the dream symbolism of stanzas 43–45 in Chapter V. The "climax" of the novel, in Chapter VI, turns around Lensky's death, the whole story of the duel, the analysis of the poet's role, and the implied delineation of the role of what we might call the lady of the house, Pushkin's Muse. Chapter VII, on the two sisters, begins with an apostrophe to winter. Chapter VIII, the denouement, is the story of the second rejected love, Onegin's. It begins with autobiography (for example, the lines in stanza 2 on Derzhavin), encompasses Pushkin's relation to the Muse (for example, stanza 4), and includes reminiscences of young manhood which frame the story (the "lost youth" of stanzas 10–11), a condensation of Onegin's travels (stanzas 12–13), and a definitive description of the reality of the ideal woman, Tatyana become a lady (stanza 14).

The shift in character and in "plot" leads to a shift in style. Onegin's appeal to Tatyana in Chapter VIII is preceded by a stanza practically in prose identifying the state of mind which produced the letter. The novelist's real friend, it turns out, is no *semblable*, is Eugene Onegin done over by the poet in this book. The question of purpose in the rhythm of the novel suddenly raises anew the issue of motivation. Contrary to the romantic notion, the beautiful, Pushkin says, is not the thing itself, necessarily, but the purity or excellence of the artist's emotion about it, of his understanding of it. In Chapter VIII, stanzas 15–16, Pushkin says he likes the word *vulgar* but cannot translate it, that it is "a new word among us." In a letter to his wife in 1833, he said, "You know how I dislike anything that smacks of the Moscow debutante, anything that's not *comme il faut*, anything that's *vulgar*." What the poet possesses is his language, and Pushkin's controversy with Shishkov (see, for example, VIII,14) followed from his effort to make the language vital so that it, too, like clothes and manners, would aptly reflect the culture of an age. A man's language is himself and encompasses him. Language goes beyond the poet and stays.

Pushkin believed what Flaubert said later, that the artist ought not to appear in his work any more than God in nature. God is outside the world of Flaubert's novels and rules that world by law; the reader must infer (as for *Salammbô* or *Madame Bovary*) the moral system. Law, for Pushkin, is inadequate and inaccurate (one of the themes of *Dubrovsky*). The god of art, much like the life force of which Pasternak speaks, *is* nature, is continually re-creating it in terms of its whole moral system, by the validity of the artist's talent: his imagination, his kindness, his courage, his skill.

> *But I withdrew from their alliance*
> *And ran far off . . . she followed me.*
> *How often the caressing Muse*
> *Enchanted me on my silent way*
> *By the magic of a mysterious tale!*
>
> (VIII,4)

In the opening stanzas of Chapter VIII, which recapitulate Pushkin's own travels, his own autobiography, homage to the Muse is equated with service to the poet's countrymen. Brodsky points out that in the fifth stanza of this chapter the manuscript contains a line, later deleted, which refers to the influence on Pushkin of the national minorities he met

in the south of Russia and to his own allegiance to social
reform:

> *And she forsook the speeches of gods*
> *For barren, alien, pagan tongues,*
> For the literature of precious freedom. . . .

Brodsky reads this as indication that Pushkin was intellectually and emotionally in sympathy with the uprisings of the
early nineteenth century. I should read it as also an acknowledgment in social terms of that freedom of which Tatyana
dreamed but which she found was inaccessible.

The novel seems to offer a moralistic finale: Tatyana
pledges faithfulness forever to her husband. Perhaps she is
not pledging herself but simply stating her condition. The
steam roller of conventions has blindly and inexorably reduced Onegin and his values to its own. The deviation has
occasioned its own disaster, mild compared to Anna Karenina's but akin to what Flaubert said of Emma Bovary: "Elle
retrouvait dans l'adultère toutes les platitudes de mariage."
This is the most painful condition: rebellion is finally subject
to the same terms as that against which it was undertaken. This
is the final irony. Onegin is left by the author in a "disastrous
moment," is turned into a move in a literary game. The catastrophe of the classical hero (Achilles, Oedipus) expresses
the preservation of the tribe or of the state; in the world of
literary realism, the catastrophe of the hero expresses the loss
of the self.

The measure of Pushkin's protest against society, the instrumentality for altering social perceptions, the source of
tragedy in the novel, is Tatyana's capacity for love, her love
affair. The beautiful dreamer, the beautiful innocent is
crushed by the distorted ambitions of people who have only a
little power and who, to live, must assert it. Man's rebellion

cannot succeed, neither Tatyana's nor Onegin's nor Pushkin's; society constrains suffering; the love affair appears in the end to have been impossible from the start. Correspondingly, the author has three roles: he narrates the sequence of events; he is friend to Onegin; he comments, as a social agent, on his own life, on his past, on Russian history and speech, on his sense of Russia's destiny. The narrative proper includes the author's ironic attitude toward the characters' motivation. Its lyric and autobiographical digressions are serious treatment of the same theme.

The novelist, to cite Auden's poem,

> . . . *must*
> *Become the whole of boredom, subject to*
> *Vulgar complaints like love; among the just*
>
> *Be Just, among the Filthy, filthy, too,*
> *And in his own weak person if he can*
> *Must suffer dully all the wrongs of man.*

The novel, which has predominated in those times and places when the individual's privacy has been publicly subverted either by social institutions or by a prevailing "philosophy," requires that the Many be suffering. The development of the modern novel, following *Don Quixote*, and of the contemporary novel, following the nineteenth-century Russians, coincides with the individual's loss of identity and his deepest illusion of freedom. Each novelist must create his own function for himself. The distinguishing characteristic of *Eugene Onegin* and of the other great Russian novels is that, in their study of society, they come to a deep and final judgment.

Onegin is the sophisticated, half-foreign, frustrated, withered, artificially passionate Byronic hero. Lensky, also half-foreign, is the impossibly Germanic romantic idealist. Tatyana is the native Russian, placid, overly simple, naïve, fresh, with

Rousseau-like natural charm, who in the end becomes grand. They are held together by the social aptness of the poet's language. Through them the poet has touched on the possibilities within which human life may occur. Intimately tied to life by the conditions under which he lived (for example, the autobiographic passages in the novel) and by history itself (*The Negro of Peter the Great*), but alienated by the disparity between prevailing norms and the final values which sanction human activity. Pushkin drew a portrait of his time and of its typically dominant figure, in which he emphasized (in eighteenth-century style) the difference between their actions and their claims and (in romantic style) the difference between their actions and their potential, and defined (in realist style) the difference between the figures and the age, on the one hand, and between the figures and himself, on the other, asserting the importance and social usefulness of his artistic labor because of its preservation of the fundamental values for human life and its exposure of all false claims and spurious understandings. Beyond the saccharine, illusioned romanticism of Rousseau's or Richardson's novels and the disillusioned romanticism of Byron's or Constant's, there is the realism of Pushkin's, reporting the intelligence of discrepancy, the final accommodation to fact.

Eugene Onegin is not just a story of a socially realistic hero, nor is it a Byronic imitation. It is the narrative of the struggle by an individual against his socially determined limitations, of the development of character in the movement determined by social life. It is "the new novel," the study of the world of the family, leaning not backward on *Adolphe* or *Don Juan* but leading forward, both by theme and by narrative expansiveness, to *Fathers and Children*, to *The Idiot*, to *Anna Karenina*—and, finally, to *Doctor Zhivago*, our contemporary "novel in prose."

A Hero of
Our Time

In Pushkin's poem "The Prophet," the *I* is the mediator and advocate to complete certain acts on our imagination's stage, as God is the agent who creates conditions favorable to the prophet's act of consummation of desire. By imitation the prophet re-creates the act of God. In the poem, Pushkin emphasizes not the agent (which the usual romantics did) but the act itself. His attitude toward the poem leads necessarily to the theater and to dramatic poetry. It leads to dramatic conceptualization of the world around oneself. Particulars of experience are not consciously sublimated, as Goethe has Faust get rid of them, or postponed, as Shelley often wanted to postpone them. They are understood to occur dramatically and in themselves to resolve the conflicts which exist. There is a way of looking at the ordinary world which is dramatic, a way in which internalized value informs on (and is informed on only by) external action. For all you talk about or around Philoctetes, for example, you cannot escape the actuality of the condition he presents. He is his own best informer.

The economy of style in prose to which this sort of conceptualization leads is most successful and powerful in the works of Chekhov, but it was discovered (in Russia, at least) by Pushkin. The perception of conflict is presented by antithesis even in details of description: "He willingly lent them to us to read and never asked for them back; on the other hand, he never returned the books that were lent him." In

45

this story, "The Shot" from Pushkin's *Belkin's Tales* (1831), the antithetical construction starts with the opening sentence, a tricky and suspenseful beginning—"Some mystery surrounded his existence"—and perseveres to the reversal at the end.

The story is a parody of the terms of romanticism, by application, so to speak, of the romantic method to other and subsequently necessary terms. The romantic pose envelops the story, but the central figure, Silvio, is a new, special kind of idealist. In no way prepared to lay down his life for a cause (unlike Rudin, who finally does), he knows the limits both of authority and of individual power in this world. Literally, in early nineteenth-century gentleman's language, he seeks satisfaction. Literarily, he acts out the conflict, shooting his walls full of holes practicing, until the Count, his opponent, by a gesture completes the dramatic sequence. That ends the story, the inversion of romanticism completing the enactment of motive. The clarity of the old romantic ideal is gone from this story. We are left with a comic, ironic, especially dramatic figure. The realness of the figure and its story is constructed by the obdurate realist's parody of sentimental romanticism.

The hero of the story, Silvio, who has said he wants to revenge himself on the Count by playing a joke, follows the proper form. The Count's continual luck in drawing lots reinforces the irony of Silvio's position. Finally the Count shoots, misses, and it is Silvio's turn. The Count's wife throws herself at Silvio's feet. The Count is, for a moment, confused. He recovers, asks Silvio to stop "making fun of a poor woman" and to fire. The Count has been committed to loss of pride at the ultimate moment. Silvio says that he is satisfied, that "I forced you to fire at me. That is sufficient." Commitment achieved, the meaning is accomplished. "You will remember me. I leave you to your conscience." Silvio then reasserts the perfection of his own technique: at random, as if setting the condition for irony, he takes a shot at the picture through which the Count's bullet passed, putting *his* shot just above the shot meant for him. He has taken the Count's game away and made it his own. His triumph leaves the Count meaningless as a man. Silvio vanishes back into the mystery of his own grandness. He has dared assert himself, and he is victorious, but the reality of the story depends on the reversal of the roles of loser. At first, Silvio has lost; then, the Count has. Gogol made all his heroes losers; only his own technique was adroit enough, he keeps saying, to "win." In Pushkin's story, there is no war between characters and author. We have the psychology of successful revenge, of the reversal that reshapes history, alters values, and supplies an unexpected, controlling idea.

We are further surprised, as with Lermontov's *A Hero of Our Time* (1840), not by the autobiographical aspects but by the degree to which autobiography is overcome by narration. As a matter of fact, Pushkin once played a role much like Silvio's. In June, 1822, in Kishinev, Pushkin dueled with an officer, Zubov: "At the duel with Zubov, Pushkin showed up with some cherries which he ate while the other was getting ready to shoot. Zubov shot first and missed." Pushkin, B. V. Tomashevsky reports, did not shoot and did not become reconciled with Zubov. The second part of "The Shot," written two days after the first part, transforms the material of biography into facts of art. What in "real life" had no end is consummated in art. Specifically, the technique of narration compels the gestures that lead to its own perfection. The five short stories called *Belkin's Tales* are, like parts of *Eugene Onegin*, deliberate, meaningful "hoaxes," manipulations of illusion, like *Tristram Shandy*. The artist sets out from autobiography to capitalize on the illusory nature of his art. He removes himself as personality, remains as talent only. He arranges a reality upon which he does not obtrude.

As an epigraph to *Belkin's Tales* Pushkin originally thought of using a saying he remembered by the father superior of the Svyatogorsk Monastery: "What will be is that we won't be." It was a joke, a pun, such as Sterne was fond of making, as Joyce was fond of. The foreword from the "editor" is the same sort of thing: a mockery of readers' habits through which to reinforce more strongly the illusion of reality. The craft of intelligence in fiction, also, is the play of language, for it is the perceived relations which stay real.

In the *History of the Village of Goryukhino* (the Belkin estate), written soon after the stories by its "owner," Pushkin makes a bold, sarcastic attack on social and political unfairness. He attacks "reality" baldly in order to reform it. Pushkin's work on the *History* was cut short by the impossibility of getting it through tsarist censorship; for the work was openly abolitionist, a brilliant and perceptive satire, a forerunner of the satire of Saltykov-Shchedrin. We see how nonfictional it was meant to be by these four headings in the final section of the plan which Pushkin drew up before writing: "It was a rich, free countryside; cruelty impoverished it; it recovered from its austerity; it declined and fell from negligence." There is no release from reality in human actions. Fiction's agency is the enactment of freedom, whether a protest against bourgeois culture or the ultimate value.

In the summer of 1831 Pushkin read *The Red and the Black*, which he thought "a good novel, despite artificial rhetoric in several places and some comments in poor taste." Stendhal may be the first of the French realist novelists, the man among us whom we, as Harry Levin says, "fully conscious of socio-politico-economic circumstance," esteem as the beginner of historic realism, but Pushkin anticipated him. Pushkin again and again defended the freedom of his creative activity from what he called "petty and false theorizing." He scorned "the dull-witted rabble," from whom he affirmed his poet's independence, and he protested limitations imposed by the court, by "high society with its critical Aristarchuses." Many years before Gide said that "the homelands of the novel are the lands of individualism," Pushkin wrote: "No law can say, write only about these subjects and no others. Law does not interfere with the privacy of the individual, . . . and so law may not interfere with a writer's subject. . . ." The novelist, like any artist, must use tradition to invest himself in office, but the talent which transforms the perceptions of experience into meaningful knowledge of motive is not merely individual but at times so personal that, like the lyric poet's, it appears solipsistic.

Literary realism is distinguished from literary romanticism or neoclassicism or sentimentalism or naturalism in that it always comes *back* to the things of this world. Romanticism supposes that we are braver than we are; naturalism catalogues our failures. But the realist presumes that we operate on principles which sooner or later are manifest and, manifested, remain always present. If we trace Lermontov's literary biography, we are struck by its close parallel to Pushkin's, but if we look at his major prose work, we notice that he presumed as operative, principles other than those Pushkin presumed. He accepts the romantic pose but, so to speak, psychologizes it out of itself. He introduces a new kind of novel, the reality of which exists in the mind of the central figure who is also the narrator.

Two kinds of novels predominated in the 1830's: the historical novel (of which we have many "generalized" examples and of which such works as Pushkin's *The Negro of Peter the Great* and *The Captain's Daughter* are "particularized" examples) and the novel of contemporary manners. "Prose," said Pushkin, "is the language of ideas." Increased peasant uprisings in the 1830's and serious efforts among the intelligentsia and the educated upper class properly to understand Russian history in the light of new, western European ways of thinking lie behind Pushkin's *The History of Pugachev*. Lermontov's novel *Vadim* (1833–34) about the Pugachev Rebellion and his *Princess Ligovskaya* (1836) are pointedly topical. In 1841 he wrote a literalistic, psychological, antiromantic sketch called "The Man of the Caucasus," began a novel called *Shtoss*, and projected a trilogy covering three epochs of Russian life: the age of Catherine, the time of Alexander I, and the period of which he himself was a contemporary. Although the trilogy was never written, portions of *Vadim* indicate the sort of book Lermontov had in mind. The novel that dealt with an historical subject was to be equally a characterization of social life:

In the eighteenth century, the nobility, having lost its former power and the means of maintaining it, did not know how to change its pattern of behavior. This is one of the hidden reasons for the year of Pugachev [1774].

The characterization of the nobility's power actually bears more sharply on the 1830's.

In *Vadim*, the Pugachev uprising is only background. The issue, as seen by the novelist, is not one of social protest or economic circumstance but one of morality, of the individual's responsibility, obligation, commitment. Like Dubrovsky, Vadim becomes a leader of rebels out of a desire for personal revenge: "Yesterday a pauper, today a serf, tomorrow an unnoticed rebel in a drunk and bloody mob." His comrades admire in him "a kind of very great vice." Vadim is personification of the demonic; his sister, of the angelic. The historical problem of the 1770's has become the dialectics of good and evil of the 1830's.

Even the putatively historical novel has become more than an attempt to suggest the intimacy of history by the dramatic reality of fictional motives. History itself is regarded as an acting out of the moral substance of human will. In *The Karamazov Brothers* Dostoevsky calls the heart of man the battlefield in the war between God and the Devil. In *Vadim,* more than forty years earlier, Lermontov asked: "Didn't the angel and the demon come from the same source? . . . What *is* the greatest good and evil?—two ends of an invisible chain which come together the farther they move apart." In "Taman," for example, and in many places in his prose and verse, Lermontov sees the world literally in black and white, though he each time sets that view within an ethical vision of the world. "Only in man," said Lermontov, "can the sacred and the sinful unite."

What is the nature of the relationship between society and the individual if a man like Pechorin, with all the accoutrements of the romantic hero, is, basically, a starved and homeless moral waif? Unlike Onegin, he is energetic, he pursues adventure, he is highly and articulately self-conscious, and he keeps the diary which is his confession, the substance of the novel.

Pechorin's abuse of other people is torment of himself. Lermontov's vision includes Pechorin's view, but reconciliation is not possible: Pechorin, the most superfluous of the superfluous men, is alienated not by failures of love or of language or by an outré idealism. He cannot conceive a task for himself, in the sense that James has the novelist Dencombe, his projected self in "The Middle Years" (1893) say, as he lies dying, "We give what we have. Our doubt is our passion and our passion is our task. The rest is the madness of art."

Both James and Lermontov had difficulty in getting free of the protagonist, James more so than Lermontov. James's passion, equally a martyrdom to art, is greater than the task accomplished, but it is a passion which lies in a rhythm the task makes true. The form cages and releases the secret grandeur. If it fails, we have not James's success but Marcher's self-pitying final whump. If it succeeds, we have perception of glory, of the grandness of vitality even in what seems the most evil gesture. "Who will communicate my ideas to the world?" Lermontov asked. "Either myself, or God—or nobody."

Erwin Rhode, in his book on the Greek romances, said that the Greek novel, or anecdotal story, was predominantly "real," that the Greek romance was, as we know, extremely idealized. Clara Reeve's *Progress of Romance* (1785) concisely differentiates one genre from the other: "The Novel is a picture of real life and manners, and of the time in which it is written. The Romance, in lofty and elevated language, describes what never happened nor is likely to happen." Hawthorne, in the preface to *The House of the Seven Gables* (1851), said that a romance was a work in which the author laid "claim to a certain latitude both as to its fashion and its material," what, in short, we would now call a novel, though Hawthorne said that a novel was "presumed to aim at a very minute fidelity . . . to the probable and ordinary course of man's experience." A romance, on the contrary, had "fairly the right to present [the] truth [of the human heart] under circumstances, to a great extent, of the writer's own choosing or creation." These distinctions find confirmation in the notion, given in René Wellek and Austin Warren's *Theory of Literature* (1942), for example, that modern prose is descended from writing which emphasized detail and from writing which addressed itself to a higher reality. If regarded as more than an indication of classification within a genre, the distinction is no longer valid. We have learned from the Russians, more than from anyone else, that the supreme fictions are what is true.

B. M. Eikhenbaum has pointed out Lermontov's development as a writer of fiction from *Princess Ligovskaya,* a story of the conflict between Krasinsky, a poor official, and Pechorin, an officer in the Guards, a story with immediate social relevance, the first serious attempt in prose to take the romance of society manners beyond romance, to *A Hero of Our Time,* a story that emphasizes the psychological portrait of an age, leaning much on the criticism of Belinsky, on the prose of Gogol (*Evenings on a Farm Near Dikanka,* 1831, *Arabesques,* 1835) and on the prose and poetry of Pushkin (*Belkin's Tales, Eugene Onegin*).

In Russia in the 1830's, Eikhenbaum has pointed out, there developed the genre of narrative cycles, each ascribed to a single fictitious author. Pushkin pretends that Belkin wrote the Belkin stories. Lermontov pretends that most of *A Hero of Our Time* was written by Pechorin. But there is this difference: Pechorin is the one, central figure. In *A Hero of Our Time*; the narrator is the chief actor. We have, as James would note, an entirely different point of view. The story of adventure has been made a psychological novel (and, as such, subsequently continued to our day). Onegin in his novel is, for a while, Pushkin's friend; Lermontov scarcely meets Pechorin. Pechorin's diary, offered after we know that Pechorin is dead, is presented with a supposedly more literal naturalism than even the "ordinary" beginning of *Princess Ligovskaya.* Pechorin's purported self-revelation is the substance of the novel, which is technically constructed on the ancient, anecdotal pattern. If we think of the modern novel as a transformation by multiplication of the old, literalistic fable, we here find the concept of novel played back against its specifics, an effort to reduce narrative to the point that only alternatives crucial for the central figure will move the "plot." The plot lies not in any action in any one story but in the pattern of the author's understanding of the central figure independent of any one of the episodes which constitute his life. (The story of the hero's "whole life," the author says, is a "thick notebook" which "sometime later also will appear for the world to judge.")

If this be so, we, like the author, are immediately pulled up short by the problem of typicality and how to gauge it (for that is what we must do). Belinsky said that Pechorin closely resembled Onegin but that, unlike Onegin, he was self-conscious, anxious to live fully, and completely sincere (he adjusts events in order adequately to confess), and Chernyshevsky later used Pechorin to illustrate what he regarded as the presentation in literature of the dialectics of the soul. In the 1840's, conservative critics adjudged the novel political, a philosophical study of its time. In a letter dated June 24, 1840, Tsar Nicholas said that the book was "harmful" and filled with examples of the author's "great depravity." Lermontov wrote a preface to the second edition (1841), stating that he had drawn not a self-portrait but the portrait of an age. We now see how the story of a man became in the reality of fiction the tragedy of an age.

The book is thematically linked to Herzen's Who's to Blame (1846), to Turgenev's The Diary of a Superfluous Man (1850), and to the discussions in the philosophical and literary groups. But, interestingly, one of the first steps the author takes to establish the probability of his hero is to undercut his time. In Eugene Onegin, in Fathers and Children, in almost all the other books in which he appears, the superfluous man is not a do-nothing but a man who is morally alienated, who has lived out all the experience his society can offer. He has used up his society but cannot alter it or affect it or be reconciled to it. As a channel marker shows the limits of navigable water, so he shows the bounds of the extremes of social behavior. He does not represent his age. He moves against it, just as this book, through its irony, its use of aphorisms and reflections, and the title itself, is directed against its time:

Perhaps some readers will want to know my opinion of Pechorin's character. My answer is the title of this book. "But that's malicious irony!" they'll say. I'm not so sure.

Lydia Ginsburg has shown, in a study of Lermontov's prose and long poems, that irony functions specifically to unite the "poetic" and "nonpoetic" elements, to extend the possibilities for naturalistic description, to allow psychological analysis of character and examination of motive—in short, to serve as the basic principle of "realism."

The structure of Russian political life in the 1830's, serfdom and the failure of the 1825 Decembrist Revolt, made inconceivable any notion of an heroic self outside sociohistoric action. The idea of the individual determined his actions; his actions shaped social life. A man's motives were considered historical agents. "Pushkin's and Lermontov's heroes," said B. V. Tomashevsky, "are representatives of a new generation for whom the heroes of Constant and Chateaubriand seem as chronologically remote as Werther and his contemporaries were for Adolphe." In this sense, the hero of the book is a product of his time—not literally, for he is no average figure, but intellectually, an individual composed of traits which the age itself constrained the novelist to treat as typical. "It's time," wrote Alexander Herzen in 1838, "to drop the unfortunate, errant notion that art depends on the artist's personal taste or on chance." If motive is an agency of history, then history, obversely, defines individual character. Vadim, and especially Krasinsky, in the unfinished novel about Petersburg, are men prepared to engage in individualistic heroics, like the Count of Monte Cristo or d'Artagnan, but only in the context of social urgency. Svyatoslav Raevsky, one of the early Fourierists in Russia, discussed the book closely with Lermontov, but social analysis of the George Sand or George Eliot sort was not possible without the elaboration of a system of prose fiction which would include the concreteness of the individual and the immediacy, not the abstract meaning, of the moral problems about extreme, institutionalized inequality. Eikhenbaum has established beyond objection that

Lermontov made secondary those problems of form which worried poets of the older generation (chiefly problems of vocabulary and genre) and focused his attention on . . . heightening the expressive energy of verse. . . . Poetry took on the form of lyric monologue, each verse appeared freshly motivated—as an expression of spiritual and intellectual excitation, as a natural means of expression. . . . The classical period of Russian poetry had to be summed up and the transition to a new kind of prose prepared. History required this, and Lermontov did it.

The role of the hero in Lermontov's work, the theme of the "fallen angel" or of the "egoist–avenger," not only ties in closely with the French, English, German, American, and Russian literature of the early nineteenth century but chiefly, as D. E. Maksimov has brought out, depends on Lermontov's own poetic "structural difference."

In this period there came new understanding of Sterne's work—how (to cite the address to the reader in V. F. Odoevsky's "Princess Mimi," 1834) dramatizing the process of making real was more interesting than the drama of the supposedly real object—the stories and sketches of Bestuzhev-Marlinsky separating the man of the late 1830's from the man of the 1820's, but above all the belief that every individual was a microcosm, "the common, daily facts" of whose life, "hidden or patent to the eye, the acts of individual lives and their causes and principles" had the same "importance which historians have hitherto ascribed to the events of public national life," to quote Balzac's famous 1842 preface to *la Comédie Humaine*.

If man is not born evil, as Jean-Jacques would have it, he is not innately virtuous, either. Is moral perfection the work of nature or of society? . . . Is virtue the result of social circumstance? What is the role of rationality and of idea, that divine emanation, in this great alteration of being?

Balzac asks this question in "Robert l'oblige," a fragment of uncertain date from the group *Comptes Moraux*. Doing Scott over, so to speak, Balzac found the form for the novel of manners—a series of episodes, or nonnarrative sketches, strung together by a philosophico-narrative device—which the Russian novelists developed to an exceptional degree. Lermontov's innovation was the use of the author himself as the narrative device in an analysis of social morality.

A Hero of Our Time consists of six parts plus the preface written for the second edition. The final form of the book evolved over several years and—to the point—only with the evolution of the stories themselves. The preface by the author protests against the critics, especially Shevyrev, who called Pechorin immoral, depraved, a figure in a dream world made up by specious imitation of western European fiction. It emphasizes the actuality of the story, its applicability to an existing society.

"Bela," the first episode, opens with a sentence in which Lermontov announces he witnessed what he will write about:

"I was traveling by stagecoach from Tiflis." The story is a version of the age-old love affair between the sophisticated hero and the simple, rustic girl, a story of which "The Apple-Tree" is probably the best known modern English version. A version contemporary to us is Charles Jackson's "Rachel's Summer," in which the pure-in-heart girl kills herself not out of remorse over her lost love but out of the despair to which she has been reduced by false rumor and social ostracism. "Poor Liza" was a sentimental version widely read two generations before Lermontov. Characteristic of popular adventure stories of the road in the 1830's, "Bela" is a literary original in that it has three points of view. It is written by Lermontov as told by Maksim Maksimych about Pechorin. It uses the extreme romantic contrasts of quest versus satiety, of violence versus beauty:

She was unconscious. We tore her dress open and bound up the wound as tightly as possible. Pechorin vainly kept kissing her cold lips—nothing could bring her round.

but the story moves with the author's, the listener's, movement along the road from Tiflis toward Vladikavkaz. Lermontov pretends that he is only making "travel notes," not writing a tale, and that the order of presentation follows the chronology of the trip.

In the section called "Maksim Maksimych," Lermontov meets Pechorin, the Bela episode is completed, and Pechorin's diary is prepared for. Here the author is a disinterested observer—that "born observer" which Turgenev called himself —who describes Pechorin by appearance and gesture. Eikhenbaum says that Lermontov deleted from this description details in the manuscript which seemed psychological, for example, a discussion of Pechorin's "soul." The portrait which Lermontov says he must present to us describes Pechorin in terms of romantic concepts—"spiritual storms," "aristocratic hand," "casual gait," "nervous weakness," "feminine softness," "noble forehead"; of naturalistic sarcasm—"like a thirty-year-old Balzac coquette"; and of dramatic oppositions, visible contrasts in dark and light which, like chiaroscuro, give perspective to a representation on a flat surface: "blond, curly hair" versus "black mustache and eyebrows, the sign of thoroughbredness in a man, like a black mane and tail on a white horse."

The author's introduction to Pechorin's diary announces irony as a literary principle and asserts that psychological facts are the essential facts. A manuscript sentence indicating that Pechorin "had prepared his notes for publication" was deleted, conforming to the principle that the vitality of confession is its assertion of privacy: "What's wrong with Rousseau's *Confessions* is that he read it to his friends." Or else confession becomes the temptation, as Stavrogin indicates to Zossima in Dostoevsky's *The Devils* (1871–72), meretriciously to celebrate oneself by cataloguing one's deviations from, and therefore superiority to, conventional moral standards. Above all, the introduction emphasizes the physical difference between Pechorin and Lermontov, that the author of the diary is independent of the author of the book.

We are brought hard against this assertion by the first story in the diary. From biographical information we know that the events reported happened to Lermontov himself in 1837 in Taman in Tsaritsykha's house. M. I. Tseidler writes in his memoirs (1889) that in 1838:

It turned out that I was to stay in the same little house that he had; the very same blind boy and mysterious Tartar were the subject of his story. I even remember that when I, having come back, was telling about it all in a group of friends, about my passion for the girl, Lermontov took a pen and on a piece of paper sketched the craggy shore and the house I was talking about.

Reading Lermontov's prose, we perceive, also, how his style has shaped a portrait, an episode, that leads toward delimitation of the reality of character and toward definition of the cognitive function of the novel. We move from the portrait of the harbor:

The moon shone gently on the restive world around, submissive to its power, and in its light I could make out, far off shore, two ships whose black rigging, like a spiderweb, was silhouetted motionlessly against the pale outline of the horizon.

to inquiry into social ethics:

I became very sad. And why had it been my fate to be tossed into the peaceful circle of honest smugglers? Like a stone thrown into a smooth-surfaced spring, I upset their calmness, and like a stone I myself almost went to the bottom!

By its language, the episode binds facts to their value. It pulls prose and verse together. Chekhov thought the story a model of prose:

I don't know a use of language better than Lermontov's. Here's what I would do: take his story and analyze it, the way they analyze stories in school, by sentences, by phrases, by clauses. That way one would learn how to write.

In a letter to Polonsky he said that Russian poets write beautiful prose: "Lermontov's *Taman* and Pushkin's *The Captain's Daughter*, not to mention the prose of other poets, at once prove the close kinship between sapid Russian verse and graceful prose." Lermontov has forced an episode from private life to yield its own and public meaning.

The biographical aspects of "Princess Mary" tend to overshadow disinterested interpretation, for Grushnitsky may be, some people say, less a portrait of Kolyubakhin than of Martynov, who shot and killed Lermontov in a duel in July, 1841. Although written as a diary, a large portion of the story is a revision and continuation of Vera Ligovskaya's episode central to her story *Princess Ligovskaya.*

In "The Fatalist," Pechorin takes on the function of narrator. Or we may say that Lermontov becomes commentator on projection into the future of incidents from his own life. The story, obviously much like Pushkin's "The Shot," is interrupted in the middle by Pechorin's reflection on us "the pitiful descendants," ideas which Eikhenbaum has shown to be a prose version of Lermontov's poem "Thought," which begins:

I sadly look upon our generation. . . .

Pechorin's monologue is in direct opposition to the cliché image of the gay young officer, suggests even that the notebook telling about Pechorin's entire life was, as Eikhenbaum asserts, unpublishable for political reasons. Lermontov, through Pechorin, has raised political opposition and moral skepticism to philosophical principle:

I like to doubt everything: this tendency has nothing to do with being determined; on the contrary, as far as I'm concerned, I've always gone ahead more boldly when I haven't known what lay ahead for me. After all, death is the worst thing that can happen—and you can't avoid it sometime!

If we number the stories as presented: preface 123456, we find that chronology has been rearranged: preface 451623. The stories are arranged consequentially according to the author's acquaintance with the hero. They move from Lermontov-the-author's eyewitness statement about traveling in the Caucasus to Pechorin-the-author's moral judgment. They complicate, by inversion, what we presume to be the usual relation of character to time. By making the hero of the novel the author, the narrator, the observer, and supposedly the only reader, Lermontov has constructed the illusion that the time of narration is identical with the chronology of the hero. By presenting the two times as one, he has tried to gull the other readers, you and me, into thinking that nothing is "fiction."

Consequently, the hero tends to impose himself on the author. And critics have commonly asserted that yes, the author and the hero are one man (where do you draw the line separating them?), that the book is autobiographical. Actually, the announcement of Pechorin's death, the introduction to the diary, the digressions in the several episodes, the preface to the second edition, the commentary and the irony—all point up that the author wishes to get free of the hero. He wants the hero to stand free of him just as he himself wants to be free of the past, to come to judgment, to be *beyond* his hero.

In a sociohistorical context, Pechorin is for Lermontov a sort of ego-ideal, an "ideal" which Lermontov, as author, wants to transcend. Pechorin is an ideal which depends not on historical fidelity or romantic literary tradition or on "typicality" so much as on the author's inventiveness, the literary skill with which he expresses his psychological examination of himself. Expression of this psychological content is the description, by incident, of a real hero, regardless of time.

The book is a series of prose stories, or *novelle*, rearranged out of chronological sequence in order to express motivational consequences of the actions of a single figure. His actions make a pattern. The pattern expresses the rhythm of his mind. He is a figure who symbolizes an entire age in his mind.

A diary is a double instrument. It is a chronicle both of

events and of a mind. It is both a confessional and a mock confessional. It must be kept either private or ironic. It must proceed from history and lean toward morality without invading or violating the province of either. Tied to the act, compelled by judgment, it must be its author's dramatization of a self beyond our history and our morality. To be successful, it must be precisely what we have here: incident, or episode, multiplied into a sociopsychological novel, that real stage in our imagination where our acts are a perfect drama.

Dead
Souls

Literature lives in its rhythm, in the satisfaction of the repetitions and variations of pattern. "Rhythm," said Ezra Pound, "is a form cut into TIME, as a design is determined SPACE." A. A. Fet, nineteenth-century Russian poet, said that "a poem and its rhythm are connected by internal necessity." He was aware of the self-generative powers of the imagination, that the work of words is to call into being the significance of what we experience. Goncharov said that literature is language in which a country expresses all it knows. For he knew that a writer's social function proceeds from his writing, not from his role as prophet or debater.

Earlier, in 1846, Belinsky had written that "Russian nationalness is not yet adequately developed or worked out for a Russian poet to be able to put its clear stamp on his work as a way of expressing ideas common to all mankind." Belinsky's point of view of the efficacy of "nationalness" is narrow, for Russian poets had long been "putting their stamp" on language as expression of common ideas. But, more importantly, Belinsky reversed the terms of the relation that a writer's social function follows from his function as a writer. At a given time, of course, the aptness of a writer's social and political attitude will in large measure determine his popularity, but in the long run his skill defines his function.

Gogol was not a politically "left" intellectual urging a program of reform. He came from an upper-class, well-off but not wealthy, Ukrainian landowning family. His father wrote plays for amateur production; his somewhat insane mother doted on him, even attributing to him the invention of steamships and the laying of railroads. Gogol's first extensive literary work, written when he was eighteen but published in St. Petersburg two years later in 1829, is a long poem entitled *Hans Kyukhelgarten. An Idyl in Scenes. By V. Alov*. Not long after having arrived in the capital to make his literary way in the world, Gogol printed his poem and distributed it to booksellers on a commission basis. Reviews were universally negative, if not hostile. The failure of the poem drove Gogol, fanatically determined to become a success, to try some other kind of writing which would succeed. As Vasily Gippius has pointed out, local-color, "folk" tales were then in vogue; there was a lack of "authentic" Ukrainian material; so, Gogol set out to manufacture it. He himself did not know the material. He borrowed liberally from Markovich's *Notes on the Ukraine* (1798) and Kulzhinsky's *The Ukrainian Countryside* (1828), a book which a reviewer said "depicted Ukrainians as Florian's Spanish and French shepherds." Gogol even asked his mother to send him Ukrainian objects from home and to explain dialect words and folk customs. He knew the literary theories and attitudes that prevailed in the capital—that the artist was above nature and that his work was different from it—and he knew the work of the writers then admired, from Zhukovsky to Irving, but he did not know the world which he was describing in his own fiction. Just as *The Inspector-General* has, in one sense, its sources in a suggestion by Pushkin, in Kvitka's play *The Newcomer from the Capital* (1827; 1840), in Weltmann's story "Provincial Actors" (1835), and in the prevailing tradition of the time, so *Dead Souls* derives from a plot for a gallery of characters proposed by Pushkin and from all the Russian and western European fiction of the road which Gogol had read. In short, he invented a world in his fancy, a world of the horrible, the absurd, the demonic, the farcical, which seemed to everybody else so much the only real world that, for example, the first English translation of *Dead Souls* was subtitled: "or Home Life in Old Russia."

Gogol is the most difficult of the great nineteenth-century Russian novelists. Many of his words are Ukrainianisms or neologisms, special distortions to fabricate impressions. A reader regularly feels tangled in adjectives, aphorisms, and Homeric similes which seem to carry him forward but which at the same time hold him still. Hard put to tell a progression from a digression, the reader is left bemused. On the other hand, if cut out from the novel and examined separately, the scenes, like stereopticon pictures, seem silly.

Gogol feared the trivial and the mediocre. He did not wish his work "reduced" to plot, and he would not wish it "read to the life." What we may say he understood he gave in the transformation of trivial typicality into essential example by carefully and consciously manipulated literary devices. Gogol's success lies in his style, in the complexity common to much late eighteenth-century and early nineteenth-century writing. Further, the romantic attitude that expressed itself in a quest for artistic freedom and that had as its corollary an attitude of social criticism politically expressed in reform movements and the events of 1830 and 1848, was artistically expressed in efforts to find a style that would assert the new social function of the novel.

Evenings on a Farm Near Dikanka, the collection of stories based on Ukrainian and on demoniacal, romantic motifs (the devil of folk narrative identified with the romantic principle of universal evil) which Gogol concocted, appeared in 1831–32. *Mirgorod* and *Arabesques* came out in 1835; "The Carriage" and "The Nose" in 1836. Gogol had created a new genre.

He may be said to have faced the world of the eighteenth century. He saw the decorum of the old world and the vegetable life of even its most powerful supporters, the shapelessness of its language and emotions, and those particular pretensions which he, like a devil, could fasten on to, use to destroy the old world's image and to resurrect himself, kinglike, on top of a symmetrical world of his own imagining. Nothing was for him so fascinating as the real or romantic horrors (figures like those in Hoffmann's stories or in Gothic tales) which presaged immortality for the clever man. Deviation was a delight; destruction, a pleasure. Both were possible because he tacitly accepted the basic order of things and of society—later, even homiletically advocated it.

In Russian the word *povest* had been used to refer to historical narrative (*The Tale of Bygone Years*, fourteenth–sixteenth centuries) and, in the seventeenth and eighteenth centuries, to exotic, allegorical narrative with an adjective to qualify the narrative's source, place, or nature: *The Coveters, an Eastern Tale* (1755), or the translation of Voltaire's *Mikromegas, a Philosophic Tale* (1756). The idea of the novel (*roman*) developed in Russia at the same time as in the rest of Europe, partly as modification of the "true-life" adventure tale (*Frol Skobeyev*) and, especially, as extension of the characteristics of the old Greek romances. Fonvizin, who in 1762 translated into Russian the first part of Abbé Terrasson's *Heroic Virtue, or the Life of Sief, King of Egypt* (1731), added a preface:

There is no doubt whatever that this book is not a novel. The events, which have the endings desired, and the important personages who, completely in despair of ever seeing each other again, meet, and the great amount of talking that goes on among them—all show that the Author did not always have a true story [spravedlivaya istoriya] *in mind but proceeded as his own ideas dictated.*

By the early nineteenth century difference in genre had become sharper and more restrictive. An analysis of the *povest* and of the *skazka* published in the magazine *The Patriot* in 1804 defined the essence of the *skazka*, the sentimental story:

To present the contradictions in one's conflict with oneself; to expose the secrets of the heart, to bring out the action of passions more intense in our time than ever before; to express by example the play of fate and the power of prejudices; finally, with the aid of concealed edification, to bring prejudice and passion, nature and society, into harmony—that is the main job of the Writer of Tales; that is the sense in which the tales themselves may be considered a school of morals and the tellers of tales teachers of mankind.

Stories of this sort had been widely popularized by the work of Florian, Marmontel, Karamzin, Guichard—work celebrating common sentiments regardless of what any of the heroes did. "The fundamental difference between a Tale and an Epic Poem," said Ostolopov in *The St. Petersburg Herald* in 1812, "is that the latter describes great deeds but the tale has as its subject a less important action, and," he added, "the action of an heroic poem is true, but in the tale it is not supposed to be true (*fabula, ficta, narratio*), not to be taken as if it were, for then it would be not a tale but a history. A tale," he declared, "can only imitate things that have actually taken place and then with names changed." The basic difference between a tale and a novel, he said, lay in elements of plot: "a novel is a binding together of several events; a tale has but one." Gogol later objected that a novel, as the term had come down from the eighteenth century, was unsatisfactorily limited by the fact that everything in it was "too much tied to the fate of the hero." Pushkin made little distinction between *povest* and *rasskaz* (short story), both with regard to his own work ("The Prisoner of the Caucasus," "Count Nulin") and with regard to others': Gogol used the term *povesti* for his *Evenings on a Farm Near Dikanka*; in a review, Pushkin highly praised the *rasskazy*. The patently fantastic *skazki*, such as "May Night" and "The Night Before Christmas," Gogol called *povesti* in order to emphasize their "realistic" side, for by the 1830's *povest* had come to designate some kind of story dealing with actual life. Belinsky said that the new meaning of the word, like the new sort of story itself, had pushed out the old. The critic Shevyrev, a conservative, writing in *The Reading Library* in 1834, said it was a "hateful form" which had succeeded because of "commercial considerations," that is, it reflected the rise of a bourgeois-like social class. Belinsky said the form was a hedgehog, but in 1846 Gogol defined it:

A *story* [povest] *takes as its subject events that really have happened or could happen to any person, events for some reason noteworthy in psychological terms, sometimes even without any intent to edify but only to focus the attention of a thinking man or of an observer. . . . A story can even be completely poetic and be called a long poem* [poema]. *. . . Sometimes even the event itself is not worth attention and is taken only to portray some separate picture, a living, characteristic, conventional feature of the age, place, and manners, but sometimes of the poet's own imagination.*

In 1836, Herzen had asked in a letter, "Can the form of narrative include science, caricature, philosophy, religion, real life, mysticism?" Herzen believed that a writer's view of the world determined his literary style. In a review in *The Contemporary* in 1836, Gogol said that new Russian literary forms would predominate over western European standards because "the environment, including the new literary forms, is so colossal and the frame for the picture has been made enormous." More than Pavlov in *Three Stories* (1835) or Ushakov in *The Veteran's Leisure* (dedicated to Gogol), like Pushkin or, later, Lermontov, Gogol tried from the first to find a method that would lead to a system of narrative, that would establish a scheme of stories. Combining types, literary styles, social and political commentary, lyric interruptions and other devices, Gogol's prose emphasized the analytic side. He involved many levels of response to define one reality. For Gogol, the office of art was not to reproduce what we have seen but to make us see what we have not. Like other nineteenth-century prose writers, he wished to "reveal" reality, but he was more concerned with the immediate, the traditional, the perceptible, the fanciful, than with internal machinations. Characters in his work seem objects of general study or of generalized significance (hence, static) made plausible by minute examination of the particulars of appearance. The stage that is the story moves, and the character, standing still, is passed through it. From the stories comes the novel.

In the early 1920's I. D. Ermakov, much influenced by Freud, published several psychological studies of Russian authors, Gogol among them. Citing Pushkin's reference to Gogol's being "melancholic," Ermakov defined Gogol as a "cyclical psychotic," at times extravagantly elated, at times maniacally depressed. As Gogol fictively ennobled his genealogy for himself, Ermakov said, so he made up an unreal world into which to escape:

He was concerned with saving his own soul and he morally became ever more closed in, since his chief task was to create and, above all, to perfect his very own self.

To be sure, Gogol became ever more convinced that, far from being the unsuccessful author recently arrived in the capital, he had been ordained by God to perform a great mission. *Dead Souls* became for him a special work, and he composed a prayer in which he regularly beseeched God for strength to complete his task "for my own salvation." Ermakov found confirmation of the fact that Gogol drew all the characteristics of his actors exclusively from within himself—from his excessive need to confess—in the adduction in Part II of entirely fantastic elements along with the banal, the trivial, the selfish, the mean, and the ugly—characteristics which Gogol had derived all his life from morbid introspection. One can readily make patterns, as Ermakov does, of the psychotically sexual imagery in Gogol's work, especially of phallic imagery suggesting a scared, narcissistic homosexuality, but it is doubtful that such patterns contribute successfully to literary judgments. "Gogol's constant characteristic was insecurity," said Ermakov. "He spent his whole life defending himself from whatever he felt exposed his weakness." His great delight, said Ermakov, was self-revelation. "The central hero of *Dead Souls*, Chichikov, is above all Gogol himself." *Dead Souls* was Gogol's *Inferno* (Annenkov, in his *Memoirs*, said that Gogol had closely studied *The Divine Comedy*). But, Ermakov sums up, none of the details of Gogol's illness and none of the failures in his private life can dim "Gogol's real, sincere, stubborn struggle for self-definition, both personal and, subsequently, national."

More recently, in his *Theory of Literature*, L. Timofeyev, expressing a modish, contemporary view, said that *Dead Souls* was written to expose the inadequacies of the landowning class, to demonstrate the good qualities of the Russian people, and to correct the vices of the time. This view reiterates in our day the evaluation of Gogol in the 1840's, when Belinsky and others canonized Gogol as a "realistic writer," the head of the "naturalist school," a canonization which Gogol considered a misunderstanding. Precisely at that time, especially during his 1836–41 residence in Rome, Gogol was becoming increasingly mystical and messianic. The freely comic and the grotesque, which others then considered elements of social satire, Gogol labeled "foolishness," and he wrote of his duty to serve the state. The digressions in *Dead Souls*, various in themselves and introduced out of various psychological reasons with various literary effects, were introduced, according to Timofeyev, to present the positive, ideal side of life. *Dead Souls*, he said, remains a paragon of edification. The lyrical digressions, Victor Shklovsky commented even more recently, were added to Chichikov's story to give a complete picture of the force of Russia.

More importantly, Shklovsky referred again to one of the central facts of literary history which *Dead Souls* exemplifies. The novel represents "a new content fighting with an old form," as, in their own way, do *Don Quixote* and *Tom Jones*. Gogol himself, in an article in 1840, had cited *Don Quixote* and *Orlando Furioso* as prototypes of edifying poems of epic stature, of precisely the sort of poem he meant *Dead Souls* to be. The alienation of the artist was to be overcome by the skill with which he carried on a long literary tradition. Said Gogol:

Schooled by loneliness, by a harsh, internal life, the artist doesn't have the habit of looking at both sides when he is writing but only involuntarily from time to time casts a glance at the portraits on the wall in front of him—Shakespeare, Ariosto, Fielding, Cervantes, Pushkin—who reflected nature as it is and not as somebody feels it ought to be.

The distinctive features of Gogol's kind of narrative, influenced by but far more complicated than the *Kunstnovellen* of the 1830's, such as V. F. Odoevsky's *Tales*, include lyric digressions apostrophizing the power of nature, the power of the artist, the power of music as expression of the heart of the people, as the purgative of the world (the morality of true art), and, beyond the concept of Pure Femininity held by Venevitinov, Galich, and other romantics, as pure form, as the source of form itself; from the crowd singling out as heroes semifabulous figures of no distinction except what is attributed to them by the author's style, the "underdogs"; a humor based on possible, instantaneous inversion into sorrow, the "comedy of tears" or what Belinsky said was one of Gogol's great successes, "drawing the poetry of life out of the prose of life"; a free, self-celebrating lyrism and its obverse, satire, the imposition of one's personal emotions on an improbable plot that does seem true, an attack by the dissatisfied self on what it construes as the spurious satiety of the world.

Gogol knew Sterne's work as well as Fielding's. Both *Tristram Shandy* and *A Sentimental Journey* had been translated into European languages shortly after their original publication. Radishchev read Sterne's *Journey* in German and said that the idea for the form of his *Journey* had come directly from Sterne. By 1800 both of Sterne's books had been translated into Russian. Sterne's popularity in Russia increased in the early part of the century following the publication in Moscow in 1801 of a book called *The Beauties of Sterne, or a Collection of His Best Pathetic Tales and Most Excellent Comments on Life*. A whole set of imitations followed, culminating in Shakhovskoy's comedy satirizing sentimentalism, *The New Sterne*. Sentimentalism, that classical romanticism with which the eighteenth century ended and the nineteenth began, most readily characterized by the work of Karamzin, had appropriated but distorted Sterne's attitude. Karamzin's *Letters of a Russian Traveler* are filled with references to and quotations from Sterne's books. In July, 1789, Karamzin's response to the seizure of the Bastille was to quote Trim's phrase from Sterne: "Nothing can be so sweet as liberty." His literary method he sometimes defended by appealing to Sterne as paragon; at other times, he set up his method as appealing, he said, like Sterne's, only "to those *sensitive souls* who have this sweet faith [in sympathy]."

Karamzin knew, as he noted in one of his *Letters*, that Sterne had learned much from Rabelais. Karamzin himself was not able to play the Janus-headed game that both Rabelais and Sterne played, nor did he see what Sterne had learned from Montaigne and Locke. However, he was never worried about Sterne's manners, as Thackeray was. He took Sterne at face value: an emotion being equivalent to its expression, the most pathetic expression (especially if with quotations from classical authors) provokes the deepest sorrow, which is to be relieved, if relieved at all, by gracefulness. The emotions in Karamzin's *Poor Liza*, for example, are poses based on an attitude of "refined" pity.

In the nineteenth century, sentimentalism in Russia declined. There developed the stories of exotic and romantic adventure that used realistic details from Gypsy or Cossack life and, also, the socially significant anecdotes and character sketches. Like Pushkin, of whose circle he was a member, Gogol picked up the half of Sterne which Karamzin had left out: the humor, the common sense, the literary gamesmanship itself, the half to which Sterne referred in a letter in 1760 when he wrote, "Reason and common sense tell me, that if the characters of past ages and men are to be drawn at all, they are to be drawn like themselves." Certain elements of style in Pushkin's *Eugene Onegin* come clearly from a reading of Sterne's *Tristram Shandy*, in particular, the use of digression to satirize and to parody the very story from which the digression is made. In *Dead Souls* and in Sterne's *A Sentimental Journey* one of the chief functions of digression is to retard and to complicate the action so that a digression itself becomes the movement of the story and a story in itself, but deliberately never complete, moving constantly and credibly from the apparently real to the apparently fantastical, each side of the mirror mocking the other.

Karamzin was a credulous sentimentalist. Radishchev's *Journey from Petersburg to Moscow*, although built up out of separate and generalized impressions assigned to sequential stops en route, is actually hung together by the author's central moral—pressing need for social reform. A. F. Weltmann's *The Wanderer* (1831–32) was the work that first marked a return to exploitation of literary methods themselves, a romantic *and* humorous book with a mixture of literary forms and a pile of "irrelevant" digressions from the thread of the story. Pushkin's "Journey to Arzrum" is an interesting and important extension of the possibilities of the device. It begins with an introduction citing an article in a French journal which lists Pushkin among the celebrants of the Russian victory at Arzrum, a citation to which Pushkin adds a couple of acerbic remarks on inspiration. The "Journey" includes quotations in several languages, digressions, political comments, descriptions—all hinged on the central, particular personality of Pushkin himself as a poet, that is, on himself in his literary role. The descriptions are self-contained fragments, but they are not presented as if they were Pushkin's emotional discoveries. Rather, they are offered as aspects of the total attitude of the poet–observer, who establishes the relationships among all the parts (a striking similarity, Yury Tynyanov showed, between Pushkin's style and Tolstoy's). The poet's understanding of the ironic and contradictory aspects of his position, both in relation to his original material and in relation to his literary work, is what moves the "Journey." The poet is, in and by his work, the center of his time.

In Gogol's work, the device of exploitation of method is the key to meaning, as imaginative critics from Andrei Bely to Vladimir Nabokov have strongly, sometimes tendentiously, argued. Connections among things are explicable (unlike a story of the supernatural, in which one basic connection is not), but the plan into which they fit is an enormous device designed to deceive a credulous sentimentalist like Karamzin or Radishchev and to mock a reader who, like Veselovsky, thinks that the digression interrupts the action (the moral becomes obfuscated). In Gogol's work, as in Sterne's, the narrative of action proceeds by means of digressions. One of the difficulties in reading him is our own natural credulousness. Gogol considered the unthinking imposition of conventional standards an erosion of life. "We have a marvelous gift," he wrote, "for making everything paltry." It seems that what he wanted to say is only implied, and that if we are to understand him we must understand simultaneously the extremes of sentimentalism and mockery commingled in his book. The emotional excesses which Gogol deliberately indulged are themselves small parts of a greater literary game.

The habitual motive behind the novel of the road or the novel of adventure—the quest for pure love or love episodes themselves—is entirely eliminated from *Dead Souls* except in parody. In Chapter IX, the morning after Nozdrev has "exposed" Chichikov's plot of buying dead souls, two ladies discuss the situation:

> *"Dead souls," said the lady, in every sense comely.*
> *"What? What?" her guest burst out, all upset.*
> *"Dead souls!"*
> *"Oh, heavens, tell me all!"*

"It's simply something concocted as a cover-up, for, really, the thing is he wants to elope with the Governor's daughter."

What we, unlike the characters, know is the *literary* terms by which to evaluate all fakes.

Gogol set up his literary traps with precision but was enraged if the reader got caught. To deceive a reader confirmed his own power, but the lack of understanding denied him a rightness and a righteousness that were the goal of his personal quest. Gogol intended *The Inspector General*, the end of which is its beginning, as a critique of the society he himself could not do without. That critics of the play's première called it "a coarse farce" Gogol considered an insult.

His famous apostrophe to the Russian language in *Dead Souls* declares the lyric *power* of writing. The power is exhibited, also, in the beginning of the tenth chapter of his story "Terrible Vengeance," a formally lyric apostrophe to the Dnepr River. The methods of literature had come to determine the writer's world view. Consciousness of the game is the first step toward the reality revealed in the method. On the other hand, unlike the sentimentalist, who either defines a reader's responses, usually by "classical" rules, or nakedly offers his own emotional or political program, the mock sentimentalist, Gogol, offers the definition or the program but then suddenly alienates himself and the reader from both by complicating the form or the perception. This is Sterne's game with the "graphs" of his plots or the blank page for the reader to write in his own description of the "indescribable" beauty, Widow Wadman. This is Gogol's game from the first page of *Dead Souls*, in which the hero enters "parked" in a rolling carriage and two workmen talk about its wheels, round as zero.

The kinds of digression are numerous. There are digressions of reminiscence both personal (childhood, youth, and school) and projected (apocalyptic, a projection of the past into the future). There are moral judgments, moral predictions, forecasts of judgments on man to come. There are stories and anecdotes within stories and anecdotes, descriptions within descriptions, and hoaxes within the hoax that the book is. (In Sterne's *The Life and Opinions of Tristram Shandy* the "life" of the hero is almost completely left out.) The demonology of the early Ukrainian tales has given way to the grotesquerie of the national novel. *Dead Souls* is about a nondescript man traveling from one absurd character to another to buy the souls of dead people. Connections are made by simile and metaphor, by parallel constructions and dependent clauses, by the author's intrusions to "explain" a point, and by appositional constructions which actually lead off in a fresh direction. There is whim, fancy, poetry, and satire. Yet over all we sense a serious morality and can ask if Chichikov is traveling among the damned in Hell or if he is himself the Devil.

Strictly speaking, *Dead Souls* is not a picaresque novel, for the "hero" does not climb the social ladder. Indeed, the hero's alienation from and opposition to society so closely parallels, by inverse definition, what society supports (Korobochka is willing to sell honey or hemp but not dead souls, "it was such a new thing, so unheard of") that society is exposed as a collection of fools. What holds society together, uniting the characters in this novel, is an invisible thread, Chichikov's buying from everyone the something that is nothing. Nozdrev's talkativeness arouses suspicion, and the denouement follows, including, however, "The Tale of Captain Kopeikin." In fact, the denouement is an exposition of Chichikov's character, starting with his flu and the camphor treatment. The exposition contrasts sharply with the sketch of him on the opening page and with Chichikov's self-announced nobility and his acceptance in the world of the serf-sellers. The denouement leads to Chichikov's history at the *end* of the novel (Part I) and to a pathetically mock-serious exclamation by the author on the necessity of "telling the sacred truth." The author refers to whatever we might call Chichikov's future resurrection, says that "there are two large parts still to come," suggesting the transformation of Chichikov in Christian terms by bringing his acts to completion; in political terms, "other nations and sovereign states will yield" to triumphant, onrushing Russia. But the image for such perfection is an inverse parody of Napoleon. Chichikov, who is literally nobody, is said to resemble Napoleon. From under the costume of false pretense by a false act comes true faith. The method of narrating the improbable reveals the belief behind it and makes it real:

Out of the many, in their own way, keen suppositions there was, indeed, one, rather odd when you come right down to it, that maybe Chichikov was Napoleon in disguise, that the Englishman had had his eye on Russia for a long time, Russia's so big and mighty, he says, and there had even been several political cartoons showing the Russian talking to the Englishman. The Englishman's standing and holding a dog on a leash behind him, and of course the dog stands for Napoleon. Just look, now, he says, and if you don't think it's so, I'll set this dog on you! And so now, maybe, they've let him out of St. Helena and here he is, making his way into Russia, as if he were Chichikov, but actually it's not Chichikov at all.

Of course, the officials were not about to believe this, but then they gave it some thought, and, each man having thought it over for himself, they found that Chichikov's face, when he would turn and stand sideways in profile, was very much like Napoleon's portrait. The Police Chief, who had been in the

Campaign of '12 and had personally seen Napoleon, couldn't help admitting that he wouldn't be any taller than Chichikov at all, certainly, and then, too, you couldn't say that Napoleon was especially fat, though not actually so thin, either. Perhaps some readers will call all this improbable; to please them, the author, too, is ready to call it all improbable; but, as ill-luck would have it, it all happened exactly as told here, and it's the more amazing because the town wasn't in some remote place but, on the contrary, not far from the two capitals.

The title of the novel is a double pun. (The censor imposed the phrase "Chichikov's Journey.") It refers to the serfs who had died since the previous census, but it is, as Koshkarev announces (Part II, Chapter III), a contradiction in terms:

"1. *The very request of Collegiate Counselor and Chevalier Pavel Ivanovich Chichikov contains a misunderstanding, for by an oversight the souls on the list have been called dead. . . . Indeed, such an appellation itself shows an empirical study of science most likely limited to the parish school, for the soul is immortal.*

"The cheat!" *said Koshkarev in self-satisfaction, pausing.* "He caught you there a bit. But admit he's got a ready pen."

On the other hand, the novel is not about those souls at all but about their owners, the souls that are indeed dead, those who, in Dante's sense, never were alive. Their perversions of human values are the substance of the book, a new kind of *Odyssey*, an *Inferno* brought to life by fiction in a physical, not a spiritual, world.

Gogol subtitled his book "a long poem," and in the first paragraph of Chapter II he calls it both a "tale" and a "long poem." Differently than in his early stories but still using folklore elements and mock eighteenth-century rhetoric, he here establishes a new style by parodying an old. In Chapter VII, for example, the romantic ideal of feminine beauty is posited but then subverted by Chichikov's game, revealing both the pettiness of Manilov and his wife and the authenticity of the idealization of that other beauty in which Gogol himself believed. (From Gogol's letters, we know that actually he found pleasing only those pages which had wide, even margins and careful lettering.)

"Aha!" He unfolded it right away, ran his eyes over it, and was astonished at the neatness and beautifulness of the handwriting. "Wonderfully written," he said, "no need even to copy it. And what a lovely little border around it! Who was it made a little border so skillfully?"

"Oh, don't ask now," said Manilov.

"You?"

"My wife."

"Oh, Lord! I'm really sorry I've caused such inconvenience."

Earlier in the novel, in a long digression in Chapter II on Selifan, Petrushka, and literary style, Gogol described reading for Petrushka in comic terms actually analogous to writing for himself:

What he liked was not what he read but, rather, the reading itself, or, one should say, the process of reading itself, the fact that, see, there was always some word or other coming out of the letters, which another time meant God only knows what.

This is emblematic of the novel as a whole, of the method by which Chichikov specifies his name and title on the piece of paper for police registration, by which the town is "described" in question-and-answer between Chichikov and the waiter in the inn, and by the round of visits Chichikov makes the next day to the Governor and the local hierarchy—by which, finally, that whole world is inverted. In the famous Homeric simile, setting out a seemingly vast space for the actors and a long distance between the author and them, of the tail-coated gentlemen around the ladies at the ball and the black flies around a loaf of sugar, the gentlemen and the flies reverse. The exaggeration is both gross and particular. What is real is shrunk; what is unreal is exaggerated; connected by "free" association, the two exchange places. The "story" is then ostensibly carried forward in a digression in which nothing actually happens, unwinding from among Chichikov's thoughts as he watches the Governor's ball. Often Gogol proceeds from an image of sound to an image of sight to a metaphor, as the whole novel proceeds from the image of the round wheels of the barouche bringing Chichikov into the story to the final metaphor of Russia, the troika, galloping into the glory of the future.

The visit to Manilovka in Chapter II involves, to the point of self-conscious, meaningful ridiculousness, an old device, of which notably Sterne was fond: digression to convince the reader that the time of narration and the time of action are identical, that the story is happening, literally, before his very eyes:

. . . *and Manilov led his guest off to the room. Although the time they will be going through the hall, the front room, and the dining room is rather short, we'll try, nevertheless, to see if we can't take some advantage of it and tell something about the master of the house.*

There follows not a characterization of Manilov, the master of the house—"only God could say what he was like"—but a partisan digression on characterization itself, in which Gogol attacks the romantic concept of idealized heroes and defends the "terrible difficulty" of his own work, delineating the characteristics of "the many ladies and gentlemen in the world who look very much alike." The passage culminates in the aphorism, "Everyone has his pet like." In the first version, Gogol's "Everyone has his own hobbyhorse" was close to Sterne's hobbyhorse, "an *any thing* which a man makes a shift to get astride on, to canter it away from the care and solicitudes of life." The concept, a modification of the old idea of "humor," resembles Pushkin's

> *Everyone has one desire,*
> *The thing he likes to do the best.*

in *Eugene Onegin*. In *Dead Souls*, however, the idea once stated is soon inverted: "In short, everyone has his own special way, but Manilov did not." Constant use of diminutives and of passive constructions shrinks the pretenses of these people and enlarges Gogol's own frame of reference to a vast, rational, comic understanding:

His wife . . . by the way, they were completely satisfied with each other. Although more than eight years of married life had passed by, each of them still always brought the other either a little slice of apple or a little piece of candy or a little nut and would say in an endearingly tender voice expressing perfect love: "Open your little mouth, sweetie, and I'll give you this little bite." Needless to say, the little mouth would open on such an occasion very elegantly. . . . And very often, sitting on the sofa, the one of them, suddenly, for absolutely no clear reason, putting down his pipe and the other her needlework, if at that moment she happened to be holding it in her hands, they would give each other such a long and languid kiss that in the course of it a person could have smoked a whole little cigar.

Femistoklyus's recitation is, like Mitrofan's in *The Minor*, a take-off on cultural ignorance. After the little boy has answered the inane questions and replied "yes" to his father's inquiry, does he want to be an ambassador, the servant wipes a big blob of snot from his nose, thereby keeping it out of the soup. This is sheer comedy, ancient, imitative, and for us plain fun.

The fun quickly turns serious. This first foray of Chichikov's has made us sympathetic to him, for he has successfully beguiled Manilov. In fact, Manilov is so overcome with delight that he symbolically inverts the social order, addressing the coachman incorrectly, and directs Chichikov (and us) into the next adventure, the next chapter:

> "But do you know the way to Sobakevich's?"
> "I was going to ask you."
> "If you like, I'll explain it to your coachman right now."
> And then Manilov explained it to the coachman in the same courteous way and even said to him once: [the formal] you.

Chapter III, however, begins with an aside to the reader, as if the reader and the author were together standing in the wings of a theater commenting on Chichikov the actor, engrossed in his newly won role. A thunderstorm follows; the travelers lose their way; Selifan gives the horses their heads, "little thinking where the road taken will lead." In the novel of adventure, all roads are equally good, the choice of any is arbitrary. The connections among events are made by the hero-author. The world ranks itself into an unalterable hierarchy, the ethics of which, says Gogol the historian of morals, are defined not by human nature but by social status. As Ivan Petrovich, the manager of the office in "Never-never Land," changes, in a manner more miraculous than Ovid dreamed of, from a Promethean eagle to something less significant than a fly when confronted by a superior in rank, so Chichikov cuts his role to fit each episode, each character, and, inverting the hierarchy, turns himself from nothing into something.

Korobochka fades out like a harmless dream—"But on! onward! why talk about this?"—and Chichikov ends up in a tavern, Odysseus-like eating, resting, and talking on. Talk, of course, is the essence of comedy. Nozdrev's game is all talk, and Gogol plays with that: on the trip to Nozdrev's estate, the conversation is too dull for Gogol to relate it to the reader. Instead, he offers a description of Nozdrev as a man also typically, exclusively Russian, ending with a pun, boisterous and pointless, the sort Nozdrev himself would make:

Nozdrev was, in a certain sense, an incidental man. Not one meeting or get-together which he was at could pass without incident.

The description ends with a generalization on clothing as mask, on the difference between psychology and appearance. And the characterization climaxes in a punning parallel between a game of (not chess but) checkers and the game of art. Nozdrev says they won't play for the money involved but "after all, only for the art involved." Chichikov says he plays badly:

"We know you and your playing so badly!" said Nozdrev, taking his turn and at the same time moving another checker with the cuff of his sleeve.

Chichikov protests; of the three he has moved, Nozdrev offers to move one back:

"Where, what place?" said Nozdrev, blushing. "I see you're really some storyteller, my friend!"

"No, sir, my friend, it's you are the storyteller, it seems, only an unsuccessful one."

The successful one is the author, who turns the hassle between Nozdrev and Chichikov into a metaphoric mock parallel of Suvorov leading a charge and brings the policeman in, like a *deus ex machina,* to arrest Nozdrev and end the chapter.

Perhaps the clearest example of the device of describing each character in terms of his mirror image is the passage on Sobakevich in Chapter V, following the digression on the relation of life to art, of the external to the internal. Everything about Sobakevich tends to take on his attributes, as if under his power, just as Gogol's world took on the shape he imposed on it. Sobakevich is described as a bear, and his clothes and even his cupboard seem to have become bearlike with him. The identification of things, of possessions, with definition of a man is complete.

The whole book is partly a mockery of power perverted by affectation to absurdity. The superior perceptive power of the artist, itself inspired by a greater, mysterious power, fractures the vulgar world by creating a "more real" illusion. The action is contrived. It is a composite of impressions collated by the author and purporting to reveal everything sequentially in the sequence of the narrative—the journeys within the journey of Chichikov, like the "sentimental" journeys in *A Sentimental Journey.* So much attention is devoted to separate items, such as the tour of Nozdrev's estate, that they are taken for the whole, the sum of the visible parts. The reader thinks Sobakevich real by virtue of the very asininity of his affectations (the dog is wagged by the tail) and the reader's own involvement in actual experience. The reader laughs at the fools he is reading about, just as the author wrote laughing at him. Near the end of the chapter Chichikov reflects on bearishness; Gogol ascribes to his hero his own reflections on character and on character development in narrative. Above all, he says in the chapter's final paragraph, the greatest, most expressive, most communicative language is Russian. The greatest power is the power of words. In short, he suggests, the greatest force in the world is his words.

Having established space for his story—the stage in the theater where the actors may play—and having made the time of action the time of narration, Gogol must, since he desires epic scope, digress to generalize the time. The seventh chapter begins with such a generalization, a lyric (the author and his story are one) apostrophe to the past, to "the days of my youth," when, the author remembers with childlike vision, he, too, like Chichikov, would arrive in some unfamiliar place, when he still possessed the potential that is now gone: "O my youth! O my freshness!" This is the genuine perception of change. The landowners' world is hierarchic and static, a decayed vegetable kingdom, the world of Plyushkin. Chichikov's journey is, at best, a delusion, a grotesque quest for the Grail. But the author's experience of change is real, keeping silent in fear and self-pity, the disinterested quiet of understanding. The episode at Plyushkin's is framed by two excursuses on time: first, the personal reminiscence of one's losses to time, just referred to; secondly, the ethical meaning of time for a man's life, the shape of the individual's future cast as the shadow of the past. Opposed to the radiance of the maple and to the completeness of art in nature and of nature in art are the decay and false lushness of Plyushkin's estate. The rottenness of man's handiwork, like Marmeladov's mindless corruption in *Crime and Punishment*—"Man gets used to anything, the pig"—arouses fear of the future, of impotency, of death:

And to what insignificance, pettiness, and dirty tricks a man can descend! And does this seem the truth? Everything seems the truth, anything can happen with man. . . . Threatening, terrifying is oncoming old age, and nothing will reverse and return! The grave is more merciful than that, for on the gravestone it says: here a man lies buried! but you'll find nothing to read in the cold, unfeeling features of inhuman old age.

The satiric digression has led back to that lyric inversion which was its impetus. The most powerful fear is the fear of nothing, the fear which underlies Gogol's entire perception of life (as, in a different way, Tolstoy's) and, here in the novel, is the serious basis of the comic digression describing Plyushkin. It is an exchange of "something for nothing," a passage in which the author introduces himself as omniscient storyteller and prepares the reader for an extraordinary occurrence or character, which is immediately nullified:

At this point our hero involuntarily stepped back and stared at him intently. He had had the opportunity of seeing many people of all sorts, of seeing even those which neither I nor the reader, perhaps, will ever happen to see; but he had never seen one like this. His face presented nothing very special; it was just about like those of lots of lean, old men. . . .

The image of Plyushkin's eyes twitching like mice poking their noses out of their holes, as vivid as the cockroaches like prunes in the first chapter, establishes Gogol's style of description, not Plyushkin's style, who has none:

In short, if Chichikov had run into him, dressed like this, outside some church door some place, most likely he would have given him a copper.

Once, to be sure, Plyushkin was regular; once everything worked; once the neighbors called on him habitually; once he was a family man. In him the past wars with the future. Like the author alone with his heroes (Chapter VII), so

Plyushkin is alone with his losses, consumed by insatiable cupidity. Propriety is turned upside down: Chichikov, in Rabelaisian delight, exclaims his surprise and pleasure at the large number of serfs who have died. They haggle over the price of invisible, nonexistent merchandise.

Like the other cardboard figures, Plyushkin has no dramatic motivation but has social prominence and, therefore, literary significance. Although the figures in *Dead Souls* suggest types and although the book is a parody of typicality, the book itself cannot be generalized. The persons, places, and things described in it are particulars without extension or motion. The whole book only seems to be wrapped in motion. It encourages the reader to *believe* that everything happens. Irrelevances are inflated, and pivotal points in men's lives are unhinged. By exaggeration, by the movement of words, and by playing off against each other the stations the characters occupy, the whole novel, the whole trick and moral appanage, are dropped on the reader's head.

Art, in this view, is a process of extracting the unusual from the most ordinary. "The more mundane the subject, the greater must the poet be in order to draw out of it everything that is extraordinary," said Gogol. The normative aspect of a character is established not by idealization (Achilles; the romantic protagonist) nor by rhythmic movement of intense emotion (Oedipus; Lear), but by attention to the character's largest and smallest idiosyncrasies, as in caricature, which are examined separately, depriving the character of continuity in space or time outside the novel. Superimposed on the reality of these established "facts" is the author's lyrical imposition of his own personality, those digressions which do not follow from methods of presentation but come directly out of the author's memory of childhood, youth, and uncelebrated manhood.

The extremes of measurement are not "good" and "evil" but the extremes of convention, that "women are stronger than anything in the world," that "there are things which women will forgive no one, no matter who he is," that language itself is the supreme convention arbitrating all others, admitting no impurity. Gogol expresses gracious awareness of the use of French in high society "but all the same doesn't dare introduce a phrase of any foreign language whatsoever into this Russian poem of his." Nozdrev announces that Chichikov has been buying dead souls: the quest is exposed as a hoax, a device, the real voyage being the author's making a poem, a private interpretation of an entire society. Basically, the author uses only the effects of actions, as Chichikov "succeeds" only as long as his story is believed, to create an absurd grotesque, a hazy world of unreality of which each piece, each scene, seems real. As A. Slonimsky said forty years ago about Gogol's style:

> *The device of the absurd runs through all of Gogol's work —weaves through the web of his language, defines the kinds of replies in the dialogue, becomes the basis of the entire comic movement, in the end breaking down logical and formal connections among things.*

Underlying the "nonsense," what Gogol himself in his later "Author's Confession" called the "whirlwind of misunderstandings," is not plot or imitation of action as the soul of drama but ego or self-perception expressed in the language of a culture focused always on a personal experience of loss, frustration, or change. In so far as the book has a plot, the plot is pointless: the hero rides in, rides through, and rides out to the "marvelous, mellifluous sound" of the troika's bell. (*The Inspector General* ends at precisely the point it began.) In so far as the book is absurd, it is true: through verbal "logic" Gogol builds a forest of "illogic," the devices of language expressing consciousness, which is what is real.

Things are exploited as signs, rather than as symbols, of ambitions, success, power, or conceits. All pretense is lampooned. Gogol ridiculed whiskers, for example, because he ascribed to them an almost supernatural power, as if they were screens or bushes behind which men hid their power—as if they were masks concealing terrible vengeance or terrible voids. Animation followed from ironic focus on inevitable and useless extensions—on, say, a man's nose. In the story called "The Nose," a barber slices his bread one morning and finds in the middle of the loaf a nose which he recognizes as that of a man whom he shaves every Wednesday and Sunday. He takes it out and throws it into the river. The man who is shaved wakes up that morning and misses his nose. He sets out after it. It becomes animated, assuming the desired functions of the man to whom it belongs. The story ends by reinforcement of the joke:

No, I don't understand this at all. I definitely don't! But what's stranger still, what's most incomprehensible of all, is how authors can choose such subjects. I confess that this is utterly inscrutable, this is precisely . . . no, no, I don't understand in the least. In the first place, there's no advantage to the fatherland at all; in the second . . . but in the second place, too, there's no advantage. I simply don't know what this . . .

However, despite all this, allowing, of course, for one thing and another and even a third . . . well, and where aren't there incongruities?—yet, for all you think about it, in all of this, to be sure, there is something. No matter what anybody says, such things do happen in the world; rarely, but they do happen.

Gogol's other stories show the same method. "The Carriage" is a digression that has no end, the kind of thing Sterne delighted in. ("Digressions," said Sterne, "are the sunshine; —they are the life, the soul of reading.") "Ivan Shponka" is a hoax within a hoax. "The Diary of a Madman" is a confusion of word associations none of which "fits." The King of Spain is used in it much as the King of France is used in *Tristram Shandy*.

Names of men themselves appear as things, something independent of the person which must be preserved if the personality is to be preserved. Gogol, we know from his biography, exaggerated the nobility of his ancestry, but in his writings he made a game of ancestry by making games of names. In the naming of Akaky Akakievich in "The Overcoat" the vaunted, desired name is replaced by one that follows from the immediate incident, from Akaky's mother's lack of concern for the church calendar. The personality of the hero follows from his name.

The action in *Dead Souls* is the protagonist's traveling through an habitual world that, as a result, becomes the book's frame of reference. That is, the story moves as the hero moves through space, and the hero moves through time with the story. Everything is connected by the hero. Since the author is in a series of ways involved with the hero and can involve himself as he pleases, almost any connection is possible and plausible. The real subjects of the books are the various moments into which the hero has moved and, by his presence, transfixed. The transpositions are the author's, his conjunctions necessary to make the continuity of art. The world is ironically animated by the author's passage through it.

The book begins in the middle of things by introducing the passive hero to the activity of his environment. The hero inside his carriage is, like the author writing at his desk, almost motionless. A landscape is pieced together by the movement of the images in the author's eye. When the eye is dull, fancy moves, associating events in a series of cock-and-bull episodes in such a way that none seems unusual, as ordinary as the activity the author observed before he invented his extraordinary art. The deception is complete.

In Gogol's work the advertisements are equally delusive. (The portrait painted in "The Portrait" disappears from the canvas. Chichikov bought names on pieces of paper. In "The Carriage," a man at a party boasts to some officers of his exceptionally fine carriage; they come to call the next day and the story ends as the officers, who find the carriage very ordinary, open the door, revealing the owner hiding on the floor between the seats.) For Gogol's characters the consequences of their activity, of their frustrations, are more serious, are often humiliating or destructive. Played out, the game is tragic. Gogol's uncertainty about the perdurability of social institutions gives his work a prevailing tone of pathos, of lurking tragedy, of despair.

Aware of this deep and egocentric sense of loss under the bright surface of the comic images in Gogol's work, one can see the limitations of pursuing a theory of "influences" or of "-isms." As Victor Vinogradov pointed out in a brief article "On 'Literary Cyclization' " in 1927, what is important to discern among literary works is the patterns of literary devices common to a time and, in particular, within each work itself:

If in [a literary -ism] one may sometimes find an "etymological" significance and a connection with some individual, usually this is an indication of a limit, of the "latest"—from a contemporary, but not historical, viewpoint (hierarchically speaking, the first)—source of the influences under which literary developments proceeded in a given period. Such were

Walter Scott, for various genres of Russian prose at the end of the twenties–beginning of the thirties; Byron, for the long poems of the twenties; Victor Hugo, for the literature of "raving" of the early and middle thirties; George Sand, for the "peasant" novel of the forties; Gogol for the "natural" school of the early forties; and so ·on. However, in these instances, too, the individuality is assigned more than is proper to it and, in any event, often not at all what, in fact, is characteristic of the evolution of its own literary scheme.

Gogol began *Dead Souls* in 1835; the first part was published in 1842. The idea of using an absurd quest as a vehicle to string together a series of episodes each about a character, or type, was suggested to Gogol by Pushkin, but literary and social prototypes existed, not only in fiction, such as Dal's, but also, Gippius says, in family histories such as his own. Gogol derived less from them, however, than from his own earlier literary discoveries. He had found that he could invent a zoo. He could create *Genesis, Inferno, Don Quixote, Tom Jones,* and *A Sentimental Journey* all in one and be triumphant master. In a review of *Dead Souls,* Shevyrev said that each of the personages was in fact an animal; Gogol himself, in preliminary plans, had referred to "the medley of freaks" he was putting together, and in a letter to Pletnev in 1846 he wrote:

The tutor who has his pupils learn the art of writing from me will be making a mistake: he'll be forcing them to do caricatures. I never had the desire *to be the echo of all that is and* to reflect in myself things as they actually are all around us.

Vyazemsky said that *Dead Souls* was a collection of caricatures "in the style of Holbein." Gippius has pointed out that Apollon Grigorev, in his articles "Russian Literature in 1851" and "Russian Literature in 1852," first applied the term "hyperbole" to Gogol's humor:

[*For Gogol, actuality takes on*] gigantic–comic *proportions given it by a passionate and petulant fantasy. Gogol's works, therefore, are true not to actuality but to the general pattern of actuality in contradistinction to the ideal.*

And Gippius adds his own view that:

We may call Gogol a realist (as long as that word, like most of our scholarly terms, is not defined precisely) in the sense that we call Shakespeare and Swift, Rabelais and Molière, and V. Odoevsky realists. . . . The prose of the naturalistic school, much indebted to Gogol, generally took a different direction; the problem is further complicated by the fact that toward the end of his life Gogol himself tended in that direction.

In Gogol's work standards for judgment do not derive either immediately or ultimately from actual life. The illusion of actuality is a pattern established and defined only by manipulation of word meanings. For example, to decide whether or not Natasha in *War and Peace* is "lifelike" or "authentic," you will readily ask if young girls do, indeed, behave as Natasha does. To decide whether or not Chichikov or Korobochka or Nozdrev is "lifelike" or "authentic," you must understand Gogol's literary construction. (In the 1840's, Polevoy and the romantics, who failed to understand it, attacked *Dead Souls* as "sheer nonsense," childish rhetoric, filth, and smut.) Since, in fact, many critics from Belinsky on have asserted for over one hundred years that Gogol's characters are "lifelike" and "authentic," we are brought round to another aspect of the position that literary realism is a function of an author's style, that is, of his or of his hero's self-perception.

The seventh chapter of *Dead Souls* begins with a digression on the traveler and the writer, an analogy set up by parallel paragraphs. It is an apostrophe to the writer, to himself, an *apologia pro vita sua* in which the successful writer is called a god. The unsuccessful writer—which every writer may be as he works along, as he takes his "next trip"—is ignored and lonely. Even the young girl, who, with her egglike face, later appears in front of Chichikov at the Governor's ball, does not embrace him. He succeeds when he brings the forms of art alive, for life does not exist in ignorance and mediocrity but in the living forms:

Each of the notes seemed to have some special characteristic of its own, and, from that, it seemed, the peasants themselves had taken on their various personalities.

The names on the list then become animated in Chichikov's mind, and the figures become real because the language has entered consciousness: Chichikov constructs a biography for the entry "Maksim Telyatnikov, cobbler" by reflecting on the set phrase "drunk as a cobbler." He addresses the list of names as if they were characters on stage, presenting their histories, challenging them, defining them. Chichikov then hurries off to see the chairman, who, "like Homer's Zeus," could "cut or expand the scenes to fit his favorite heroes' wrangling." The image, again, is that the omnipotent, successful writer *is* god.

The writer is above his heroes as long as they are playing their parts in his play. In "real life," he is his heroes. Moreover, he is the reader, too. He is, he says, not the "upper-class readers from whom you won't hear a Russian word," but the reader for whom he "ought to describe the offices our heroes walked through, but the author has a great fear of all such official places." His heroes are undistinguished; his reader is insignificant, one who does not know the offices of important people; the author is the third figure in the trinity and, by identification with both hero and reader in an experience of repression, brings the reader and hero together. The joke of the hero's catastrophe is the other side of the author's perception of genuine loss; together they make the book real for any reader. In the same way, the town is not so aptly characterized by Chichikov's round of visits as it is by the literary measure of its life, "who reads Karamzin, who reads *The Moscow Record*, and who reads nothing."

As the book unwinds, slowly coming round to its beginning, the manners of writing are put against the manners of the town—Selifan and Petrushka journey right out of the story to get a drink; the ladies fail to make all the real (Russian) words good, half their talk being in bad French; the modish verse appears in an anonymous letter; the Governor gives another ball and the pretense is superlative: "This was no province, this was the capital, this was Paris itself"—all measured by the manner of writing, by Gogol's putting his novel against the fashionable novels of his day:

. . . *but there was something said with great courtesy in that spirit in which ladies and their consorts address each other in the stories by our secular writers who like very much to describe drawing rooms and to show off their knowledge of class, rather in the spirit that, if they capture your heart that way, there won't be any room in it, not even a crowded little corner, for those whom you have pitilessly forgotten.*

The ladies' charms are made pointless: "None of this had the intended effect on Chichikov." Chichikov becomes more and more different from the people of manners, more and more isolated. Toward the end of Chapter VIII, Gogol increasingly uses impersonal pronouns to cloud the issue, to separate Chichikov from the others and to set himself, as author, off from them all. The fantasies invented by the officials in Chapter IX to explain Chichikov to themselves, following Nozdrev's revelation, a plot within a plot, assign them a point of view which completes Chichikov's alienation. The circle is completed with the question, "Who was Chichikov?"

Chapters X and XI, like the final scene in a play with all the actors on stage, are a little novel within the novel. Gogol calls Kopeikin's story "a whole poem, in its own way, for some writer," as, one hundred years later, Mann used the Gregory legend in *Doctor Faustus* and then made it into a whole novel. Gogol proceeds to define Chichikov's story by analogy, the means of art. The postmaster's story is historical ("after the campaign of 1812"), allegorical (the Captain was wounded, maimed, and set out to St. Petersburg in quest of a pension), literal (the description of the capital parallels description of Chichikov's provincial town). Kopeikin, unsuccessful, hungry, thinks always about eating; throughout the novel Chichikov's success is symbolized by eating and drinking. The story is moral—or, rather, antimoralistic: the farther it goes, the farther it gets from relevance, the more it becomes a story for its own sake. As Gogol writes, "here begins the intrigue of the novel." It has been a question of costume, of action, of faith (the Napoleon reference), of making something from nothing, until the story of Chichikov's quest has been perfectly reversed into the story of the quest for Chichikov.

Like Don Quixote at the end of his road, Chichikov experiences reversal of the usual terms of judgment which his journey has effected, but, unlike the Don, he is entirely isolated from society. The Don was himself transformed by his quest; Chichikov, like a catalyst, is unaffected. His supposed departure, equally supposedly the end of the story, is fouled by details. As in the beginning, the town as the setting is described, and the capping irony occurs: there is a funeral. Literally, the prosecutor is being carried to his grave. Chichikov, who failed in his quest for dead souls, at the end meets a dead man and thinks to himself, "It's good luck, they say, if you meet a dead man."

The coda of the book begins with a long digression on the author's lyrical sense of history, on "the road itself is something wonderful," on the function of the artist to describe life as it is, not as it may be. This leads to the author's own and final story, the exposition of the motivation of the hero. He gives a résumé of the gestures of Chichikov's quest and reveals the quest to have been, in reality, a flight—literally, from the customs office, but allegorically out of the past into the future. After a few jokes, the ironic reversal completed (that Chichikov thought it all up), the author identifies the future of *any* hero with that of the nation.

Gogol strongly supported the society he ridiculed; he insisted on decorum and the propriety of form. His attitude to art is perhaps most clearly and most seriously put in a letter he wrote his mother after he had seen the Marienkirche in Lübeck:

*On one wall of the church there is an unusually high clock.
. . . When twelve o'clock comes, a huge marble figure on top
strikes twelve times. The doors above open with much noise,
and from behind them there file out one after the other the
twelve apostles, each the usual height of a man, singing; each
bows as he passes the statue of Jesus Christ, and then passes
on in the same order, through the opposite door. The door-
keeper greets them with a bow, and the doors close shut be-*

hind them. The apostles are so artfully made that you could take them for living men.

Against prevailing confusion and mediocrity, Gogol insisted on sensibility and form, the proportions and perceptions of beauty. He held a tragic view of life, the view of a man withdrawn from it who contemplates it only as artist, who wants to be great and brilliant but who fears his own failure and is depressed by everything he sees:

I always feel sad when I look at new buildings which are constantly being put up and on which millions are spent. . . . Involuntarily there comes the thought: Has the age of architecture passed without hope of return? Will grandeur and genius never visit us again?

More than death, he feared the pettiness and the grubbiness of self-satisfied mediocrity.

In an essay written before *Dead Souls*, he wrote a sentence which anticipated the crisis later in his life. Music for him was the supreme, ineluctable *form*, and he identified it with God:

The Great Architect of the world sent to our age, which is both young and yet senile, mighty music so that it would rapidly turn us to Him. If, then, even music should forsake us, what will become of our world?

Gogol disliked France; arriving in Italy, he felt as if he had come home.

As he aged and the world impinged on him, he drew closer and closer to his mystic vision. Ten days before he died, in fever, he burned his corrected copy of the second part of *Dead Souls*, destroyed his "sinful work," leaving only his notebooks behind. In *Selected Passages from Correspondence with Friends* he had written:

We can no longer serve art for art's sake no matter how beautiful such service may be, without having first comprehended its highest purpose and without determining what it is given to us for. We cannot repeat Pushkin.

By the end of his life, he believed that beauty was not an end in itself but, rather, an instrument for salvation, that it led to ultimate grace. He said in his own way what Dostoevsky said about twenty years later, that "beauty will save the world." He came to feel a tragic helplessness in western European society, to feel that it was decaying and diseased. Unexpurgated sins, he felt, were ruining it. Russia, he thought, had a special role to play:

Why does Russia alone act as prophet? Because she feels more keenly than others the hand of God in everything that comes to pass within her and senses the approach of another kingdom.

Gogol's Chichikov set out from a *besoin de voyager,* both adapting himself to his vehicle and choosing a vehicle to suit himself. He is an extension of Gogol at a safe distance, and, like the other characters, a sentimental figure belonging to an inventor who only at times is sentimental. But having animated all the hobbyhorses and having set up the machinery of irony, Gogol kept coming in in the middle of the game, was repeatedly frightened by his actors' motions—and suffered. His own delusion caught him. The world which he felt obliged to see as a kind of Hell from the beginning became a real Hell. He died tormented by the spirits he himself had tried to exorcise.

What remains, however, is not Gogol's preaching but his perception of pattern, Chichikov's fantastic quest which, circular, cyclical, carried rhythm in language beyond language itself to define a world view. Precisely the formal elements of the "long poem" *Dead Souls* shaped Gogol's philosophy. As we ourselves have devices and habits for making pretend, so Gogol had devices and habits for making real. The pattern of these devices is the life of consciousness and the rhythm of his novel, a fantasy of the rational imagination which the specifics keep real.

Oblomov

Swift said in a letter to Pope that life is a ridiculous tragedy, which is the worst kind of composition. Life is self-contradictory, which is not only awkward but, from the viewpoint of a novelist, unsuccessful. To make good art —to compose, through use of images or symbols, a non-self-contradictory entity including and exceeding experience—you must get away from life without, obviously, ignoring or denying life. You may take any attitude toward life, toward what you have, provided you simultaneously affirm the negation of existing reality—ultimate freedom. You write satire because you don't like what you have but know that you need it.

The word *satire* comes from the Latin *satira* or *satura* meaning, says Webster's, a poetic medley or dish filled with fruits, coming from *satur* meaning full of food, *sated*. Satire takes in all human folly and vice, the distinguishing, individual tricks of men, and measures man's complement or satisfaction against his common performance.

The satire that is *Oblomov* takes all the habitual stunts of satirists and disguises them more than usual. Swift is candid in denouncing arithmeticians and politicians: he presumes man is merely the prey of his own delusions and that by being sensible man can resurrect himself in societal life. The life of the world is tragic because it is not at all ridiculous; or ridiculous because it is not really tragic. A man is turned into a fool by revelation of the discrepancy between his ambitions and his achievements, not because of the nature of his ambitions themselves. Man is silly or comical or the object

103

of satire in so far as what he does makes him an exaggeration of himself.

Oblomov, Goncharov tells the reader, makes this sort of revelation of self-exaggeration by his division of reality:

Life was divided, in his opinion, into two halves: one consisted of work and boredom—for him these words were synonymous—the other of rest and peaceful good-humor. This was the reason why his chief field of activity—government service—proved an unpleasant surprise to him. . . . "But when am I to live?" he would repeat in distress.

At the end of the novel, Stolz apotheosizes Oblomov:

"He was as intelligent as other people; his soul was pure and clear as crystal; he was noble and affectionate—and yet he did nothing!"

"Why? What was the reason?"

"The reason? What reason was there? Oblomovism," Stolz said.

"Oblomovism?" the writer repeated perplexed. "What's that?"

"I'll tell you right away. Let me collect my thoughts and memories. And you write it down; it may be useful to somebody."

And he told him what is written here.

The novelist asserts the moralistic nature of his comedy. He insists on pretending, even at the end, that the book "happened," that the book is "real" and normative. He says that he made his book to tell men what he thinks of them. Ironically, both as part of his message and as device in the book, he pretends that he got it all from men themselves.

Goncharov's personal life and career do not fit our usual image of the nineteenth-century Russian writer as a fiery intellectual antagonistic to the autocratic hierarchy and advancing, in sophisticated circles of conversation, the brightest French ideas. Or I suppose that that is our image. Our popular biographies surely overdramatize the writers' histories, and we forget the facts of real life, just as schoolchildren seldom take note that Julius Caesar was one of the richest real-estate speculators in the Rome of his day.

Goncharov came from rich gentry in Simbirsk, went to Moscow University, and had a long career in the civil service, serving as censor after 1856. He wrote and published relatively little, his chief works being: *A Common Story* in 1847, much praised by Belinsky; *Oblomov's Dream* in 1849; *The Frigate Pallada* in 1857; *Oblomov* in 1859; and *The Precipice* in 1869. For the last twenty years of his life he asserted that Turgenev and Flaubert had stolen ideas and material from him. And although in the 1840's he had been sympathetic to the ideas and the work of Belinsky and all the new writers around Belinsky, he was and remained a "liberal conservative," more concerned with describing the existing social structure than with trying to effect the sort of social change for which Belinsky was arguing. As N. A. Dobrolyubov, the young critic of the late 1850's, said about *Oblomov*, "Goncharov doesn't come to, and obviously doesn't want to come to, any conclusions. Life as described by him is . . . an end in itself."

On publication in 1859, *Oblomov* caused a sensation. "Like a bomb," said A. M. Skabichevsky, "it landed among the intelligentsia right at the moment of the greatest social unrest, three years before the manumission of the serfs, when all of literature was preaching a crusade against daydreaming, inertia, and stagnation." Grigorev said that the novel was overdone, drawn out, undramatic. Turgenev, who had heard it read in manuscript, wrote Nekrasov that the book contained long, dull passages but that "it's a really fine piece of work, and it would be excellent if you could get it for *The Contemporary*." The figure of indolent Oblomov, symbolized by his bathrobe and slippers, as archetype of the Russian landowner, remains still canonical in some contemporary commentaries:

In Oblomov the reader can see how the conditions of the nineteenth-century social structure and the gentry's way of life caused the hero to be apathetic, without a will of his own, indifferent to everything. Oblomov has concentrated in him, like a focal point, all the qualities of a man brought up under that system. . . . In fundamental and psychologically convincing terms, Goncharov has shown Oblomov's road to recognition of his own pointlessness, to his lack of independence, and, in the final analysis, to the disintegration of his personality.

The book is a satire, and the term to which it gave rise, "Oblomovism," remains a satiric reproach. Although the social implications of the satire may be (as they were) read as similar to those of *Dead Souls*, the terms in which the satire is cast are basically different. One can see this by putting *Oblomov* against still another and successful satire, *The Golovlev Family* by Mikhail Saltykov-Shchedrin.

Saltykov-Shchedrin wrote mostly satiric sketches of our habitual vices. His little book *The History of a Certain Town*, called in the book Glupov, or Stupid Town, is a parody of Russian history through the microcosm of provincial life with its petty ambitions and bickerings. His later tales, for all their power, are in the same way affected by a severe topicality, always the most obvious limitation on satire. On the other hand, of course, like all who opposed the status quo, he had to write in Aesopian language to circumvent the censorship.

The Golovlev Family (1872–76) is a social novel which chronicles the history of a provincial family like all those who, "having no work, no connection with public life, and no political importance, were at one time sheltered by serfdom but now, with nothing to shelter them, are spending the remainder of their lives in their tumbledown country houses." It is a sardonic, savage attack on the moral disintegration and brutishness of the acquisitive "culture" of the formerly serf-owning class. Spread through the novel, as if splayed on pins in a museum, are the ursine people who are given to coarseness, vulgarity, greed, spite, and mere brutality for no reason but the failure of their artificial social system. They have always fed on society; now, serfless, they feed on each other.

The novel falls into two parts: the Golovlev manor before and after the abolition of serfdom. In the first part, the story, such as it is, turns around Arina Petrovna, a selfish, domineering, steel-willed matriarch. When her oldest son, Stepan Vladimirovich, returned from Moscow a bankrupt failure, she met him on the back steps and had him taken to his father through another entrance.

"Ah, my boy, you've been caught in the old hag's clutches," he [the father] called out when his son kissed his hand. Then he crowed like a cock, laughed again, and repeated several times, "She'll eat you up, she'll eat you up!"

. . . Stepan's forebodings came true. He had a room assigned to him. . . . The doors of the sepulchral vault opened, let him in, and slammed shut.

The old virago loses her authority to her favorite son Porfiry Vladimirovich, nicknamed Iudushka, or Little Judas. This little bastard is the brightest and ablest of them all. He is an unctuous and pious son of a bitch who, for the joy of conversation, continuously mouths hypocritical cant. He is not hypocritical, says the author,

in the sense that Tartufe is or any modern French bourgeois who goes off into flights of eloquence on the subject of social morality. He is . . . simply a man devoid of all moral standards. . . . He is pettifogging, deceitful, loquacious, boundlessly ignorant, and afraid of the devil.

"We Russians," Saltykov-Shchedrin goes on, "have no need to be hypocritical for the sake of any fundamental social principle and do not take refuge under any of them. We exist quite freely, that is, we vegetate, babble, and lie spontaneously, without any principles."

Both of Iudushka's sons die through his callousness: when the younger one needs money to pay off gambling debts, Iudushka, now the wealthiest landowner in the district, says, "God took from Job everything he had, my dear, and yet he didn't pine, but said, 'The Lord gave, the Lord hath taken away—Blessed be the name of the Lord.' That's the way it is, m' boy." Both of Iudushka's nieces, who fled the estate to win useful careers as actresses, get caught in the mire of vulgarity and end up as whores. A scandal follows. One poisons herself. The other turns to taking care of Iudushka, by now a demented aging miser who with her is always half-drunk. He drinks to drown his conscience and hates "the whore, who so coldly and impudently probed his wounds, but is irresistibly drawn to her as though something still remained unsaid between them, and there were more wounds to be probed."

The story limns the extremes of human depravity: the men and women in it, unlike Gogol's characters, are more nearly animals than people. All that remains is their passion, like hope intense to the end. The book seems to be as close to the horrible and the deformed as satire can come.

Satire is an inversion of the lyric, a denial of romantic experience. It comes from disillusion, and it tries to disillusion those who come to it. It asserts the personal against the social in a world or at a time when society disregards the functional values of the individual or when the age is inimical to poetry. It has at least three elements in it, three stages by which it alters the connection or associations we ordinarily limit ourselves to: it is a sermon, a monologue, a distorted (because personal) instruction for regulating life; it is a disconnected, therefore distorted, chronicle of social events; as parody, it is a distortion of the understanding of the experience of actuality. The sequential movement of time is fractured, and the author's private, disfigured vision of the present is put forward as if it were Hell—or an inverted utopia. Satire is as close as the novel can get to a legislative function and still remain a novel.

The bulk of Chernyshevsky's *What's to Be Done?* (1865) is too programmatic to be rescued for fiction even by satiric elements. N. A. Nekrasov's novel, *The Life and Adventures of Tikhon Trostnikov* (1843; pub. 1931), for all its elements of social protest and utopist vision, is built around the old, very popular adventure novel (the second part is even subtitled "The Adventures of a Russian Gil Blas") with its digressions, separate stories, humorous tone, wit, satiric attitude, and lively sketches. Nekrasov felt that there were two Petersburgs, the rich and the poor. Whatever political change he argued for, he proceeded from his own experience of an irreconcilable opposition in the life of the present.

Oblomov proceeds not so much from antagonism to prevailing social conditions as from a new, special idea: it parodies, by taking to the extreme of success, the idea of individual freedom, which underlay fiction from about 1830 on. The protagonist or supposed hero of the book, Oblomov, a symbolic character, evaporates explicitly at the end into the idea he has been taken to represent: Oblomov becomes Oblomovism, which is held to be more important, just as in Molière's comedy *The Miser* the idea of avarice is the central figure, not the avaricious man. The semblance of realism the author imposes on you, the reader, is only a trick, like the use of a "hero" and the novel form itself, to attract you to his moral and to keep you involved, or at least interested, in the process of his narration, which itself has no narrative interest.

The usual understanding of hero is that of the great actor, Achilles or, by formal extension, Falstaff. Goncharov plays his "hero" off against both concepts: the classical or romantic idea of a great man who by acumen and power manipulates his own destiny and that of his followers and, secondly, the comic use of a moral condition as the measure and determinant of a man's stature. That is, in Goncharov's book both the man and the idea of the man function as we require a hero to function. That neither can be heroic, as Aeneas had to be, is part of the book's intent.

Dobrolyubov perceived what we now call the "intentional fallacy." In his article on *Oblomov* called "What Is Oblomovism?" he asserted the independence of the book from any particular intellectual presumptions. For him, Oblomov was the end of the line of literary figures from Onegin and Pechorin to Manilov and Rudin. Oblomovism Dobrolyubov thought a typically Russian *social* defect in that, as a result of serfdom and patriarchal ways of life, it had infected the bureaucracy, the middle class, and the nobility as well. The book's author, Dobrolyubov said, "guarantees only its correspondence with reality."

Dobrolyubov read the book in two ways: inside out and outside in. By that I mean that he was careful to distinguish his political pleasure with the book from the value of the book as a sample of literature. He insisted that the book carried its own system of meaning independent of any external constructs; that the organization of the book was "esthetic" or imaginative, not logical; that it was made from art rather than from life, as Cimabue had said all art is made. On the other hand, Dobrolyubov read back from the abstraction to the conditions of life as he himself found them, and, in these terms, consciously imposed on the book a kind of political propriety as standard. In this, he read *Oblomov* as a clue to many riddles of Russian life. And in this he was helped by Goncharov himself, who said, in a little article written after the publication of *Oblomov*, that this idea for the book had come from observation of Russian provincial life. What Goncharov meant, I think, is that the condition of moral delusion—as Joyce, for example, uses it—is the actual content of human activity. What he *made* is less apparent.

Those politicians who, like Lenin, take the legislative aspect of the satire as a typical reality mistake the art of the book. Believing the images, they dislocate or misplace the values. They read *Oblomov* as an image of actual life. This in turn they try to reform. Other, more responsive Russian critics in the early twentieth century went further: Oblomovism was not only psychological conservatism, an escape from reality, and a complex of immaturity with the subsequent idealization of infantilism, but also a sign of Oriental fatalism. Oblomov does not want to be, according to them, an agent in the historical process; he reflects the attitude of many Russians who thought individual intervention in current events useless and even silly.

Oblomov is a symbol—or, rather, we read *Oblomov* as a symbol, taking that word loosely for the moment—of some of our desires and of part of our total, real condition. The specific features or relevant, contemporaneous attitudes Oblomov has are Russian, but neither as figure nor as man is he, as writers on Russian literature keep trying to make him, typically Russian. Oblomov's book is not at all objective in the common usage of that word. Like other satires and comedies, it could not be and still be comic. It *must* be a distortion. Part of satire's success in its exaggeration is the degree of impartiality or verisimilitude it can pretend, thereby to make you believe it, for the more you believe it the more efficacious it is. A comedian is a preacher.

Our desires for ease and peace, for much food and sleep, are represented in the history of art by such images as those of the Saturnian Realm, Arcadia, the Land of Cockaigne; that is, by a world in which we can avoid the first condition of our actual life: prevailing scarcity. Here in this world everybody must work and many must be deprived of basic necessities because we, purportedly rational creatures, cannot organize ourselves any better. But in Oblomov's world of unreality, in the land of his Dream, everything happens as man subjectively desires it would with the least inconvenience to himself:

A *heart worn out by troubles or completely unfamiliar with them longs to hide in this secluded spot and live there happily, unnoticed by anyone. Everything there promises a calm, long life until the hair turns from white to yellow and death comes unnoticed like sleep.*

It is the life of absolute freedom as men here in this life imagine it: absence of all restraint, repression, or want. No pain, no passion. There, nothing can be disturbing. Time goes on and on with no significant distinctions. There, as we dream, we lose our sense of time, our consciousness. All the monotonously pleasant moments perish, and everything would seem to have lasted for ages. The only reality this fanciful world has is that we do, in fact, each privately dream it: an everlasting world in which we would have real meaning, real importance, as distinguished from the celebrity or fame we seek in this. In that world we would be perfectly adjusted to our nature, we would be exactly what we dream ourselves to be. In this world, we are to others only what we have done. No one else can see, as Oblomov has it, what we see as the exceptional sensitivity of our own perceptions.

What Oblomov has is what we all pretend we want. Since he has it, he has nothing to do. *He has no need to do anything.* He moves along with time, refusing to commit himself to anything that is, from his point of view, superfluous. He continually retreats from what we think the vital status of manhood. He reaffirms, from our point of view, his own superfluous nature.

We like him, I think, because he is a kind, well-intentioned, harmless person, but we do not, in the end, like his point of view. He disaffects us from our ideals of tranquillity and happiness, and encourages us in our illusions of virility. We like him because he does not seem to do anything—to us, or against, or for us. Maybe he is ultimately alarming because his problem is ours, we know, when we endure moments similar to the moments of his whole life. His problem is not that he has no will power. He is not, as some critics called him, a "negation of the efficacy of human will." He does not *know* what to do because he is completely satisfied. As a mask of a real person, a plausible figure in a novel, he isn't satisfied, but as a dreamer he is. This satisfaction is given as his real condition. He approximates it more and more successfully as he moves through the book.

In his youth he kept a few notions of service and of contribution; these vanished when he no longer felt a need for them, just as Olga vanished when he ceased to need the responsibility of love. In a sense, Olga seemed stubbornly to impose on him an awkward but plausible change. His rejection of her, however, doesn't turn on the fact that *she* seems to require something of him. *He* who wants to be cared for, to be attended, refuses to return the responsibility. He loses the need to care for someone else. He rejects Olga because he can't extend himself to her or even honor her. What he discovers in himself is a need for irresponsibility. He knows that he wants some impersonal figure to look after him; he knows he can't tolerate any love and still retain the reality, or even possibility, of his dream of freedom. If it takes him an hour and a half to get out of bed—or not to get out of bed—that is because he doesn't have to do it in less time. He need not work because he doesn't need money and because he has the conviction of his satiety.

If in the progress of the book he is represented as acting, his effort nonetheless, even in commitment, is to escape all devotion or sacrifice or power. Having met Olga in the park, in reply to her question,

he was silent. He would have liked indirectly somehow to let her know that the mysterious charm of their relationship had disappeared, that he felt burdened by the concentrated effort which she had wrapped herself in like a cloud, as if having withdrawn into herself, and he didn't know what to do, how to behave with her.

But he sensed that the slightest hint of this would provoke a look of astonishment from her, would then make their treatment of each other colder, and perhaps put out entirely that spark of involvement which he had so carelessly extinguished in the very beginning. It had to be ignited again, quietly and carefully, but how—he had no idea at all.

He vaguely understood that she had grown up practically as tall as he, that now there was no going back to a childlike trustfulness, that before them lay the Rubicon, and their forfeited happiness was already on the other shore: one had to cross.

But how? Supposing he crossed alone?

He did think that he loved Olga, but when he came to know that he desired neither to love nor to be loved, he advised her to go. Ultimately complete in himself, he cannot know or keep love because he cannot want it. In the same way he ceases to think of work and fritters away all his money. It is not that he knows to do nothing, but rather that he can know nothing to do:

He frowned and sleepily looked around. She looked at him for a moment, then put her needlework into her basket.

"Let's go to the grove," she said, giving him the basket to carry, opened her parasol herself, straightened her dress and set out. "Why aren't you cheerful?" she asked.

"I don't know, Olga Sergeyevna. Why, indeed, should I be? How?"

"Do something, see people more often."

"Do something! A man can do something when he has a goal. What goal do I have? None."

Time for Oblomov passes ever more slowly until, through his effort to overcome any need for Olga, it seems to stop altogether:

He decided that until he had positive news from the country he would see Olga only on Sundays with others present. Therefore, when the next day came, he didn't start thinking in the morning of getting ready to go see Olga.

He didn't shave, didn't dress, lazily leafed through the French papers borrowed from the Ilyinskys the week before,

*didn't keep eying the clock and didn't frown at the fact that
the hands didn't move ahead for a long time.*

Although Oblomov's life appears to be suspended, it is
not. He continually advances toward fulfillment. As he does,
he moves farther and farther from conventional existence or
conventional happiness. Or closer. The relationship is, in a
sense, paradoxical. The closer he is to ordinary activity, the
less successful his activity is. The further he is from ordinary
activity—the more involved he is in the conventions of his
own habits—the more successful his activity is. If looked at
in terms of usual and real standards of accomplishment, instead of usual and unreal standards, the process is reversed.
To his friends, Oblomov comes to resemble an eighteenth-
century actor. His gestures seem to be extensions of Lomonosov's *Manual of Rhetoric*, specifying the *poses* of expression
and communication, or of Lafatère's *Physiognomical Fragments for Affecting Human Knowledge and Love of People*,
in which the author asserts that the nature of a man and his
merit are definable by his facial features.

As Oblomov knows more and more about his possibilities,
he knows less and less to do, since the potential is absolute
freedom—specifically, no activity or commitment whatever.
Similarly, if we were completely free we wouldn't know what
to do to be happy. This is the dilemma—or paradox, since it
is presented as a function—we catch from Oblomov's sleepy
laboring toward meaning.

All the images in the book revolve around Oblomov's
understanding of life and reinforce the semblance of realism.
China, for Oblomov, is "a chest filled with old lumber."
Oblomov's dressing gown becomes a dramatic symbol of the
internal, intellectual conflict between obligation and liberation. The smallest details of actuality are itemized and per-
sonalized to make them seem real and to give them meaning.

They become aspects or extensions of Oblomov and take on, in that setting, the exaggeration that he is.

It is these facts of actuality which impinge on Oblomov's satisfaction, as he implies in his letter to Olga. He says there that she doesn't love him, though of course she thinks she does, but what she really has is an unconscious expectation or need for love, for passion. He doesn't, and he knows he doesn't. He is ready to face those who will laugh at him for seemingly running away.

If Oblomov could run away from reality he would. But he can't, and it discourages him and mocks him. Stolz stands against him, much as Iago stands against Othello as we usually remember the play. Only, Stolz isn't very interesting, and Iago is. And Agafya stands in contradistinction to Olga, and so on. The book is well made and painstakingly made. Oblomov's great charm, distinguished from the world's rather baked-apple face, is his belief

in friendship, in love, in a man's honor. However many mistakes he made or might still make about people, although he suffered, his conception of goodness and his faith in it were never shaken.

The book satisfies us doubly. It demolishes by ridicule the preposterous ignorance and uselessness of Oblomov and, by analogy, our impossible ideals of complete peace and perfect freedom. We don't mind this mockery, really, because our ideals, being ideals, are inaccessible. The book supports us and our institutions in admiring the successes of hard work and devotion to discipline and self-sacrifice. Stolz is not much of a man, even in novelistic terms; he is not a paragon, either. Oblomov is the hero. We are given to know everything about him as an aspect of ourselves exaggerated into story, and we find it, inevitably, intolerable. Oblomov's position is self-defeating. He destroys himself as a man. He takes away his own dignity. He stands at the end of the line of the men wholly alienated from society, who can neither know nor need to render social service nor fulfill a social function.

Fathers and
Children

Every age imagines the one which preceded it as having been halcyon, or, at least, harmonious. We always suppose that our grandfathers lived with a sense of purposefulness and orderliness which we cannot manage. In fact, every age is, in some ways, a mess; in other ways, a dream which cannot last. The eighteenth century was a time of political confusion, economic transition, and social contradictions, but, unlike the centuries before and after it, it had a common notion of the orderliness of art, based on a belief in the absolute nature of beauty. Art and philosophy lay outside the movement of history. The poet was to try to accomplish a perfect solution of a final task. "The correct solution of the set problem was regarded as actually absolute, that is, unique," said Gukovsky in his "Russian Classicism" (1928), and every problem was assumed to have a perfect solution; "there could not be two correct, differing solutions."

By the middle of the nineteenth century this attitude had gone. Faith in hierarchy had been supplanted by faith in progress, and although society was slow to reorganize itself its artists and intellectual speculators could not construe even historical events except in individual terms (as *War and Peace* makes clear). Between the esthetics of the 1750's and the 1850's, between Sumarokov and Turgenev, between great-grandfathers and great-grandsons, lie the 1840's, that special period in which romantic esthetics and political theories of social change came to form a single point of view. Herzen's

119

1842 essay "The Dilettante Romantics" is a good example of this new outlook by which what the eighteenth century regarded as autonomous, ideal literary style had come to be considered inseparable from the social and political aspects of a world view.

Herzen called his view "realism," elaborating on the difference between it and the romanticism of the 1830's, the basis of which, he said, was transcendental spiritualism, and according to which, he said, "individuality, insignificant in the classical world, had won limitless rights. The aim of art had become not beauty but sublimity." This romanticism, like the greater and more productive classicism which preceded it, Herzen said, was unsuccessfully partial and inadequate. Realism, in Herzen's understanding, Lydia Ginzburg writes in "Herzen and the Esthetic Issues of His Time" (1963),

encompassed all spheres of human activity including art. The new realistic trend in art was based on the forward movement of history, on the idea of progress which Herzen understood in the spirit of utopian socialism as a movement toward a just organization of society. . . . The realistic synthesis in art was advanced not metaphysically (spirit and matter, the infinite and the finite), not typologically (the two eternal principles of the human soul), but historically.

The nineteenth-century novelist could not avoid coming to political judgment. The virtue of art, of course, is to judge. To make no judgment meant finally to be criticized for irresponsibility or, worse, irrelevance. To make disinterested judgment, as Turgenev in *Fathers and Children*, for example, claimed to have made, meant to risk being criticized for failing to be partial to social reform, as Turgenev was criticized. The nonaligned novel that he hoped would define an age became, on publication, mired in party politics.

Turgenev's first idea for the novel came during a visit to the Isle of Wight. He thought of writing a novel with a tragic hero, extending the Onegin–Pechorin tradition (which he himself had labeled in his story "The Diary of a Superfluous Man") and offering as hero an "Everyman," a figure whose ordinary life contains the seeds of his tragedy. As Turgenev once said, "We are all condemned to die. Can there be anything more tragic than that?" The image of the hero which occurred to him first was of a dying man born ahead of his time, a man who by the necessity of his nature did not fit into the prevailing social structure. "My whole novel," Turgenev later said, "is directed against the nobility as the foremost class in Russian society." One proof of Turgenev's sincerity about his plan and about his attitude toward the hero of the novel, Bazarov, is his dedication of the novel to the memory of V. G. Belinsky.

Turgenev worked on the book during 1860–61. It appeared in serial form in Katkov's *Russian Herald* in 1862. Published after the manumission of the serfs, it narrated events which had occurred before. Some response was favorable. Dostoevsky, for example, compared the book to *Dead Souls* and said that it was worth all of Turgenev's previous work together, but, then, Dostoevsky was using Turgenev to fight Chernyshevsky and Chernyshevsky's influence on Nekrasov, editor-in-chief of *The Contemporary*, of which Chernyshevsky had become criticism editor in 1856. M. A. Antonovich, reviewing Turgenev's novel in the March, 1862 issue of *The Contemporary*, said that the book was badly written, "a political treatise in dialogue," and that Bazarov was "a monster with a tiny head and an enormous mouth." An allusion by Antonovich to Turgenev's relationship with Pauline Viardot caused Turgenev finally to break with *The Contemporary* and with Nekrasov personally as well. Chernyshevsky agreed with the opinion predominant among the radicals, adding that Bazarov was a caricature of Dobrolyubov, who had died in late 1861. Although Turgenev said, some ten years later, that the model for Bazarov had been not Dobrolyubov but a young country doctor he had known, he had alienated himself from the radical group. His assertion that he shared all of Bazarov's views except those on art (Bazarov to Anna Sergeyevna Odintsova in the novel: "You said that, because you don't suppose I have any artistic sensibility, and, indeed, I really don't.") and his equation in the novel of the concept "nihilism" with the failure of the idea of revolution brought him under very heavy attack. The man who in 1852–53 had been exiled to his estate for his politically suspect encomium of Gogol and whose *A Sportsman's Notebook* was said to have influenced Alexander to enact the manumission now found himself opposed by the people whose champion he had been all through the 1850's. Attacked, Turgenev expressed regret, said later that he should have been aware of the political consequences of the book, especially because in 1862, when he returned to Russia for a visit, the nihilists were being accused of setting fires in Petersburg. Turgenev felt he had failed and vowed never to write again. Of course, he did write again, taking up in other novels and stories the very themes of *Fathers and Children*.

Goncharov believed that the political and quasi-moral exhortations and homilies of the radicals could neither give birth to the new man nor help shape a new art:

I am no longer in agreement with those esthetics of the new generations which fix the end of art by certain utilitarian aims, demanding that it merely reflect life teeming with day-to-day troubles, that it portray the passing heroes and heroines who are here now and gone tomorrow, and that it encompass every trifle, every detail. . . . Strict and serious art cannot portray chaos, corruption, all the microscopic things of life. This is the province of the lowest art, of caricature, epigram, light satire. . . . The old people, like the old habits, have outlived their time; the new paths have not yet been laid out. . . . The new life itself is still unformed. Turgenev in A Sportsman's Note-book, *Pisemsky, Grigorovich, have immortalized the customs of the peasant under serfdom . . . Ostrovsky has defined once and for all the entire merchant way of life. . . . The re-forms are at the most fifteen years old, some only ten—and only when they have set up a new life and this life has taken on a set form and a definite atmosphere will countless portraits become clear. . . . Only then will there be abundant harvest for the future Turgenevs, Pisemskys, and Ostrovskys. Until then one must not reproach us old men, as I have been re-proached, for portraying only the old way of life. The new life and the new men have not yet pecked their way out of the shell.*

In Russia, as in other Western countries, for all the variety of critical commentaries and analyses, there have been three basic attitudes toward literary criticism. One attitude, which is now often associated with the work of such men as B. V. Tomashevsky, B. M. Eikhenbaum, Yu. Tynyanov, V. B. Shklovsky and V. M. Zhirmunsky in the decade after World War I, but which goes back to the eighteenth and early nine-teenth centuries, is the view that the force of literature comes from its compositional pattern, that literature consists of ele-ments ("devices") which it is the critic's job of work to an-alyze. Another attitude, connected with thinkers and critics as different and as remote from one another as Skovoroda and Berdyaev, Zhukovsky and Vladimir Solovev, Sumarokov and G. I. Chulkov, asserts that literature affirms life by being the revelation of transcendent ideas, that the truth is superior to the everyday world and independent of it. A third attitude, which arose about the middle of the eighteenth century and is particularly clear in the critical and programmatic prose of Novikov, Radishchev, and Krylov, in the fiction of the great majority of nineteenth-century novelists, and in the scholarship of men such as P. N. Sakulin, G. A. Gukovsky, V. V. Gippius, and Yu. G. Oksman, regards a work of art as inextricably bound to and in part explained by social processes contemporary to it. Russian literature of the nineteenth century is characterized by objective technique going hand-in-hand with the author's social message. Belinsky's critical writings in the 1840's are still excellent samples of this attitude, especially, perhaps, his essay "The Idea of Art," in which, reshaping Hegel, he identifies the actions of any individual both with social progress and with absolute truth:

Art is the immediate contemplation of truth, or thinking in images. . . . The starting point of thought is the divine absolute idea; the movement of thought consists of the growth of this idea from within itself in accordance with the laws of higher (transcendental) logic or metaphysics. . . . Thinking, as an action, essentially presupposes two opposite things— the subject and the object—and is inconceivable without a reasoning creature, man. . . . Nature is the initial moment of the spirit striving from potentiality to become actuality. . . . Nature is a sort of mode by which the spirit becomes actuality and perceives and cognizes itself. Hence its crowning achievement is man. . . . Civil society is a mode for the development of human individuality. . . . Every important event in the life of mankind occurs in its time, never before or after. Every great man performs the deeds of his time. . . . Man is reason incarnate. . . . The focal point of his thought is his I. . . . All phenomena of nature are but the particular manifestations of the universal. The universal is the idea.

Belinsky was careful to single out and to emphasize the "genuineness" of a literary work. He was able to accept a new book in these terms, without worrying over fashions or ranks in a literary hierarchy. His sincere criticism, though it lacked deep perception, helped the development of Russian literature and greatly helped the development of a social attitude favorable to literature. Belinsky pointed out that

the public . . . looks upon Russian writers as its only leaders, defenders and saviors against Russian autocracy, orthodoxy, and nationality, and therefore, while always ready to forgive a writer a bad book, will never forgive him a pernicious book.

For Belinsky, esthetic judgment followed ethical, to use Norman Foerster's distinction. Although the pleasure or excellence involved in a book was an ultimate value on which decisive judgment rested, first judgment was of the book's capacity to imitate life and to extend the reader's knowledge of human nature. Literature for Belinsky was "the record, in terms of beauty, of the striving of mankind to know and express itself."

Beyond Apollon Grigorev's "organic criticism," a view that literature must be an organic outgrowth of the national soil and that life, like art, was a complex, self-conditioned unity—"Life is something mysterious and inexhaustible, an abyss that engulfs all finite reason, an unspannable ocean, the logical conclusion of the wisest brain, something even ironical and at the same time full of love, procreating one world after another"—the new attitude presumed the rational power of the intellect and the possibility of unlimited human progress. Belinsky did not closely follow Hegel, accepting neither Hegel's exaltation of Greek art nor his prediction of the death of art. Belinsky believed literature tied to life, the expression of a national spirit:

Even today there are still many good people who, repeating the outdated ideas of others, very naively assert that art and life go their separate ways, that there is nothing in common between them, and that art would degrade itself if it descended to contemporary interests. If by contemporary interests is meant the fashions, the Stock Exchange quotations, the gossip and trifles of high society, then indeed art would degrade itself if it descended to contemporary interests. That is what happened to art in France when it compelled the heroes of ancient Greece and Rome to indulge in contemporary court gossip. No, this is not what we mean by the historical trend in art. It is a modern view of the past, the thought of the age, the sad reflections, or the radiant joy of the times—not the interests of a class but the interests of society, not the interests of the state but the interests of mankind. In a word, it is universal, in the ideal and lofty sense of the term. . . . It is absurd to think that progress must cease because it has now reached an extreme point and can proceed no farther. There is no limit to human progress, and never will mankind say to itself: Stop, enough, there is nowhere farther to go.

For Belinsky, art, concerned with the eternal truths of human existence, is subject to the process of historical evolution, to given sets of historical conditions. It is like life, but it is not a substitute for life. It cannot be essentially fantastic; it must be "natural," "national," "genuine," "real." In a work of art "reality must have passed through imagination," and imagination "must create something whole, complete, unified and self-contained." A novel is to be the narrative of understanding of an imagined, real world, not merely a document of the habits and events of the world of the newspapers.

Belinsky saw no contradictions between historical and esthetic criteria or between esthetic and social demands on a writer. It is easy, according to Belinsky, for art to be reconciled with social service: "Art is social, yet it serves society by serving itself. Art purifies reality." Art for art's sake Belinsky thought an absurdity, a dreamy abstraction which, in fact, had never existed:

To deny art the right of serving public interests means debasing it, not raising it, for it means depriving it of its most vital force, that is, the Idea, and making it an object of sybaritic pleasure, a plaything of lazy idlers.

Scientists and philosophers by their statistics prove a condition; the artist, by an appeal to his audience's imagination, shows pictures of a condition.

The former are listened to and understood by few; the latter, by all. The highest and most sacred interest of society is its own welfare, equally extended to each of its members. The road to this welfare is consciousness, and art can promote consciousness no less than science or philosophy.

The aim of criticism, as Belinsky first distinguished it, was to differentiate the temporal from the eternal, the historical from the artistic. Later, he came to think this the task not so much of the individual critic as of the historical movement of society itself. In a series of articles he said that Pushkin had become obsolete because of the forward movement of Russian society and its literature. New artists, he said, satisfy a new and necessarily superior time. Critical judgment itself is formed only by the processes that happen in time. The chief determinant of an artist's work is the society which supplies him his materials. Every society is responsible for its art.

In the 1850's, especially during the Crimean War and after the death of Nicholas in 1855, political necessity altered the quality of philosophic inquiry and sharpened political distinctions among writers and literary trends. The merit of speculation tended to be measured by practical consequences. One often hears mention, therefore, of the predominance of utilitarian principles in the decade surrounding the manumission. The liberals of the 1840's yielded in importance to the radicals of the late 1850's and the 1860's. N. G. Chernyshevsky was the active center of tolerated political opposition at this time, a very strong voice in decisions taken by *The Contemporary* after 1855, and an outspoken advocate of social change, effected by political activity or, if necessary, by force. The men around Chernyshevsky felt that new political conditions required overt response. As a letter from one of them (V. P. Pertsov-?) to Herzen in May, 1858 makes clear, they did not assume any efficacy in argument and they believed that there existed a profound social schism which could be bridged only by thorough social reform. The "Letter from Petersburg" to Herzen in London said that:

It's now very clear here that the government is on the side of the landowners' party, that it would be delighted to say no to its own innocent notions in this business of freeing the serfs and to leave things as they are, if only somebody could show it a sure way of going on without change and without provoking peasant unrest. Fortunately, there's no such way, and that's where our hope lies, not in any noble nature on the part of the government.

Chernyshevsky and the radicals around him hoped that the government would bungle the job of playing the liberals and the landowners off against each other and cause a political catastrophe "which would set Russia on the road to open class struggle."

Chernyshevsky's views on art and the function of literature were corollaries to his political outlook. The spirit of a nation is awakened, he said, not by books but by events.

Literature induces a peaceful and reasonable disposition in the mind aroused by events. Literature is a surrogate for life, a passive mirror of society. Art is an inferior reproduction of reality. What is beauty? Beauty is life. Words are always general, hence pale and feeble. A woman walking the Petersburg streets is more beautiful than the Venus de Milo. Poets write their autobiographies. Why then art? Because our imagination is feeble, and we need reminders of what we want to keep. The most art can be is a handbook for those studying life.

N. A. Dobrolyubov argued similarly that "literature only reproduces life, it never portrays what does not exist in actuality." Literature helps clarify existing tendencies in society. It may help give "greater fullness to the conscious work of society." It is "an auxiliary force, the importance of which lies in propaganda." He also believed, however, that artists become the historical leaders of mankind, that, like Shakespeare, they may symbolize an entire phase of human development. The social types in a novel, he said, are revelatory of the author's world view, regardless of the author's conscious intentions.

In the living images the poet creates, he may, imperceptibly even to himself, grasp and express an inner meaning long before his mind can define it. It is precisely the function of criticism to explain the meaning hidden in these images.

Like Chernyshevsky, Dobrolyubov demanded social reform and demanded that the novelist produce for society the "new man" who could direct the reform and express a positive attitude toward his experience of human nature in the Russia of the 1860's.

It was in this period of philosophic disagreements and

strong political antipathies that *Fathers and Children* came out.

Now, more than one hundred years later, most readers, if asked to choose, would say they prefer Dostoevsky or Tolstoy or Pushkin to all other Russian writers and would absent-mindedly deny Turgenev the exceptional role he played in the literary world of preemancipation Russia and even in French and English intellectual life in the late 1860's and the 1870's. One forgets, also, how politically conscious Turgenev was, in the deepest sense, how, in his time, politically contemporary. On May 24, 1862, in London, a few days after a long political and philosophic discussion with Turgenev and Botkin, Herzen wrote a note, now in Yu. G. Oksman's collection and recently published by him, clearly reaffirming, as Oksman says, Herzen's "sociopolitical views, an expression symbolizing his faith." The note, written in French, states:

The powerful thought of the West, the end result of its long historic development, is the only thing that can germinate the seeds dormant within the patriarchal structure of the Slavs. The artel *(the workers' guild) and the rural commune, the sharing of produce and of land, the communal assembly and the unification of villages into self-governing administrative units—all that will serve as a base for our future regime of national liberty. But this base is as yet no more than widely scattered stones, and without the thought of the West the house of our future will never be more than that.*

To this N. P. Ogarev added:

All outcomes are possible, but it is for the future to decide which will take place. All I know is that the greatest utopia is the utopia of preserving the status quo, witness the six thousand years which mankind has existed. Everything has passed —the empire of Xerxes and the Roman Empire, Alexander and Charlemagne, the gods of Egypt and the gods of Olympus. Everything has passed like the ichthyosaurus and the mastodon, yielding to other kinds of organization. The elements are the same but the chemistry of society, like physical chemistry, changes the combinations once their cohesion becomes impossible.

Turgenev strongly protested against Herzen's and Ogarev's inadequate evaluation of western European capitalism and against their insistence on Russian socialism. Herzen declared, Oksman informs us, that his "Russian socialism" complemented the "Western socialism" of which "the first representatives . . . in Petersburg were the followers of Petrashevsky. . . . After them there appeared the powerful figure of Chernyshevsky." In connection with this debate, Herzen expressed many of his notions and opinions in a series of polemical articles in *The Bell.* Turgenev formulated his response in his novel *Smoke* (1867), in which Potugin sums up what, corroborated by letters and memoirs, may be regarded as Turgenev's views:

"Yes, yes, I'm a Westerner. I'm devoted to Europe, . . . devoted to its cultural standards, to those cultural standards which people here poke such delightful fun at nowadays—its civilization—yes, that word is still better. And I love it with all my heart, and I believe in it, and I have and will have no other belief. That word: civ-i-li-za-tion . . . is comprehensible and clean and sacred; but all the rest of it, the nationality, for example, and the glory stink of blood. . . . Let them go."

"Yes, but Russia . . . your country—do you love it?"

"I love it passionately, and I hate it passionately."

"That's an old song . . . that's a platitude."

"Well, so what? Is it the worse for that? . . . I know a good many platitudes. For instance: freedom and order—why,

do you think it's better the way things are: hierarchy and disorder? And besides, aren't all those phrases which intoxicate young heads so much—the contemptible bourgeoisie, the souveraineté du peuple, *the right to work—aren't they all platitudes, too? And as for love, inseparable from hate——"*

"*That's Byronism . . . the romanticism of the thirties.*"

"*I'm sorry, you're wrong; the first to point to such a mingling of feelings was Catullus. . . . I quote it from him, because I know a little Latin. . . . Yes, I both love and hate my Russia, my strange, dear, rotten, precious country. Now I have abandoned it; I had to give myself a little airing after sitting for twenty years . . . in a civil service building. I've abandoned Russia, and here I'm very comfortable and happy; but I'll go back soon; I feel that.*"

The first half of Turgenev's literary life was closely connected with *The Contemporary*, the magazine which Pushkin had founded in 1836, which Pletnev had taken on after Pushkin's death. Eclipsed during the decade after Pushkin by the livelier and more strong-minded *Moscow Observer*, Kraevsky's *Notes of the Fatherland*, and even Senkovsky's *The Reading Library*, toward the end of 1846 *The Contemporary* was taken over by a group of men led by Nekrasov and Panaev: N. A. Nekrasov, poet and editor, one of the ablest and most "advanced" literary men of the nineteenth century; I. I. Panaev, a columnist; V. G. Belinsky, who had moved to Petersburg in 1839, who had been writing anonymous criticism for *Notes of the Fatherland*, and for whose criticism Nekrasov wanted to establish a regular vehicle—to give Belinsky "a magazine of his own"; V. P. Botkin, critic and editor; and Turgenev, whose first published work had been the poem "The Old Oak" in *The Contemporary* in 1838, who had moved in the discussion circle around Stankevich (died 1840), the Pokorsky circle described in *Rudin* by Lezhnev, and who was to become the

dominant man of letters in the period from the rise of Dostoevsky (1845–46) and Tolstoy (1852) and Gogol's death
(1852) to the liberation of the serfs (1861) and the formulation of new, radical or "populist" social and political aims, as
presented in such novels and stories as Chernyshevsky's
What's To Be Done?, V. A. Sleptsov's *Hard Times* (both
published in 1865), and G. I. Uspensky's *The Morals of
Rasteryaeva Street* (1866).

In 1857 Turgenev contracted with Nekrasov to publish in
The Contemporary everything he wrote, although Nekrasov,
conscious of the new sociopolitical possibilities for Russia after
Nicholas's death, had split with the liberals the year before.
Turgenev remained for several years on terms of personal
friendship with Nekrasov, but his political opinions were
somewhere between those of the French writers, whom he in
disgust felt had a materialistic and uncivic attitude, and the
new Russian "left," as personified by Chernyshevsky, whose
manner and whose ideas (*The Esthetic Relation of Art to
Actuality*, 1855) Turgenev could not tolerate. Turgenev was
on the other side. As Tolstoy wrote to Botkin in 1858:

*What would you say now, when the filthy stream of politics
is trying to swallow everything up and to dirty, if not to do
away with, art—what would you say to those who believe in
art's independence and its amorality getting together and
demonstrating this truth both in deed (creative writing) and
word (criticism) and trying to save what is eternal and independent from accidental, one-sided, all-pervasive, political influence? Why shouldn't we be they? That is, Turgenev, you,
Fet, and I, and all who share our opinions.*

In 1859 Turgenev broke with Goncharov; in late 1860, with
Nekrasov; in 1861, with Tolstoy, famously; in the 1870's, with
Dostoevsky and with Fet. By the late 1860's his work had be-

come widely known in Germany and France; by the middle of the 1870's it had been translated into English and published both in England and America. Oxford awarded him an honorary degree in 1879 even as critics and writers were turning to Tolstoy, especially because, they felt,· Turgenev's portrait of the radical, such as Bazarov, did not describe the actual radicals of the post-reform period. After his death in 1883, despite his importance for James, Howells, and Conrad, Turgenev yielded in popular interest to Dostoevsky as well and became considered, chiefly for nonliterary reasons, a tame Westernizer who had abandoned his fierce, passionate people.

When *Fathers and Children* came out in 1862, D. I. Pisarev, radical and nihilist, wrote an article on Bazarov, whom he hailed as the representative of the new man. Perceiving that Turgenev had an ambivalent attitude toward his hero, that he did not "sympathize" with either the fathers or the children, Pisarev treated Bazarov as an extension of himself, for he shared Bazarov's bitter, ruthless negations. For him Bazarov was a symbol. Pisarev's criticism was not literary criticism but, as René Wellek called it, a radical's act of self-knowledge.

There is no doubt that Turgenev meant Bazarov as a radical, a man who fails through the very qualities the radical critics believed would guarantee his success. His self-confidence leads to careless error and a too costly mistake. His devotion to his ideal, his nonconformism, leads to emotional sterility, to a pointless and unrewarding removal from ordinary life. His faith in and commitment to not the present but the future (the essence of any radicalism) is the source of his "tragedy." "I dreamed of a dark, wild, large figure," Turgenev wrote to Sluchevsky, "semiautochthonous, strong, vengeful, honorable—and yet doomed, nevertheless, to perish because he stands on the threshold of the future." The poignancy and

the irony of Bazarov's life come from the fact that his attributes, which he most needs to make a life for himself in a
society from which he is naturally alienated, destroy him. His
faith in the community of mankind isolates him from men.
When the hope of accomplishing what he promised is gone,
he, like Quixote, can at best only assume the responsibility of
dying with dignity.

The novel begins with a scene of expectation set on May
20, 1859. Nikolai Kirsanov at the local coach stop is waiting
for his son, Arkady, to arrive, to return home. The conflict
between generations (the theme of the novel) is immediately
given by the characterization of the servant Petr, "a man of
the newest, up-to-date generation," and, in the beginning of
Chapter IV, by reference to Kirsanov's living room "furnished
in the latest style." The father's story, from the civil service
in Petersburg to family life on the estate, describes the circle
of place and of time within which the novel happens. To give
the history of a man, Turgenev assumes, is to reveal his character. "What is character," asked Henry James, "but the de-
termination of incident? What is incident but the illustration
of character?" The device recurs also on the introduction of
Odintsova into the novel, her character having been determined by the pattern of her past, the deaths of her parents,
and her marriage to the rich Odintsov. Of the main characters
only Bazarov acts before his past is revealed; for him, history
lies only in the future. Turgenev focuses on the differences between the past and the future, between Kirsanov's thought
that his wife "had not lived to see the day" of their son's return and his reflection that, like himself once, "his son . . .
[was] a graduate . . . Arkasha." The difference is made
morally striking in the judgment passed on Pavel Kirsanov's
hopeless pursuit of Princess R. (a kind of shadow of Turgenev's
pursuit of Pauline Viardot), which ruined his career. The

contrast between the two brothers is simple and strong. For Nikolai, "ten years passed like a dream"; for Pavel, "ten years passed . . . colorlessly, pointlessly, and quickly, terribly quickly." The stage is set for the arrival of a man of faith and devotion, the incarnation of one's image of an intellectual, a man of "self-confidence and intelligence." But Bazarov does not speak to Nikolai Kirsanov's greeting; he tips his cap. A moment later he does speak, and the first thing he says is to order the coachman: "All right, get a move on, bushy beard!" The ambiguity of the several characters' positions is confirmed after a few minutes by the inversion of the father–son relationship. Arkady, the prodigal, forgives his father, the begetter of Fenichka's child. Against this inversion, affirming the order of nature underlying human order, Turgenev fits Arkady's reflections on the land, as he rides home past the lush fields, into the processes of spring, as if in classical fashion setting the hero into nature, both an identification with nature and a consciousness of difference which is supported by the citation from *Eugene Onegin*, turning literature back to life through literature:

> How sad I am when you are here,
> Spring, Spring, the lovers' season,
> How . . .

Hardly a dozen pages into the novel, we are already aware of the basis of the book's structure and of the sort of conflict the characters will be involved in. The older men have made compromises which, whether successful or not, assert an undercurrent in life stronger than any socially defined relations. The younger men, still in the spring of their lives, full of idealism and energy, seem overshadowed by the probability of failure, for even in one's happiest moments, we feel, one is aware of the end, of an endless and unfathomable tragedy.

The most convenient and most easily comprehended human change, other than biological, is political, precisely what Turgenev turns to with the irony of Bazarov's first speech: "There's an English washbasin in my room, but the door won't lock. Still, you've got to encourage that—English washbasins, I mean. That's progress!" The details of discord in the political world are echoed by the discrepancies between what the actors are capable of and the material they have been given to work with. The discrepancies recur throughout the novel. "All children are quiet in my arms," says Bazarov to Fenichka, "I know how." And Dunyasha says, "Children sense who loves them." On the other hand, Bazarov says to the stable-boys, "You and I are just like frogs." "A good chemist," he says, "is twenty times more useful than any poet." Arkady, who embraces his father, refuses to pass judgment on him; Bazarov, he agrees, is a nihilist. Bazarov subsequently declares that "two times two is four, and all the rest is nonsense." "We act according to what we consider useful," says Bazarov. "Nowadays negation is the most useful of all—we negate." He does not hesitate to tell Arkady that his father is a "nice man, but he's behind the times." In the name of truthfulness, Bazarov calls Arkady's uncle an idiot; Arkady, full of family sentiment, says Bazarov is unfair. The difference between good and evil, Bazarov tells Odintsova, is only the difference between healthy and sick. Moral illness, he says, comes from a bad environment, "from the hideous state of social affairs." Political change will correct the deformity.

As Arkady has been defined by his four university years, so Pavel and Nikolai Kirsanov, brought together in late middle age by private losses, are defined by the time gone by. Pavel wants to forget; Nikolai looks back with nostalgia. Against them and their empty time stands Bazarov, faithful to the future, opposed to romanticization of the past, who declares that "every man must educate himself." Time in the novel not only defines the characters psychologically—Anna Odintsova's feeling of being old, the very notion that Bazarov is a man ahead of his time—but is also an objective condition. Space in the book, like that in Dostoevsky's *The Devils*, is carefully circumscribed, limited to four scenes under the shadow of the university and the world of Petersburg: Kirsanov's estate, the town, Odintsova's estate, Bazarov's parents' estate. Each character's concept of what he has made of his life or must yet make of it is set against what, in these several environments, he does make of it. Psychologically, or naturalistically, a man is happiest when he loses awareness of time:

Time (everyone knows) sometimes flies like a bird, sometimes crawls like a worm, but a man is especially happy when he does not even notice whether it goes swifty or slowly. Arkady and Bazarov spent fifteen days at Odintsova's in just such a state.

Beyond such psychological definition is the concept of time as a rhythm, a recurrence of events in pattern, an idea of "interval" relating what are otherwise unrelatable, because imperfectly communicating, selves. Two events in the novel illustrate two aspects of time as such an objective condition.

In Chapter XVI, at Odintsova's, Katya plays Mozart's C-minor sonata–fantasia. The music brings Arkady to Katya. It establishes the beginnings of a profound relationship between them, not because she, who is attractive, has played the music well (which is all that Arkady can express either to Katya or to himself) but because of the expression through the music, itself the essential, esthetic expression of time, of the objective condition underlying life:

The final part of the sonata especially overwhelmed Arkady, that part in which, in the middle of the exquisite gaiety of

the lighthearted melody, there suddenly come bursts of such
a mournful, almost tragic sadness.

The two young people briefly comprise a society by partici-
pating in the society of music. Music, as an ideal condition,
is contrasted to that ideal condition of political society to
which Bazarov is devoted. To perceive the world's sadness is
to be in harmony with the world, as an analogous and beautiful scene in Turgenev's *A Nest of the Gentry* (1859) suggests.

That novel is the story of an intelligent, rather orthodox,
somewhat Slavophile man named Lavretsky, who made the
mistake of marrying an enticing but selfish and fickle lady.
Having found out her adultery, he pensions her off, as it were,
and returns from Europe to his estate in Russia. He falls in
love with a forthright, innocent girl named Liza. His affection for her helps persuade her not to marry Panshin, a West-
ern-oriented, unattractively ambitious, talented young man.
But the novel ends in sadness. Lavretsky's wife returns with
their daughter. Lavretsky arranges for Liza to meet her. Liza
abjures her declaration of love to Lavretsky and insists that
he forgive his wife. The wife joins Lavretsky, and Panshin
becomes a visitor. Lavretsky goes away; Liza enters a convent. Years later, Lavretsky, a "superfluous man," returns to
the house where Liza lived and watches young people playing
in the garden by the tree where he confessed his love to Liza
and received hers. He visits the convent where she lived:

Stepping down from choir to choir, she walked close past him.
She passed with the even, meekly hurried gait of a nun and
did not glance at him. Only her eyelashes quivered slightly
and the emaciated face bent still lower and the fingers of her
clasped hands entwined with the rosary were pressed tighter
still. What were they both thinking, what were they feeling?
Who can know? Who can tell? There are such moments in
life, such feelings. One can but point to them—and pass on.

There had previously been in Lavretsky's life one similar moment. It occurred just after he had told Liza that he loved her and she had, in effect, agreed to marry him. He was in a state of ecstasy. And as he passed the house where old Lemm lived, the very old German musician who gave Liza piano lessons, he heard "a mighty flood of melody" streaming from the windows upstairs. He shouted at Lemm to let him in. The old man did. He made Lavretsky sit down, and he went on playing his latest composition.

It was long since Lavretsky had heard anything of the kind: the tender, passionate melody gripped the heart from the very first note. It was all aglow, languishing with the fire of inspiration, joy and beauty. It rose and melted on the air. It spoke of everything that is precious, unutterable, and hallowed on earth. It breathed immortal sadness and ascended, dying, to the heavenly spheres. . . . The music seemed to clutch at his heartstrings, still quivering with the tumult of new-found love. It pulsated with love itself. "Again," he whispered as the last chord died away. The old man glanced at him sharply, tapped his chest with his hand, saying slowly in his own language, "I have done this, for I am a great musician," and he played his wondrous composition again. There were no candles in the room; the beams of the rising moon fell through the windows; the soft air was vibrant with sound; the poor little room seemed a holy place, and noble, and the old man's head loomed inspired in the silvery half light. Lavretsky went up to him and embraced him. At first Lemm did not respond to the embrace; he even pushed him away with his elbow; for a long time he sat motionlessly, with the same stern, almost surly expression and only mumbled twice, "Aha!" At last his transfigured countenance relaxed, and in response to Lavretsky's ardent congratulations, he first smiled faintly, then burst into tears, sobbing weakly like a child.

"It's remarkable," he said, "that you should have come just at this moment. I know, I know everything."

The other event in *Fathers and Children*, in Chapter XXIV, on Kirsanov's estate, turns time into a joke on history, gives it the independent authority of irony, and threatens its consummation, death. The scene is Pavel Kirsanov's challenge to Bazarov and their duel. "My view is that you're superfluous here," Pavel tells Bazarov. There then follows the conflict between generations as expressed by social manners revealing class allegiance and moral and philosophical values.

In *The Devils*, published serially in the same *Russian Herald* nine years later in 1871, Dostoevsky assigns to a partly ridiculous Stepan Trofimovich, a man of the 1840's, views which he himself, Dostoevsky, had held in the 1840's and which, he is aware, stand in sharp contrast ·to the views of the 1860's. Analyzing Stepan Trofimovich, the narrator says:

There's no doubt that for a while he, too, belonged to the remarkable pleiad of certain social activists of the generation now gone by, and, for a while—though only for the briefest moment—many people in their hurry then spoke his name practically in the same breath as those of Chaadaev, Belinsky, Granovsky, and the just-emigrated Herzen. . . .

He returned from abroad and excelled as university lecturer at the tail end of the forties. . . . Also managed to defend a brilliant dissertation . . . [which] smartly and sharply cut to the quick the Slavophiles of the day. . . . Then—however, after he had lost his chair—he managed to publish (as a kind of little revenge and just to show them whom they had lost) in a progressive, monthly magazine, which translated Dickens and preached the doctrines of George Sand, the beginning of a very profound study, something about the causes of the extraordinary moral goodness of some knights at some point,

or something of that sort. . . . People said later that the con-
tinuation was quickly suppressed and that even the progres-
sive magazine suffered for having published the first half.
It's very possible, because just about every sort of thing hap-
pened then, didn't it?

There follows an account, told by the narrator Mr. G—v and
similar to Dostoevsky's own biography, of Stepan Trofimovich's involvement in a discussion circle in the 1840's, in a
group of about thirty who "were said to be thinking of actually translating Fourier." A poem which Stepan Trofimovich
had written some six years previously, in the style of the late
1830's, and which circulated in manuscript, was picked up
and found "dangerous." Mr. G—v's account of its excessively
romantic, utopian socialist contents—"a sort of allegory in
lyricodramatic form reminiscent of Part II of *Faust*"—makes
the poem an historical joke, for "in our time" it is "absolutely harmless." The list, in Chapter VI of *The Devils*, of
topics of conversation among "the new men" of the 1860's,
ranging from idle gossip about events in Petersburg and spite-
ful comment on Kraevsky's house to discussion of political
redivision of Russia on nationality lines and arguments for
women's rights, underlines the historical change. The ex-
igency of events has made old dreams ridiculous. Political action has superseded moral inquiry. "Your group never loved
the people," Shatov says to Stepan Trofimovich, "neither
Russia nor the people. . . . You can't love what you don't
know, and you never had the slightest understanding of the
Russian people." Bazarov tells Pavel Kirsanov the same thing:
"You don't even know how to talk to a peasant."

The conflict between social attitudes, given as the con-
test between generations or the incompatibility of fathers
and children, is reduced in the duel scene to "the brother"

versus "the friend," the uncle versus the guest—is reduced, as if through gears, to nonsense. Pavel's argument, like the attitude on which it is based, is ridiculous. Just as Stepan Trofimovich's idealism is cut down to political life-size by being labeled ineptly imitative of unsuccessful and unreal drama, so Pavel's gestures, undertaken to proclaim a special, aristocratic world view, amount only to bad fiction. They represent, not real Russian life, nor even the life of Russian realism (which is Turgenev's job of work), but artificial, French fancifulness.

"Splendid," said Pavel Petrovich and stood his cane in the corner. "Now for a few words about the terms of our duel, but first I should like to know if you consider it necessary to resort to the formality of a brief quarrel which might be the provocation of my challenge?"

"No, no need for formalities."

"I think so, too. I also assume it is unnecessary to go into the real reasons for our conflict. We cannot abide each other. Need there be more?"

"Need there be more?" Bazarov repeated ironically.

"As for the actual terms of the duel, since we shall have no seconds—for where can we find them?"

"Exactly, where?"

"I therefore have the honor of suggesting the following to you: to fight early tomorrow, let us say at six, beyond the grove, with pistols; the barrier at ten paces. . . ."

"Ten? So; at that distance we'll hate each other. . . ."

"Two shots apiece, and, just in case, each to put in his pocket a note taking upon himself his own death."

"Now, I can't quite go along with that," said Bazarov. "It's starting to look somewhat like a French novel, unreal somehow."

The farce of the preparations yields to dramatization, to the "acting out" of the internal opposition between, or across, generations. Anticlimax of the farce is selection of Petr, the representative of "the newest, up-to-date generation," as witness. "But won't you agree, Pavel Petrovich," Bazarov asks, "that our duel is unusual to the point of being ridiculous? Just look at the expression on the face of our second." Pavel replies that he does not deny the oddness of their duel but that "I consider it my duty to warn you that I intend to fight in earnest."

Differences in value are differences in time. Time is defined by the pistol shots. The older generation shoots while the younger waits. The bullet whizzes by Bazarov's ear. Bazarov shoots without aiming—not to shoot would be to insult Pavel in fact—and accidentally wounds Pavel in the thigh. The shot reverses their roles. Bazarov has behaved nobly, endangering his life though knowing better. He wins and becomes doctor to Pavel. Pavel acts out a scene of dying, urges his brother to marry Fenichka, "dabbed his forehead with eau-de-cologne and shut his eyes. Lit up in bright daylight, his handsome, emaciated head lay on the white pillow like the head of a corpse. Indeed, he really was a corpse." He does not die biologically (he later goes to Moscow on business and then to Dresden "for his health") but he, the incarnation of the effeteness of his generation, is sexually, emotionally, and morally dead. The pistol shot marked the end of his time. Afterwards, the "interval" between him and Bazarov, as between the 1840's and the 1860's, is defined wholly in Bazarov's terms.

If one thinks of Pushkin as a "novelistic poet" in *Eugene Onegin*, one might call Turgenev a "poetic novelist" for his insistence on the specificity of things experienced and the symbolic nature of their meaning. His stories are, on the whole, basically narratives of the breaking-up of an impossible love triangle. Chulkaturin in "The Diary of a Superfluous Man" is dispossessed of inaccessible Liza by Prince N., who never intended to stay with her, anyway. Rudin hovers between Darya Mikhailovna and Nataliya Alekseyevna, as Nataliya Alekseyevna hovers between Rudin and Volyntsev. In "First Love" Voldemar is only Zinaida's page; his father, her lover; Zinaida herself, always lost, alone in a world of admirers, exquisite and tragic. In "A King Lear of the Steppe" Kharlov is betrayed by his two daughters, who come finally to hate each other and to be almost fantastically isolated from the world around them. In "Spring Torrents" Sanin wins Gemma from Klüber, leaves her for Mariya Nikolaevna, who has a husband, and in the end is about to depart on the actual journey of which Gemma has long represented the symbolic fulfillment. In *Fathers and Children* all the love affairs express loss. Pavel Kirsanov is alone. The incompleteness of Nikolai's affair with Fenichka is pointed up by recollection of his past happiness with his wife. The joy with which Arkady enters his new life with Katya has required surrender of his old ideals and proceeded, in the first place— witness, specifically, his proposal to Katya—on the immediacy of Bazarov and Anna and their self-consciousness of failure.

> *"Your friend, Arkady Nikolaich, has come, [says Odintsova] and I've fallen back into my old rut, into my real role."*
> *"What role is that, if I may ask?" [says Bazarov]*
> *"The role of aunt. . . . But, mainly, he's young, so young . . . not like you and me, Evgeny Vasilyich."*

Bazarov dies. Odintsova marries a man "as cold as ice." Ironically, she has lost the capacity to love at precisely the age love is most exotic (*Antony and Cleopatra*). Her story is a history of purposelessness. Bazarov's story is an account of inappropriateness. The stories of Nikolai Kirsanov and of Arkady are psalms of accommodation, of adjustment, of passive response to the force of life, manifest in nature as well as in, say, Odintsova's face, which "expressed a kind of tender and gentle force." We are not moved by the stories themselves. We are moved by the perceptions of character, the "intervals" among the characters which the events of the novel uncover. We are moved by Turgenev's mind in the excellence of its literary craftsmanship.

We may regard the construction as a series of fractured triangles or as a series of oppositions, in concept like but in technique unlike Dostoevsky's "doubles." We may think of the time itself as "before" and "after," as a triadic past-present-future, or as a vivid conflict of opposites in every moment. The setting of the novel, primarily triadic (the three estates), is equally opposition between "here" and "there," the difference between where one is and where one wants to be. More often than not, a character responds to or behaves toward another in terms relating to a third: the duel between Pavel and Bazarov, which makes Petr blanch, is undertaken to define the conditions of the new life, that is, ironically, for Petr's benefit. What finally will hold Arkady to Katya is their child, the next generation, as, at the beginning of the novel, Arkady held his own father to the memory of his mother. Alone in his grave, fenced in, marked by two firs (unlike Pushkin's monument, in the poem after Horace, to which the people beat a path), Bazarov holds his parents togther who "have nothing left." Whether we cast the relationships in triangles or in "doubles" is irrelevant. Characters in pairs—Arkady/Bazarov, Pavel/Nikolai, Odintsova/Katya—relate each to the other through a succession of still other people, each relationship forming a temporary triangle, each triangle imperfect, for the basic pair is constructed of complementary, not identical and not antagonistic, figures. The third person's action always in some sense splits the original pair. The sources of these pairs are characteristics of actual people recombined into fiction. "In order for me to give birth to a fictional character," Turgenev wrote N. A. Ostrovskaya, "I have to choose a living person who can, in some way, serve me as a kind of conducting wire. That is the reason I have never tried to do a historical novel." Once the combinations have been constructed and the characters seem real, Turgenev wrote Maikov, "I introduce them into a web of various actions, and so there grows in my mind a whole and separate little world. Then, without my expecting it or wishing it, there comes the necessity of giving visible form to this little world, and I do, with pleasure and delight. Consequently a *preconceived bias* never directs my work in any sense." Whatever social or moral "message" a reader finds there (as André Mazon, in his study *Turgenev's Parisian Manuscripts*, found that in the later social novels Turgenev "projected the thesis before setting to work, and the work showed evidence of his doing so"), the work appeals to our pity, our response to experience of loss and the hopelessness engendered by change.

A careful writer, "a man of taste and order with regular habits," as Mazon says, Turgenev was profoundly melancholic. The excellence of the play of his mind lies in the picture composed, as the excellence of a painting lies in color. Form is color, said Jonathan Edwards. Structure is the gestures of excellence. Ideally, as in the following excerpt from "Kasyan from Krasivaya Mech" (1851), the eye traces a form built by imagination:

It's a wonderfully pleasant thing to lie on your back in the forest and look up. You think you're looking into a bottom-

less sea, that it stretches out far and wide underneath *you, that the trees don't rise from the ground but, like roots of huge plants, drop down, fall perpendicularly into those glass-clear waves. The leaves on the trees are sometimes as translucent as emeralds, sometimes opaque in a golden, almost black greenness. Somewhere far, far away, at the end of its slender twig, a single leaf stands motionless against a blue patch of pellucid sky, and beside it another one sways with a movement like the play of a fish on a line, a movement that seems spontaneous and not produced by the wind. Like fairy islands under the sea, round white clouds float quietly up and quietly away—and suddenly the whole sea, the radiant air, the sun-drenched branches and leaves, all begin to ripple and tremble with a transitory brilliance, and there comes a fresh, thrilling murmur, like the interminable, faint splashing that follows the rising of a sudden swell. You gaze without stirring, and no words can express the gladness and peace and sweetness that catch at your heart.*

The prose invents gentleness, with an overtone of gentility; there is this sort of calm only in leisure. Only in leisure is there disinterestedness, which is a prerequisite for successful communication, the disinterestedness of the spectator, the clever but casual observer, which Turgenev considered himself. As he said to Flaubert, apropos of the Paris Commune, "We have some hard moments to live through, we others, we born spectators."

The moment of harmony exposes to a man the meaning of life, this book says. That man delights in being one with the world but is conscious of continual losses. Many readers have tagged Turgenev "sentimental"; still more have called him politically anachronistic. But, as in the following passage from *Fathers and Children*, political activity about the future and harsh political judgment on the past lead to the understanding that none of it remains, that mortality is a limit which only beauty can only briefly offset. At the governor's ball the gentry speak bad French and the protagonists of the novel act like antiheroes: the modern Arkady dances badly; Bazarov, trusted by the servants and more nearly one of them than a gentleman, does not dance at all. Did Bazarov's death affirm his ideals or, as Turgenev puts the question, are his parents' prayers and tears pointless? Nikolai Kirsanov, walking in his garden, reflects on the two young men:

They have something we don't, some advantage over us. Youthfulness! No, it's not just that. Isn't their advantage the fact that they show fewer traces of gentleman's behavior than we do?

Nikolai lowered his head and ran his hand over his face.

But to deny poetry? he thought again. Not to feel art, nature?

. . . It was already turning evening; the sun had gone down behind a small aspen thicket lying a half-verst beyond the garden, its shadow stretching endlessly across the still fields. A peasant was trotting on a white horse down the dark, narrow path beside the thicket. . . .

He remembered the first time he had seen her [his wife]. He was still a student then. . . . And later there were the first, shy visits, the hints, the half smiles, and bewilderment, and sorrow, and outbursts, and, in the end, that panting joy. . . . Where had it all flown? She had become his wife, he had been happy as few on earth are. . . . But, he thought, those sweet, first moments, why couldn't they live an eternal, immortal life?

How can they be accommodated to the fact that in the present one generation reads Pushkin's "The Gypsies" and another generation reads Büchner's *Matter and Force*?

For Bazarov, negation is a principle of assertion, a philosophically functioning concept; it is also a procedure of action. The crucial sociopolitical question of Turgenev's day, one to which Bazarov addresses himself, was how to treat the *obshchina*, the peasant commune. Turgenev's crucial question was how to connect a necessarily revolutionary response to that question with an antirevolutionary understanding of the beauty and sadness of life. Partly, he answers his question by retelling the past as a series of stories within the novel, regularly using one character as witness or narrator of another character's actions or surroundings. Frequently he does it by opposing to that commentary, and to the lyricism (or compassion) which he finds in love and in loveliness, dramatic irony. Perhaps the best, conspicuously and provocatively nonpolitical gesture is Bazarov's contracting typhus. Bazarov, the new, rational man, struggles not to go mad. The doctor of the future turns into the patient of the past—bitterly, ironically, the patient when Odintsova gives him the final kiss:

> *Anna Sergeyevna bent down to him.*
> *"Evgeny Vasilyich, I'm here."*
> *He instantly took her hand and raised his head a little.*
> *"Farewell," he said with sudden strength, and his eyes sparkled with a final brilliance. "Farewell. . . . Listen. . . . You see, I didn't kiss you then. . . . Blow on a guttering lamp and let it go out. . . ."*
> *Anna Sergeyevna pressed her lips to his forehead.*
> *"And that's enough!" he said and sank back onto the pillow. "Now . . . the darkness. . . ."*

Bazarov could not become a Nietzschean superman. Life precluded the possibility. Dostoevsky in turn could not let the rational rebellion of Ivan Karamazov, say, triumph in revolution and blasphemy. He could not let man become his own god. Life does not allow the possibility. Such self-assumption or self-assurance issues inevitably, in his novels and in Turgenev's, in despair or destruction. No man can presume so much and live.

Turgenev like Dostoevsky supposes that life is ultimately nonrational and that it can be dealt with significantly only in nonrational ways—self-denial, self-purification, love, and prayer. The assumption contradicts Belinsky's assumption behind his statement that "Society's tyranny demands heroes to combat it."

Belinsky assumed that society exploits its members for benefits which are not theirs; that this repression and exploitation can be opposed and overcome; and that only outstanding men with courage and prescience are able to resist tyranny and to persuade others to follow them. He presumed that man alone torments men, a torment which can be eliminated by compelling men to understand the sensible, the natural, the rational way of living together in mutual respect and helpfulness. (Opposition to tyranny, the arbitrary exercise of absolute power, always argues for a rational division of labor and a rational distribution of power.)

Both Belinsky and Turgenev believed in the necessity of establishing the hero as a power and as a symbol, in literature and in life. They sharply disagreed on what life was. Turgenev said that real life was irregularly visible, was spiritual, was manifest in the thousand crooked ways a man expresses consciousness, was almost incommunicable. Belinsky said that real life was everywhere obvious, was material, was continually dramatized in the conflicts between the oppressor and the oppressed. As Dobrolyubov said, the only activity worthy of man was "true and effective struggle against environment." Belinsky was certain that "the source of all progress and advance lies in human nature," and that man's intellect, the battleground in the war of ideas, could determine the mode of his existence. Turgenev wanted men to live more wisely; he knew that their novels must be political, but his intellect could not allow him to infer the necessity of progress from experiences of amelioration or wishes for love.

"The deepest quality of a work of art will always be the quality of the mind of the producer," said Henry James. "In proportion as that intelligence is fine will the novel, the picture, the statue, partake of the substance of beauty and truth." This criterion for excellence, measured only and finally in the execution, points to the center of Turgenev's talent. Episodes from his own life, of course, lie behind many of his stories and many scenes in his novels. "I never try to improve on life; I merely try to see and understand it. . . . Every line I have written has been inspired by something that has actually happened to me or come within my observation," said Turgenev. To read Turgenev's stories back to the life, to try to label their "sources," seems inappropriate. The moral dilemmas of Tolstoy's life are enacted in his prose. Turgenev's personal history becomes, in his prose, a literary pattern, the work of the organizing, visionary intelligence—of that "fine mind." Close friend of Flaubert, Turgenev belonged to a circle in Paris which included Daudet, Zola, the Goncourts, and young Henry James. One discussion, according to James, was about

questions of taste, questions of art and form. . . . The conviction that held . . . [the speakers] together was the conviction that art and morality are two utterly different things, and that the former has no more to do with the latter than it has with astronomy or biology. The only duty of a novel was to be well written; that merit included every other of which it was capable.

The criterion for Turgenev is taste. He considered *L'Assommoir* spoiled by Zola's desire to tell "what Gervaise felt rather than what she thought. What difference does it make to me," Turgenev asked, "whether she perspires in the middle of the back or under the arms?" As for his own work, he meant notations of characteristics to define essential character. The two were one. James wrote about him:

To describe him in the fewest terms, he is a storyteller who has taken notes. If we are not mistaken, he notes down an idiosyncrasy of character, a fragment of talk, an attitude, a feature, a gesture, and keeps it, if need be, for twenty years, till just the moment for using it comes. . . . He has no recognition of unembodied ideas; an idea, with him, is such and such an individual, with such and such a nose and chin, such and such a hat and waistcoat, bearing the same relation to it as the look of the printed word does to its meaning.

James thought of him not so much as a realist—those he called the "grandsons of Balzac"—as a "romanticist of realism." Turgenev excluded the difficult, the dirty, the vile, the perverted, yet the sadness of his perception of them lies like a shadow over everything he wrote. As James said,

the element of melancholy in his nature was deep and constant. . . . [He] gives us a peculiar sense of being out of harmony with his native land. He loves the old and he is unable to see where the new is drifting. . . . [He] strikes us as a disappointed man. . . . The fermentation of social change has thrown to the surface in Russia a deluge of hollow pretensions and vicious presumptions, amid which the love either of old virtues or of new achievements finds very little gratification.

As he grew old, tired, haunted by the fear of death and

the pain of dying, depressed by the despair of late middle age, believing there was nothing more to do and nothing to expect, Turgenev turned gently to a notion of Russian nationalism. The French and all the Latins were, he maintained, *hommes de la loi*; the Russians, *hommes de l'humanité*, who had a deeper and warmer social awareness, an indifference or irreverence for merely human regulations, a devotion to what was ultimate, real, and radical. Russians did not fear simplicity. And once he remarked that Russians were liars because they had so long been slaves, but that they demanded in art what life had so long denied them—truth and freedom.

Literary activity in nineteenth-century Russia expressed social understanding. To think was to do. And in an essay, "Hamlet and Don Quixote," Turgenev divided men into two sorts of idealists: the socially impotent rationalists frustrated by their own ideas, and the fanatical dreamers driven by faith to translate their ideas into acts. Pushkin and Lermontov by their stories and novels, Griboedov and Vyazemsky by their letters, Davydov by his autobiography, introduced into Russia a fresh way of thinking in prose; Zagoskin's historical romance *Yury Miloslavsky* (1829), Pogorelsky's humorous tales, Bestuzhev-Marlinsky's *Ammalat Bek*, prepared the ground for the Russian fiction we especially remember Given the fact of alienation, the unstereotyped typicality of the heroes of this nineteenth-century literature surprises us. But Onegin, Pechorin, Oblomov, Lavretsky, Bazarov, Ivan Karamazov, Levin, express, each in his own way and all by irony, a unified social consciousness and a passionate desire for freedom and personal significance. "Art comprehends all our activity from boat-building to poetry," said Joyce; in nineteenth-century Russia, everyone agreed that it did.

There was wide literary activity—poetry written, essays composed, journals and papers published, dissertations assembled—increasing steadily from the middle of the eighteenth century. In 1861, *The Contemporary*, a first-rate magazine, had a circulation of over 7,000. Writers like Turgenev, knowing that the "forever" of art depends on its "now," transcended provincialism and nationalism as, Turgenev said, the Greeks had, by focusing on them. Life determined its own fidelity. Turgenev did not impose his feelings on what he perceived but, instead, derived his feelings from it.

Art, of course, begets art. Young Giotto painted sheep not as he saw them but as Cimabue painted them. The great artist is the one who changes tradition and, by that, life. In that sense, developing ever greater mastery of the forces in the material world and continually adjusting to this, man has been becoming a greater and greater realist. The contributions of the writers like Turgenev come from a heightened awareness of the terms of this reality and from a tradition continually adjusted to an ever greater actualization of character. These writers represented man in society as a lonely, naked, frustrated, hopeful, selfish, kind, practicing visionary, a figure living as it had to but, in the incompleteness of its life, always imagining a different way it ought to live. Against the censorship, the policing, the overt repression, and the crass inequality of tsarist Russia, their work was all the more important. They emphasized the transformational nature of man's understanding, not only the transmutation of thought in symbol but also the transformation of man himself, of his values, by the use of his natural, intellectual faculties in useful social service. Understanding of failure was even more important than achievement of success. They were intent not on describing the motion and material of a thing but on seeing its purpose.

Turgenev, among them, revealed purpose through description of things. He insisted that he owed allegiance only to his vision of truth and to the integrity of his work. "Art," he said, "is such a great thing that the whole man, with all his faculties, including the intellect, is hardly enough for it." The artist's experience seemed to him partly like the thinker's, partly like the seer's:

You walk among the heroes of your novel; you see yourself among them, and at the same time you realize the difference between that self and your ordinary self. It is thus that in a dream you know a man to be Ivan Fedorovich, although he looks like someone else, a fact which does not bother you at all.

The novelist's great strength, he asserted, is understanding: "Instinct, however nearly it approaches genius, is unworthy of man; reason—simple, sound, ordinary reason—is our true heritage, our pride." He stood his talent up to nature, measured what he saw, adjusted as well as he could, and wrote at a remove, like any artist, because he could not adjust completely. Even less than Henry James could he hide in his art: "I have always avoided themes which are too subjective; they embarrass me."

Flaubert in Paris was at home. James there was an expatriate, an ambassador like Strether, embarrassed of his home and burdened by a mysterious but portable wound, irresistibly attracted to European charm and antique culture. Turgenev, who wrote in Russian, constantly lamented that he was not at home, said that he could not be, and identified fundamentally with everything that was born, grew, and died in Russia. In a letter from Germany he commented:

I understand very well that my remaining abroad hurt my literary work, but this cannot be changed. . . . One can write well indeed if one is living in a Russian village. There the air is thick with ideas. Here you remember the past, and nothing living or vital can come of it.

Toward the end of his life he said that "there has been something tragic in the fate of every Russian writer who was at all prominent; with me it has been absenteeism."

All the same, the series of rendezvous and encounters that are the bones of his novels yield an informed consideration and sympathy for the conditions of life of ordinary men, specifically, Russian men. Turgenev sees their unhappiness and unjustifiable suffering against a background of a vision of beauty and reason, a classical, intellectual symmetry deriving from, and giving life to, all nature. An image of this occurs in *Rudin*, when Lezhnev describes a discussion circle:

Philosophy, art, science, life itself—all this was for us just words, or maybe just concepts, tempting, beautiful, but incoherent, disjointed. We weren't conscious of, we didn't sense, any common bond among the concepts, any universal law, although we vaguely talked about it, made every effort to realize it. . . . Listening to Rudin, we at first thought we had finally seized it, this common bond, that at last the curtain had been lifted. Suppose he wasn't speaking his own mind— what does that matter? A harmonious order was established in everything we knew; everything that was incoherent suddenly fitted together, formed a pattern, and rose up before us like a building; everything shone brightly, there was spirit in everything. . . . Nothing was now meaningless, fortuitous; everything manifested a rational necessity and beauty, had an obvious and at the same time a mysterious meaning; each separate phenomenon of life resounded with one accord, and we ourselves, with a kind of sacred awe, with a sweet quivering in our hearts, felt ourselves living vessels of eternal truth, its implements summoned to something great.

Turgenev wrote from affection for life and its values with a deep, quiet talent which expressed the inside through the forms of the outside, which spoke always of consciousness by the expression it wore. Ultimately, perhaps, this is to say that Turgenev, like the other very great Russian novelists, convinces us that he understood that the meaning of a man is his function, as meaning is a function of a word. This is a perception of purpose, an inquiry into value. Pressed, in turn, to its ultimate, it is ineffable, like that moment of mystery in "Spring Torrents" when Gemma and Sanin are literally and symbolically inseparable from the entire universe although they have no rational understanding of it (they cannot use what they have experienced) and are therefore only the more keenly aware that what seemed fulfillment was actually loss: "the deep silence set in again."

Crime and
Punishment

In January, 1846 Nekrasov published Dostoevsky's *Poor
People* and *The Double*. In February, Belinsky reviewed
them, praising one extravagantly, associating Dostoevsky with Gogol, but querying if, in the second tale, Dostoevsky had not exceeded his own abilities and good literary
taste. By late autumn an almost paranoid Dostoevsky had
split with Nekrasov and *The Contemporary*, blaming, above
all, Belinsky and Turgenev. Since then, forgetting Turgenev
and Dostoevsky's temporary reconciliation in the 1860's and
remembering Dostoevsky's caricature of Turgenev as Kar-
mazinov in *The Devils* (1871–72), people have often talked
about two lines of Russian fiction in the nineteenth century,
one including Pushkin, Turgenev, Tolstoy; the other, Gogol
and Dostoevsky. We tend to forget the close literary connection between Pushkin and Gogol and between Pushkin and
Dostoevsky, on the one hand, and, on the other, the prove-
nance of the distinction itself.

Chernyshevsky's public defense of his Master's thesis, *The
Esthetic Relation of Art to Actuality*, in the summer of 1855
and his "Outlines of the Gogolian Period of Russian Literature" split the writers associated with *The Contemporary* into
two camps. Druzhinin, Grigorovich, and Annenkov, with the
sympathy of Botkin and Turgenev (who was still on friendly
terms with Chernyshevsky, "a man who understands the requirements of our contemporary world"), started publishing
their work elsewhere. For, in January, 1855, Annenkov had

published his edition of Pushkin's *Works.* "There once more arose," said N. V. Izmailov, "forgotten since Belinsky's days, those general questions about the direction literature was to take, about the meaning of creative writing and about its social significance." The fight devolved into debate over two contrasting trends in literature, each of which was labeled, Izmailov points out, with the name of a great and recent author. The so-called objective tendency, or the harmonizing and unifying of details in a work of art by means of formal specifics, was associated with Pushkin; Gogol's name was tied to the so-called subjective tendency, the emphasizing of contradiction and idiosyncrasies by emotional heightening of perception. That this distinction was only a mark covering a political and cultural argument is affirmed by the fact that Turgenev's early work, especially A *Sportsman's Notebook*, falls under the "Gogol" heading, though Turgenev himself, partial to the "Pushkin" faction in the argument, said that the artist must encompass both sides. "A poet must be a psychologist," he told Leontev, "a hidden psychologist. He must know and feel the roots of appearances, but he can present only the appearances themselves, either in their blossoming out or in their fading away." Furthermore, understanding of the terms of the debate lets us understand two of Dostoevsky's statements, one from *Poor People* in the mid-1840's, to the effect that Gogol's "The Overcoat" was an unrealistic caricature but that Pushkin's "The Stationmaster" was vivid and natural, and the other, from *Crime and Punishment* in the mid-1860's, that Pushkin and Turgenev were the great realists. Gogol's stories, such as "Nevsky Avenue" and "The Nose," opened new subjects and new techniques to Dostoevsky (and supplied words to be borrowed and comic effects), but, as Strakhov said, Dostoevsky's first writings were "a bold and definitive emendation of Gogol." "The art of the psychological tale," says K. Mochulsky, "Dostoevsky learned from Push-kin." In short, a literary hassle of 1855, masking a profound political divergence, gave rise to a wrong-headed cliché about different literary traditions.

Dostoevsky's first writing was an imitation of Schiller, an unpublished, unacted play called *Mary Stuart*, which he destroyed. His first published work, in the winter of 1844 shortly after Balzac had visited St. Petersburg, was a translation of *Eugénie Grandet*. And he meant for Varvara's story in *Poor People*, her dreamlike "confession" of her "happy" childhood (and the deleted description of serf life) and her subsequent pathetic humiliation to evoke romantically sentimental sympathy, as Eugénie's story had. *Père Goriot*, so popular that it was published in translation in *The Reading Library*, defined for Dostoevsky the type of ridiculed, middle-aged official of which Devushkin and Pokrovsky were his first examples. In Russia, "according to A. Tseitlin's count," Gippius writes, "in the 1840's there were some 150 tales about a poor official." "Balzac is great," Dostoevsky wrote his brother; "his characters are creations by a universal intellect." Under the spell of E. T. A. Hoffmann and German romanticism, in a following letter he said, "I have a project in mind: to become a madman. Let people go mad, be cured, let them do something intelligent. If you've read all of Hoffmann, then you remember his Alban. It's terrible to see a man who doesn't know what to do, who makes a toy of God." At seventeen Dostoevsky had written, "I think our world is a purgatory for heavenly spirits bewildered by a sinful idea. I think the world has taken on a negative signification and that out of lofty, elegant spirituality there has come satire." Including the characters and themes derived from the literary and political interests of his day, a chronological survey of Dostoevsky's novels and stories would be a history of his life, dramatized and deepened by the electricity of faith between the poles of glorification and suicide, between dreams of beauty and experiences of ridicule.

The change in Dostoevsky's political views following his exile—his shift from utopian socialism (he said that in his youth he might well have been an atheistic supporter of Nechaev) to Orthodoxy and monarchistic nationalism—accounts for his polemics with the nihilists in *Time* and *Epoch*, magazines he and his brother published, but it does not embrace the dilemma which *Crime and Punishment* dramatizes. Raskolnikov is "a man of the new generation," as typical in the 1860's as Pushkin's Herman in "The Queen of Spades" was typical of the 1830's ("an extraordinary and regular Petersburg type," Dostoevsky himself states in *The Adolescent*), the young intellectual tempted to murder to assert the power and the freedom of individuality. Historically, the idea that mankind consists of rulers and slaves goes back to earliest political theorizing and lecturing—back to Aristotle, for example. In the early nineteenth century, it was expressed by Hegel in his *Philosophy of History*, which Dostoevsky read in Siberia, by Carlyle, by Napoleon III's *History of Julius Caesar*, translated into Russian and published early in the winter of the year Dostoevsky worked on *Crime and Punishment*, 1865. The romantic concept differed from the classic in that the ruler, Hegel's "subject" of history, Carlyle's "hero," was said to have the obligation of living by laws different from those for the ruled, the objects of history. He was beyond morality, the human mover of the world. Scholars and researchers, such as V. V. Danilov, L. P. Grossman, G. I. Chulkov, have commented on the suggestiveness of this material for Dostoevsky, on his use of popular mid-nineteenth-century histories and novels which expressed in broad, social terms the individual's new political self-consciousness.

Social activity was supposed to guarantee personal liberty. Dostoevsky, through Lebezyatnikov and Luzhin, parodies the socialist thinking of the century, insisting that an individual act is required to validate any theory and that liberty must be expressed in that act, as Raskolnikov reflects in a landscape symbolic of the novel's "argument." It is tempting to us to interpret the Neva as the water of life, as a mother-fertility symbol, as that "river of living water" in *Revelation*, one of Dostoevsky's favorite books; to note that the sun, especially the hot July sun, is the external world from which Raskolnikov by theory has removed himself and to which he returns to act; to point out that in the following passage the sun is setting, that it is red, suggesting the murder to occur the next day. But most important is the almost inexpressible liberation anticipated through the murder but which presents itself first, ironically, as relief from the idea of the necessity of murdering:

Crossing the bridge, he calmly and quietly looked at the Neva, at the brilliant sunset of the bright, red sun. Despite his weakness, he did not even feel tired. It was as if an abscess on his heart, festering all month, had suddenly broken. Freedom, freedom! He was now free of this witchcraft, of the necromancy, the fascination and the obsession!

But the idea lives on in his head:

A strange idea kept pecking inside his head, like a chick coming out of an egg, and very, very much interested him.

The conversation between the student and the officer identifies the dilemma and puts Raskolnikov back into it, as if into prison. Only the act will liberate the idea and liberate him from it: "And *then*, that means, that's how the sun will shine!"

What surprises about the relation between *Père Goriot* and *Crime and Punishment* is how superficially Rastignac and Vautrin are like Raskolnikov and Svidrigailov/Porfiry, how, finally, they are deeply different. Grossman, Chulkov, and after them Mochulsky, Lukács, and Philip Rahv have cited Dostoevsky's borrowings rather than his changes, although Chulkov, a symbolist and mystical anarchist, said that Dostoevsky had a mythology which Balzac lacked and which made Raskolnikov's moral problem tragic. I assume he meant that Dostoevsky's Christianity was less perfunctory than Balzac's. Even as one cites parallels, starting with physical description, one sees deviations:

RASTIGNAC: . . . *whitish skin, black hair, blue eyes. His figure, his gestures, his habitual posture, indicated the son of a noble family. . . . Ordinarily he wore an old frock coat, a sorry-looking vest, and the miserable, faded, badly tied black tie of the student. . . .*

RASKOLNIKOV: . . . *he was extremely good-looking, with beautiful dark eyes, dark-haired, taller than average, slim and well-built. . . . His hat was tall, round, made by Zimmermann, but already worn out, all rust-colored, full of holes and covered with stains. . . .*

RASTIGNAC: *His responsive mind, his lofty ambition, made him see right . . . into the heart of his family. . . . As with all great souls, he wished to gain nothing except by his own ability.*

RASKOLNIKOV: *"And what about me? . . . What did you actually think about me? I don't want your sacrifice, Dunyechka, I don't, Mama! It won't happen as long as I live, it won't, it won't! I don't accept it!"*

VAUTRIN: *Rastignac could not long live thus under fire from Vautrin's batteries without finding out whether this man was his friend or his enemy. . . . [Said Vautrin:] "My idea*

is to go live a patriarchal life in America, in the South. . . .
I am a great poet. I don't write my poems: they consist of ac-
tions and feelings."

Svidrigailov: *"This is the whole question: am I a monster*
of cruelty, or myself a sacrifice? Well, if I am? You know,
suggesting to the object of my affection to go with me to
America or to Switzerland, maybe I had the most honorable
feelings. . . . Reason, after all, serves passion; maybe I hurt
myself even more, so help me!"

"That's not the point at all," Raskolnikov cut him off in
disgust, "it's simply that you're repulsive, whether you're right
or wrong, and so they don't want to have anything to do with
you, and chased you away, and so get!"

Rastignac is a student, lives at night whether he be dancing
or studying; Raskolnikov lives in the dark—his room is a
"closet"—and "does nothing." Vautrin says that the source
of great fortunes is often a crime "forgotten because it was
aptly done"; Raskolnikov accuses himself of, above all, ineptness. Madame de Nucingen needs money, and Rastignac,
enmeshed in Vautrin's plot to murder Taillefer's son, goes
out gambling, wins, gives her the money and saves her honor;
after the crime, we learn that before the crime Raskolnikov
had supported a dying student, had helped his family, and
at great personal risk had rescued two children from a burning apartment. Rastignac believes in God; although Raskolnikov tells Porfiry that he believes in God, in jail during a
Lenten service the prisoners accuse him of being an atheist.
Contradictory statements, a frequent device in Dostoevsky's
work, force us to look deeper for meaning. As Vautrin's
scheme takes place, Rastignac behaves wildly, his medical-
student friend, Bianchon, thinks him mad, says, "You have
fever"; Raskolnikov behaves like a madman until there begins
the solution of the moral paradox which has followed his at-

tempted way out of his dilemma, and Razumikhin, the sensible student friend, which his name indicates, says, "Rodya, you're out of your mind." But the most striking deviation is in the relation between Vautrin–Rastignac and Svidrigailov/ Porfiry–Raskolnikov. Raskolnikov has picked up, if it may be put this way, Vautrin's assertion of the amorality of power and of the necessity for the individual to test it. Vautrin says to Rastignac, but it might well be Raskolnikov thinking to himself, that "A man is all or nothing. . . . A man is a god when he is like you. . . . You are a superior man." Dostoevsky has split Vautrin, an escaped convict, an insinuating and malicious middle-aged homosexual, into two parts. Svidrigailov is dark, erotic, incomprehensible; Porfiry Petrovich is no less insistent but entirely rational, communicative. Vautrin is a predatory beast; he tells Rastignac: "You are a handsome young man, sensitive, as proud as a lion and as obedient as a young girl. You'd be a good prey for the devil." Svidrigailov and Porfiry are parts of Raskolnikov himself. Rastignac felt that he had made a pact with Vautrin, as Faust had with Mephistopheles; Svidrigailov says to Raskolnikov, "Well, didn't I tell the truth, saying we were birds of a feather?" They are dramatic extensions of what Raskolnikov is aware of in himself. Always surprised to see them, as if staring into a mirror at half his face, Raskolnikov never denies them. Their conversations with him describe the limits within which he has moved both in theory and in act. They are the high noon and black midnight of his daily existence. Their violent, dramatic conflict in him must be solved (or the whole play scrapped) for him to be able to move at all—either to live or to die.

Dostoevsky has not set the "mandarin" problem, which Balzac set for Rastignac. Rastignac and Bianchon cite the problem from Rousseau, but it is a general example of a moral dilemma: if, in order to inherit the wealth of a very rich man whom you have never seen—say, a Chinese mandarin—you had only to press a button and he would be dead, and no one would ever find out who was guilty, what would you do? *Tuer le mandarin* means, then, cynically to commit a criminal act for one's own benefit at no personal risk. "If you mean to do it," says Bianchon to Rastignac, "you have to be an Alexander or else you'll be hanged." But Dostoevsky makes clear, before and after the murder, that fear of apprehension is irrelevant. As he wrote to Katkov in September, 1865, he was working on the psychological account of a crime:

Action is contemporary, takes place this year. . . . About a month [in the final version, just over a week] goes by afterwards [after the murder] until the final catastrophe. Nobody suspects him, and there is no reason to. Just at this point the whole psychological process of the crime unwinds. . . . And it ends with his having to inform on himself. . . . Juridical punishment for crimes scares a criminal much less than lawmakers think, partly because he himself requires it morally.

Balzac can pose the question as if the alternatives were real because he is dealing with the Euclidean geometry of a romantic Paris, a city of elegance and squalor, a kind of detailed stage setting for the melodrama of love, sex, intrigue, perversion, murder, political ambition, and noble idealism which he sprawls out across it. Dostoevsky changed the question.

In fact, Dostoevsky changed the reality which we assume behind the question. The different question suggests different alternatives. These apply to a different geometry. And we know that precisely what we have in *Crime and Punishment* is a non-Euclidean space, a world of space-time in which all the events occur in consciousness (wherever else they may *seem* to occur) and the intervals among them are determined exclusively by acts in consciousness, that is, acts without formal cause, acts that follow only from the "logic" of discourse or dialectics, and acts that lie outside any concept of causality whatever, acts that are sheer coincidence. We as readers can quickly follow Madame de Nucingen's carriage down the Parisian boulevards or the slow trip of the undertaker's hearse to Père-Lachaise. The city spreads out before us like a brightly lit map, and we follow the actors through chronological time measured by the clock of social life and the biology of growing old. Dostoevsky gives us the sense of a whole city though he describes only a fraction of it.

Dostoevsky makes the clock no more than a symbol of coincidence. That Raskolnikov sleeps until late morning shows not how indolent he is but how inadequate are the usual measurements of industriousness. It shows that Raskolnikov is different, beyond measurability. He is, in our everyday sense, outside time, just as he is, in his tiny garret, outside the space of the ordinary, sunlit world. Six o'clock symbolizes an important moment of rendezvous—the old pawnbroker is to be home alone—but it has been picked up by coincidence and it leads to a meeting, a murder scene, which is itself entirely coincidental: that is, basically there is no adequate explanation for it. In short, Raskolnikov follows neither the clock nor the avenues of our usual world. His dreams impinge on his waking life; he cannot keep the two apart. He counts 730 steps from his place to the pawnbroker's, but he cannot define the location of the one except by reference to the other. He frequently finds himself in places unable to understand how or why he got there. He travels along lines shaped by the geometry of his consciousness. And the picture we get of Petersburg—the city which Peter imposed on the swamp and of which "The Bronze Horseman" is an ever-present symbol

—the picture we get, however vivid the details may seem, is a picture of a vision in Raskolnikov's head:

There was still the same oppressive heat, but he greedily breathed in this stinking, dusty, city-infected air. His head had just started spinning a little; a kind of wild energy suddenly shone in his inflamed eyes and on his emaciated, pale yellow face. He did not know and did not even think about where to go; he knew only "that all this had to be finished today, . . . that otherwise he wouldn't go home, because he didn't want to live like this!"

Dostoevsky has taken notions and characters from the world of literature and dramatized them back to life. In his letters to Katkov before writing *Crime and Punishment* he kept insisting that the ideas with which he was dealing were contemporary: "Our papers are full of traces of the unusual instability of ideas urging [the young] on to terrible things." He cites the examples of a university student and of a seminarian. When, after publication of the novel, a young man committed a crime much like Raskolnikov's, Dostoevsky felt that he had been prophetic. It reminds us that, in genesis, the novel had about the same relation to the life which it measured as the general theory of relativity to the motion of the perihelion of Mercury. A passage from Dostoevsky's article "Petersburg Dreams in Verse and Prose" (1861) shows, among other things, that he had discovered the organic, autonomous, parthenogenetic life of the mind. He is looking at the heart of the city from across the Neva:

It seemed, finally, that this whole world, with all its inhabitants, strong and weak, with all their dwellings, the hovels of the poor and the gilded palaces, in this evening hour was like a fantastic, magical vision, a dream, which in turn will right away vanish and rise like steam up to the dark blue sky. A strange idea suddenly stirred inside me. I shuddered, and my heart in that moment seemed to be flooded with a hot stream of blood, suddenly boiling up in the onrush of a mighty but previously unknown sensation. In that instant, I seemed to have understood something which had until then only been stirring in me but not intelligibly; to have perceived something new, some absolutely new world, unfamiliar to me and known only from certain vague rumors, from some mysterious signs. I think that it was in precisely those moments that my existence began.

Dostoevsky has not only removed robbery as a motive for murdering the "mandarin" and involved Raskolnikov in the life of the victim, both by the pledges tendered and money borrowed and by the bloody effort to kill the woman, but also he has redefined our notion of actuality. Actuality is neither "this world" nor "the next world" but the world where things happen. Unlike Atlas, or Alexander, Raskolnikov does not carry the world on his shoulders. He carries it in his head.

We cannot be so concerned with Dostoevsky's sources, which are literary, as with his transformation of them. We are interested that, unlike the sound of the sea for Paul in *Dombey and Son*, Dostoevsky's motifs take on symbolic significance only with reference to the world of the novel, as Raskolnikov's hat symbolizes Raskolnikov but cannot be extrapolated and given social meaning. In *Père Goriot*, Vautrin asked, "A feeling is the world in an idea, isn't it?" Dostoevsky reverses this perverted romanticism. To be conscious, Kirillov says in *The Devils*, and Stavrogin repeats it, is "to feel an idea." Consciousness excludes nothing. It is the man himself in all his plasticity. Dostoevsky sets no limits to consciousness; also, there are no limits dividing the "real" from the "fantastic," *is* from *seems*. He focuses on the moments of alternation. Dolgoruky, the narrator of *The Adolescent*, confesses his dramatic uncertainty and self-contradiction:

How does it happen that with an intelligent man what he says is always stupider than what he retains? I've noticed this about myself many times even in social intercourse with other people during this whole past fatal year and have been tormented by it.

And in *The Devils* Fedka the convict says that Petr Verkhovensky may call a man a bastard and a fool but "maybe I'm just a fool on Tuesdays and even Wednesdays, too, but on Thursdays smarter than him."

The basic theme of all of Dostoevsky's novels is self-knowledge, not so much self-transcendence through faith or love of God/Christ as awareness of guilt. (R. P. Blackmur has said that Dante would have punished Raskolnikov in Hell by having him search forever for a mirror.) Says Stepan Trofimovich in *The Devils*, "indeed each of us is guilty toward the rest for everyone and everything." N. M. Chirkov in his book *Dostoevsky's Style* (1963) said:

In Dostoevsky's work the ego, on the one hand, clearly proves its worth and affirms itself; on the other hand, it intensely seeks its "main half" in the struggle of a great number of spiritual potencies, in the contradictions of various possibilities, in the shifting of various aspects.

Crime and Punishment began in Dostoevsky's mind in 1859. Subsequently the plans for two tales (*povesti*) "The Drunks" and "The Confession" were combined into one novel (*roman*). Marmeladov's story and Raskolnikov's were fitted together. Svidrigailov was added. Sonya was changed from a passive, rationalistic defender of the Russian people to an actor connecting the two dramas, which ring a circle around Raskolnikov, the center. From the opening paragraphs the reader knows that a murder is in preparation. The first six chapters describe Raskolnikov's planning of it and detail plausible motives. In Chapter VII the murder occurs. The remainder of the book is the story not of the crime but of the transgression, the psychological drama of the murderer and all the persons involved in his life. Dostoevsky originally conceived of that story as a first-person narrative beginning, "I am on trial and will tell everything," but found that the necessary bias of such a narrative would render improbable aspects of the story which he considered essential.

Most of Dostoevsky's stories and novels are narrated in the first person as a memoir by a participant (a confession) or by an insignificant observer (a diary). The narrator begins by alluding to a dilemma which is crucial for him and which must be solved instantly if there are not to be terrible consequences. Usually it turns out that there is no solution or that the solution taken was not a final solution. The narrator, as in "The Christmas Tree" or *The Devils*, ends as alienated from the action he has described as he was in the beginning. He is catalytic. Mr. G—v is confident to Stepan Trofimovich and exposes aspects of Stepan Trofimovich which supply motives for actions which we could not otherwise see. At one point, when this function is minimal, when Mr. G—v is only recording action, he actually slips out of the novel, and Dostoevsky writes as omniscient author. The style by which Mr. G—v, or any Dostoevskian narrator, makes events in everyday life become events in his mind translates them for us into events in our minds and liberates him from those events. When the narrator and the central actor are identical, we have a confession, presented either as a secret document for the reader (*The Adolescent,* "White Nights," the excised chapter of *The Devils*) or as a revealed correspondence (*Poor People* or, as parody, "A Romance in Nine Letters"). What seem to be the most fantastic events of the everyday world are made plausible by the conventions of art.

In an essay on Maeterlinck, A. A. Blok said that creative writing "is all delicate flowers" and berated literary critics for "leaning their elbows on them and delivering lectures about how Ivan Karamazov's 'way out of contradictions' is found in Christianity." The viability of Dostoevsky's novels and stories does not depend on his religious philosophy, ultimately, "to bow down and kiss the earth." It does not depend on eschatological concepts or even on the symbols associated with each character. Raskolnikov's room is a closet, a coffin, without windows; Sonya's is a "distorted shed," with (transparently) three windows; the pawnbroker lives in a spiderweb— which is Svidrigailov's image of eternity, infinite but bounded:

"We keep imagining eternity as an idea which can't be understood, as something enormous, enormous! But why necessarily enormous? Suddenly, imagine it now, instead of all that, there'll be just one little room, sort of like a country bathhouse, with spiders in all the corners, and that's eternity."

Nor does viability depend on "story," in almost every instance melodramatic, that is, speciously emotional. In each novel it depends on a dramatization of an inevitable conflict among the "selves" of a central character, a dramatization as refined and as complex as possible. Knowledge, for Dostoevsky, means comprehension of the philosophical paradoxes into which a man is driven by the necessity of seeking freedom. In a letter to his brother in October, 1838, still very young, he wrote:

What do you mean by know? *To* know *nature, the soul, God, love—these are known by the heart, not the mind. The mind is the conductor of thought through the dura mater into the soul. Intelligence is a material capacity; the soul, or spirit, lives by thought whispered to it by the heart. . . . Thought arises in the soul. The mind is a tool, a machine, moved by the spiritual fire.*

One must not suppose philosophy is only a simple mathematical problem where the unknown is nature. Note that the poet in a burst of inspiration divines God, consequently carries out the task of philosophy. . . . Consequently, philosophy is this poetry, only the highest form of it.

But what propels the drive for knowledge (all his heroes are highly active, intellectually ambitious men) is a need to solve a basic, unjust contradiction in life, exploded for everyone to see by the forces which the French Revolution released. As Saint-Just said, "If you wish to found a republic, you must be concerned with extricating the people from a state of poverty which corrupts them. There are no political virtues without pride; there is no pride in poverty." This is the bottom of *Crime and Punishment*, the starting point of the book. Against this we see clearly the intolerably bitter irony of the set phrase, also the title of an Ostrovsky play, several times repeated by Marmeladov: "Poverty is no vice." The point is that by its very nature it *is* vicious. Raskolnikov's dependency on his family deprives him of the right to be free, but he proudly insists on being free. He is impotent, but he insists on inventing an act of supreme power. Driven out of society by exercising the attributes of intelligence and will under the dehumanizing condition of poverty ("Man gets used to everything, the bastard"), he who can neither alter the conditions nor accept them inverts his attributes. He wills to climb over himself by asserting the superiority of individual will, even in destruction, above all social institutions.

The book is a study of the relations between an alienated individual and the social institutions through which he must work out his life. In this sense, it is a modern novel. The modernity excites us, especially the first time we read the book. The detail impresses itself on us. We discover our involvement in the nature of crime. We become aware of the meaning of punishment. The impact of the book is the impact of crime. Life, said Laforgue, is *"vraie et criminelle!"*

Crime is a violation of a "public right," says Webster's, a "gross violation of human laws," an "evil act or sin." Given man's alienation, any anti-institutional act is an anarchic, criminal act. Rousseau said that the evil men do proceeds chiefly from the institutions they have established, that mankind is corrupted in civilization. More strongly, as Trotter put it in *Instincts of the Herd in Peace and War* (1953) (and as Dostoevsky analyzed it), both the good and the evil are in the same establishment:

. . . *we seem almost forced to accept the dreadful hypothesis that in the very structure and substance of all human constructive social efforts there is embodied a principle of death, . . . that the intellect can provide no permanent defense against a vigorous barbarism.*

The individual's conscience, his essential consistency, his "most cherished moral agency," Herbert Marcuse says in *Eros and Civilization* (1955), is "permeated with the death instinct." Suppression by the superego is a self-destruction in socially useful activity. The greater the assertiveness of the ego, the greater, correspondingly, is the required repression. That is, Marcuse says, "the very progress of civilization leads to the release of increasingly destructive forces." Human institutions arise to counteract these forces, to oppose archaic domination, and to enforce primal domination for the "good" of the whole society, even if the primal dominator himself be ultimately liable for what he has done ("The Grand Inquisitor"). The experience of domination and the effort to overcome it is still necessarily part of civilized existence. From his own viewpoint, the individual, typically Raskolnikov, whom Dostoevsky makes not average, not normal, but typical of his generation, has not forfeited his paradise by sinning against God, as the institutional taboo insists. He was deprived of the "paradise" which was rightfully his by domination by his fellow men, who are themselves at least as guilty as he. We enter Raskolnikov's crime through this ambivalence. What Raskolnikov does is what we are liable to—and for. In symbolic terms, there is no distinction between desire and fact, between temptation and act. As long as the repressed material returns, the individual is punished for what he has long since ceased trying to do. Raskolnikov's story is actual.

The image of the garden, symbolizing paradise, the state of spiritual grace in which the soul and the intelligence are in harmony, unites the several situations in the novel. It is the image of the Golden Realm, projected as New Jerusalem, frequently referred to in Dostoevsky's work from the earliest writings to the latest, from Vasya Shukov's dream of universal happiness in "heaven on earth" ("A Weak Heart," 1848) to "The Dream of a Ridiculous Man" (1877), prefiguring the resurrection of contemporary Europe through love of Christ. Frequently presented as a vision of an orderly garden or of a peaceful landscape, it is several times associated with Claude Lorraine's painting "Acis and Galatea," the children of sunlight in what Stavrogin calls " 'The Golden Age,' I don't know why." In his confession, "At Tikhon's," Stavrogin says he has dreamed back to the cradle of European civilization of 3,000 years ago, to "beautiful people, happy and innocent," and he cries tears of delight for such bliss, the dream ending with a vision of a "tiny reddish spider" on a geranium leaf, associated with Matresha's death forced by Stavrogin's violation of her. In *Crime and Punishment*, after Raskolnikov has given a résumé of his article "On Crime," Porfiry Petrovich asks Raskolnikov if he really believes in New Jerusalem, and Raskolnikov says he does, as well as in the raising of Lazarus and the existence of God. The New Jerusalem is "the holy city . . . coming down from God out of heaven, prepared as a bride adorned for her husband. . . . Behold, the tabernacle of God is with men, and he will dwell with them." (Revelation, XXI, 2–3) Previously, on his way to the pawnbroker's to commit the murder, the crime of false transcendence, Raskolnikov appropriates to himself, also, the role of divine gardener, charged with beautifying and harmonizing the earthly city, *viz.* Petersburg:

Passing the Yusupov Garden he was even filled for a moment with the idea of building tall fountains and of how well they would cool and freshen the air in all the squares. Gradually he came to the conviction that if the Summer Garden were extended the length of the Champs de Mars it would be a beautiful thing and very useful for the city.

The force of the garden is the force of life. Spiritually it is Eden; physically, it is the power of growth and regeneration as manifest in green leaves. The symbol of Raskolnikov's perversion of this force is his isolating on the wallpaper in his room one white flower at the moment his friends talk about Lizaveta, also, having been murdered:

Raskolnikov turned to the wall where on the dirty yellowed wallpaper with its little white flowers he picked out one grace-

*less white flower with some sort of little brown streaks on it
and started examining how many leaves it had, how many
notches there were and how many streaks. He felt that his
hands and feet were numb, as if amputated, but he did not
try to move and persistently stared at the flower.*

Parallel with the levels of imagination and of intellect
are the levels of narrative and melodrama. All are kept going
throughout the book. The killing of the old woman was an act
of liberation; it was an expression of social good; it was the
first climax in a murder plot involving consequences and devices for telling it; fourthly, Lizaveta, the supernumerary, was
pregnant.

At the end of the novel, linking the epilogue to the book
(however lamely) is Raskolnikov's dream of "the whole world
sacrificed to a terrible, unheard-of and unprecedented plague
sweeping out of the depths of Asia across Europe. . . . Only
a few people in the whole world managed to save themselves,
and these were the pure and elect." The dream is an allegory
of conscience, but its image of purification, connected to the
physical illnesses of both Raskolnikov and Sonya, leads into
Raskolnikov's vision of the "garden." It is very like the vision
in "The Little Hero" of the mowers working in the green fields
across the river, a story Dostoevsky wrote while jailed in the
Peter-and-Paul Fortress in 1849. It is a vision, dated shortly
after Holy Week, projecting the time of Abraham forward
into the Christian kingdom:

*Raskolnikov went out of the shed onto the bank itself, sat
down on the logs piled by the shed and began looking at the
wide, vast river. From the high bank the land around stretched
out a long way. Singing could be heard faintly from the other,
distant shore. There on the sun-filled steppe, stretching farther
than the eye could see, nomads' tents were barely visible black*

dots. There there was freedom, and other people living there, not at all like those here; there time itself seemed to have stopped, as if the age of Abraham and his flocks had not yet gone. Raskolnikov kept sitting there, motionlessly looking, not turning away. His thought turned into daydream, into contemplation. He was not thinking about anything, but a kind of longing bothered and tormented him.

Descriptions of nature do not merely set the tone for the action or locate the story. They express the convictions of the characters. They reflect the characters like a millpond, showing the effects of their actions on a passive element. They are instruments for Dostoevsky's plot of ideas. "Closely connected to the descriptions of nature," said Chirkov, "are not only the elements of the story which have a thematically functional significance (character description, action, the overall emotional tone) but also its separate and characteristic details."

Raskolnikov's symbolic conception of the murder "beforehand," when the idea comes to him on its own, offers him in his intense pride and desperation a total freedom in which he imagines his dreams actualized. Murder is the necessary tool for transcending degradation, for asserting the extraordinary over the ordinary. He puts it to the life. He makes and becomes his crime: oppression, rebellion, and the suppression of rebellion commingled in one life. He goes beyond the ordinary world. His mind, without reference points, becomes disorganized. He seems mad, but he is still driving toward the freedom which rationally ought to be his. He is wild and sane at once. Although almost unconscious of what he is doing, for example, he kills the old pawnbroker with mechanical efficiency. His first reflection, as he grubs through the old woman's skirts to make pretend robbery, is: "Lord! Am I going mad, is that it?" This is the reverse of Petr Verkhovensky's statement in *The Devils* that, "I went there—Littré's thesis was truculently pushed, that crime is insanity; I get here—and crime's not insanity but good common sense, practically a duty, at least a noble protest." Stavrogin confesses that after his crime he felt himself "in an unbounded freedom" threatened and tempted by self-destruction. "Who knows really," Raskolnikov exclaims, "maybe I actually am mad and everything all these days—maybe everything is just my imagination!" His mind works excellently, but he cannot come to judgment: "Either it's all a mirage, or else *they know!*" We can say of him, as of Lear:

> O *matter and impertinency mix'd,*
> *Reason in madness.*

The rest of the book after the murder dramatizes the reorganizing of Raskolnikov's mind.

Its final reorganization lies outside the novel itself. It is given as a picture, that is, as a description of an effect, in the nearly incredible epilogue, which stands to the real novel as a platitudinous moral stands to a fable. The epilogue presents a picture of composure which the forces unleashed in the book declare absurd. We understand the meaning of the web of secret impulses of the man who does a violent act, and we see that the intellectual effort to reorder the tensions of confusion, despite the absence of a new social order, including complete social revolution (which is the subject of *The Devils* but not of this book), must be frustrated. The intellect, Dostoevsky believes, must rely on grace. The completion of an act lies beyond the terms in the name of which the act was undertaken. Theologically, Dostoevsky seems to say, the guilt of mankind, engendered by Adam's sin, cannot be expiated by the noblest individual gesture toward freedom. The most one can do, as

Raskolnikov does, is to define consciousness of one's own guilt so that, with grace, the catastrophe and epiphany may occur in the same moment through the same action, so that disaster and discovery may lie in the one gesture. The actual condition for salvation is suffering. In suffering one has the vision of salvation, as Marmeladov hopelessly parodies it by announcing that he himself "should be crucified." In Christian terms, crime is sin. Punishment is the suffering (the solace, Forese said to Dante) that leads to grace. Crime and punishment are coincident, as the coincidences in this book emphasize. There is no rationally justifiable explanation for their falling together, but neither occurs outside the other.

Apart from each other, neither is real, there is neither crime nor punishment. When Raskolnikov's sister Dunya shouts at him, pressing him to her and kissing him: "Aren't you, going to your suffering, washing off at least half your crime?" Raskolnikov shouts in sudden madness, "Crime? What crime?" The crime, he maintains, was its own expiation: he killed a foul, pernicious, useless louse "for killing which forty sins are forgiven." What, by standards of habit and law, is called a crime may, by the very principles on which those standards are based, equally be fulfillment of the law. The social shame to which Raskolnikov considers himself obliged to submit—the obvious expiation—is not a consequent of, or even an aspect of, the essence of the crime either as idea or as actual murder. Marmeladov's humiliation leads only to accidental and meaningless death. The idea of the crime remains unaffected by the murder. The murder of the pawnbroker, like the superfluous murder of the sister, turns out to be not an enactment of the idea at all. The idea of murder seemed to Raskolnikov to have come independently of his will. Complete as idea, the murder seemed to him to have occurred in his mind before he committed it. The failure of the crime, then, was neither ethical nor practical. The idea did not go bad. The murderer was not detected. It failed esthetically. The crime was not beautiful. It was not artful perfection of the idea. It provoked no immediate or disinterested pleasure, no moral exaltation. Committed, it turned out to be not an independent and self-subsistent product of the creative imagination, but, as if it were a coincidence, something preordained. Far from stimulating delight in itself, it was liable to the same deformity which it was intended to reform.

We may read *Crime and Punishment* as the first of Dostoevsky's post-exilic works dealing, as if in crescendo, with the means by which an individual can locate himself in the universe. The first stage is willful anarchy, the solipsistic destruction of anything opposing one's own infinite grandness. The first step (given in this novel as dramatically as possible) is to refute all alien claims by daring to assert that the right to live is unique, that is, that it was Adam's; now it is mine. That Dostoevsky's novels follow in order of an ever more refined study we can see by Tikhon's announcement in *The Devils* that

Crime, by its nature, is ugly. Crimes, no matter what they may be, are more, so to speak, picturesque and impinging the more blood and horror there is, but there are crimes which by their nature are shameful, disgraceful, beyond any justification by horror;

and by the succession of novels in which a central crime is located ever more deeply in human life: *Crime and Punishment*, intellectual novel, one man—one problem; *The Idiot*, social novel, two families—"marriage"; *The Devils*, political novel, one town—revolution; *The Karamazov Brothers*, family novel, father and four brothers—blood feud. The contrary to anarchy is assent, not agreement or the "community of worship" on which the Grand Inquisitor has built his empire, but the assent of supreme naïveté. This is Sonya's naïveté; better, at the highest level of consciousness possible, it is Myshkin's in *The Idiot.* This is the force of soul by which the individual transforms not only himself but also the whole world and its institutions into another Eden. In an essay on James, Blackmur said:

Force of soul is what we see when great naiveté is joined with conscience, and it has something to do with that reality which T. S. Eliot says we cannot bear very much of, but which we must seek, and when we find it must find destroyed.

The problem of a man's regeneration which, at the end of *Crime and Punishment,* Dostoevsky says lies ahead, is split among an earthly trinity in *The Karamazov Brothers.* One goes mad (which Raskolnikov does not); one goes to prison to be tormented to purify his soul (like Raskolnikov); and one goes to the monastery to enact his faith (of which Raskolnikov has only the first degree, love). Dostoevsky projected but never wrote the novel of the man of faith. He referred to subsequent volumes in a planned trilogy, *The Life of a Great Sinner;* also, in his notebook he left a line saying he intended to do a life of Christ. I suppose that that would have been his supreme fiction, a Dürer "Veronica" in prose.

In Raskolnikov's world, which is our world, the idea and the act do not fit. Neither is appropriate to the other, although each may be said to "exist" only in the other's terms. Theoretically, murder in the name of humanitarianism and progress is necessary; practically, the wisdom of moral improvement is justice. In individual terms, it is conscience. The limitations of human life, however, deform either the concept or the act. Raskolnikov takes the measure of these limitations. He finds that they are, indeed, untransgressable borders and that the geodesics of a man's life bring him back on himself. About to submit to what he calls useless shame, he sees clearly, he says, "the whole absurdity of my cowardice. . . . I'm determined [to submit] simply because of my baseness and mediocrity." He wanted the good for men, he says,

"and would have done hundreds, thousands of good deeds instead of this one stupidity, not even stupidity but simply blunder, since this whole idea was not at all so stupid as it now seems in failure . . . (in failure everything seems stupid!). . . . But I, I did not sustain even the first step because I'm—a no-good bastard! That's the whole problem!"

If he had succeeded, he says, he would have been crowned; because he has failed, he is in a trap. What he did is not at issue; how he did it has led directly to his catastrophe. That's not it at all, says Dunya. But Raskolnikov insists sharply:

"Ah! Not the proper form, not such an esthetically beautiful form! Well, I absolutely don't understand: why is throwing bombs on people in regular siege a more respectable form? The fear of esthetics is the first sign of weakness! . . . Never, never have I been more clearly aware of this than now, and more than ever I do not understand my crime."

What he understands, in one sense, is that, in another sense, he cannot understand it. The idea does not fit, but there is no "reason" for its not fitting. Having lived to experience its inappropriateness and the mysterious discord engendered, Raskolnikov finds that the most significant response is to assume that he, as agent, was the source of the distortion and to take on himself responsibility for the incongruity. This makes the incongruity corruption; the crime, not an imperfection but a sin. Having failed as an artist, Raskolnikov is required to become, at least, a man.

In the magazine *Time* Dostoevsky once wrote:

We believe that art has its own complete and organic life. Man has a need for art, just as he has for eating and drinking. The need for beauty and creativity is inseparable from man; man longs for beauty, accepts it under any circumstances, and just because it is beautiful.

In *The Devils* Stepan Trofimovich says that "man can endure without science, without bread—but not without beauty." "The world," says Prince Myshkin in *The Idiot*, "will be redeemed by beauty." "Beauty," says Dmitry Karamazov, "is a terrible and awful thing." The lack of any necessary connection between the beautiful and the good is terrifying. The heart of man is the battlefield between the Devil and God. If man's world is to be saved (Dostoevsky believes that it is), only beauty will save it. The task of man's rebellion is to save beauty.

The pathos of "A Gentle Creature" is that the rebellion has failed: the girl kills herself physically and remains as a moral force; the narrator destroys himself morally by insisting too much on preserving his vision of the beautiful. His vision has blinded him. Mr. Prokharchin's rebellion—the effort to establish harmony for himself—is frustrated by its ineptness. His friends think him a queer fool; we see him as a tragic joke, a man whose device for realizing beauty according to his vision of it is inadequate to the actual world.

In most of Dostoevsky's work, certainly in the work of his later years, the focus is on the idea. The idea is presented as both form and content. It is made into a story or a novel, not into a play, because it is close to Dostoevsky himself. He cannot allow it the impersonality which the stage requires. The idea does not carry itself, because it is not a normal or "real" idea: it is a conjuring up in the mirror of the mind. To be expressed it must be interpreted. Dostoevsky does not give long descriptions of his characters, nor does he digress to comment on them or on their "ideas." He develops action and assigns his characters parts in a drama of ideas. Each acts out an aspect of Dostoevsky's central idea. Dostoevsky's way of thinking (men have ways of thinking as they have ways of walking), which sees Ivan Karamazov or Polzunkov as protagonist, cannot invent the way of thinking which sees Lear or Falstaff as central figure, for the dilemma which the thought represents can never be described by action. Lear's story of love is acted out partly by himself and partly by Cordelia and the Fool, but it is acted out. One person confronts another. Ivan's story of love is recited by him as the poem of the Grand Inquisitor. It is dramatized introspection. One person confronts himself.

Man's soul, Dostoevsky says in *Notes from the Cellar*, is not subject to the processes of actuality. Both good and evil are nonrational, but evil leads to putrefaction of the spirit, and good, to the purification of the spirit from whatever evil has been done. The first step in achieving either is rebellion, extreme self-assertion for personal benefit over the false standards which the world has set up in ignorance and cupidity. Man essentially cannot avoid the good; if, caught in corrupting passions, he does deviate from it, then his soul (which is purely good, purely himself, purely natural) begins to pain him. He suffers pangs of conscience. To reject one's best nature is to distort the rebellion, to try to affirm oneself above everything true, as well. Defiance leads to self-annihilation. Ivan Karamazov's understanding of man and of God, symbolically presented in his poem, cannot withstand the pervasive, implicating intelligence of the devil. Ivan goes mad. His personality is shattered. A criminal is a man who fails in his quest for self-affirmation and freedom. More than other men, he has mistaken his own best interests and destroyed himself as a man. "How many great powers have perished here for nothing," Dostoevsky writes about the Siberian prisons in *Notes from the House of the Dead.* "One must admit that, indeed, these were unusual men, perhaps the most talented, the most forceful, in the whole nation." The struggle for freedom is a kind of dialectic at every stage resolving itself into a further refinement of the perpetual dilemma between thinking and doing, between our excellences and our vulgarities.

The beautiful is accessible only to excellence. The most absurd manner, the most grotesque deportment, may, by parodying itself, realize the opposite. This is the sadness of Marmeladov's farce. This is the tragedy of the joke Raskolnikov has played on himself. This is what Dostoevsky's dreamers are after. The "Ridiculous Man" reports a fantastic vision of the Land of Cockaigne which, we are then told, he personally perverted. In "The Little Boy at Christ's Christmas Tree" the perversion of an innocent soul by the actualities of this world precedes that soul's redemption in fantasy, a fantastic vision of harmony in heaven for only the pure-in-heart. A number of Dostoevsky's stories deal with children at precisely that voluptuous age when temptation is a real force, when they are aware equally of good and evil and, like the girl violated by Stavrogin, are committed to neither. Like Sonya, they are innocent. They see the world from a passive, personal point of view, but the world cannot touch them, just as the grossest physical violations cannot affect Sonya. Raskolnikov demands of himself that he be active, that he *be* his idea of man.

From the beginning of the novel, we follow the development of the idea in inverted terms. Drunk, in the tavern, with no place to go, his daughter a whore, Marmeladov says to Raskolnikov:

"Doesn't matter, sir! Doesn't bother me, this nodding of heads, 'cause everybody knows everything now, anyway, and everything secret's becoming clear; it's something I don't object to but accept. Let 'em! Let 'em! 'Behold the man!' Let me ask you this, young man: can you . . . no, wait, got to put it stronger and more forcefully: not can you but will you dare, looking at me right now, say affirmatively that I'm not a pig?"

The quotation is from John, XIX, 5. Like all of Dostoevsky's literary references, it reflects not his wide reading but his single-mindedness, how he focuses all action and all thought on a center of human behavior. What illuminates this passage is the context from which the citation comes when put against the context in which it is cited. Marmeladov mimics the idea of Christ's crucifixion; he courts martyrdom; he mocks himself; he is guilty of self-humiliation; but his pathos is his self-awareness, which he states artistically—that is, analogically—refusing to pass judgment on himself or on any man. He taunts Raskolnikov by asking for judgment, but "the young man did not say a word." Like Christ, Marmeladov is abandoned to the vengeance of his fellow men. John, XIX, 5–7 reads:

Then came Jesus forth, wearing the crown of thorns and the purple robe. And Pilate saith unto them, Behold the man!
When the chief priests therefore and officers saw him, they cried out, saying, Crucify him, crucify him. Pilate saith unto them, Take ye him and crucify him: for I find no fault in him.
The Jews answered him, We have a law, and by our law he ought to die, because he made himself the Son of God.

Marmeladov has made himself mankind's Fool; he dies. It is a parable for Raskolnikov, who would make himself mankind's King.

Between the fool and the king, both of whom act for the good of man, is the devil, whose resources for evil are mysterious (unknowable) and limited only by human corruptibility. Like Ivan Karamazov, Raskolnikov has a dream of the devil as a middle-class gentleman, the essence of harm in the mask of irreproachable mediocrity. Immediately after the dream, Svidrigailov enters. Although Raskolnikov, too, like Svidrigailov, "at least considered death by water," as George Gibian says, Raskolnikov does not imitate Svidrigailov; he does not make a pact with him. Svidrigailov is Raskolnikov in another form, is Raskolnikov's subterranean self, is the man in the cellar. Svidrigailov is the ultimate abnormality, the "absolute" corruption, the representative of the dark and destructive "other" self suppressed in normal life. Dostoevsky noted down about him, Ernest Simmons reminds us, that he "is conscious of mysterious horrors within himself which he will tell no one but lets slip out as facts." His power (its power) is the contamination that is temptation. Even when the temptation is consummated, as Dunya consummates it by aiming the revolver and firing, one knows only that the response was or was not complete. One does not know what it means. The power is always beyond understanding. It is mysterious, like Svidrigailov himself, the way Stavrogin, Dostoevsky said, was meant to be.

Although portrayal of Svidrigailov as incarnation of this force makes him seem grotesque, like a demon in an allegory, at times almost a gargoyle, he is entirely human, and his power is, also. He, in one way, and the criminals in Siberia, in another, stand for that aspect of self which Raskolnikov killed when he killed the old woman. They are part of a man. Svidrigailov makes this clear by quoting Terence in the beginning of his talk with Raskolnikov: "I am a man *et nihil humanum*," he says, breaking off. The full line reads: *Homo sum, et nihil humanum a me alienum puto*. Again, the context illumines meaning. For the source of evil is not that portion of the world untouched by God, as some of the Church Fathers would have us believe; it is, says Dostoevsky, in the very center of man himself. It is man's torment of himself. In this sense, his crime is his self-punishment. Svidrigailov acts the idea out to its extreme: he consummates self-temptation by suicide. He is, like the title of Terence's play from which the line comes, *Heautontimorumenos*, "The Self-Torturer." The point is not: what was Dostoevsky's source? but: he created meaning by dislocating (parody, the grotesque) the context in which the citation occurs. These constant dislocations give Dostoevsky's novels the power of high drama, although *rationally* the actors are dull folk and the plots are teary melodramas.

Razumikhin (whom Luzhin, in a Freudian slip of the tongue, once addresses as *Rassudkin: razum*—reason, mind; *rassudok*—sense, intellect) can understand his friends, Raskolnikov or anyone else, only by outward signs. To restore Raskolnikov to health he urges him to work and to dress properly. He assumes that external signs are adequate indices of spiritual conditions. He would quickly agree with de Tocqueville that "morality is the best security of law and the surest pledge of freedom." He would have grasped the relation between freedom and the desire for equality expressed in social action. But he would not have understood the limits of the idea that "the same effort which makes a man violently shake off a prevailing error, commonly impels him beyond the bounds of reason." For him, the reorganization of Raskolnikov's mind is no more complicated than recostuming him, giving him a fresh and sensible role to play:

"It's something, believe it or not, old man, that's been bother-
ing me very much. And then, we've got to make a man of you.
To business: we'll start at the top. You see this headpiece?"

Raskolnikov rejects it. He knows that the first condition of
life is the humiliation of the stinking city, in which human
life hardly exists. This is where he begins. He is involved with
Marmeladov, ruined and foul, by interest, by compassion, and
by necessity. Marmeladov plays a game with him analogous
to Porfiry's. Raskolnikov finds himself in a Slough of Despond,
a human swamp, which he must go through in order to define
himself, but he does not know how to get through and doubts,
in the pride of his intellect, that he has the ability to get
through finally. When he reads in his mother's letter that
his sister Dunya is to marry Luzhin, that she will do the
ordinary thing for him which he cannot, the self-destructive
compromise which he will not allow himself, he knows he
has lost all "reason" for existence. At that moment the idea
of murder returns to his mind as if by itself as an independent
necessity. It requires that he actualize it and thereby complete himself. The preparation for the murder allows it to
ripen, as Blackmur says, allows the murderer and the victim
to fall together, to be coincident.

Suddenly he shuddered: a certain, also yesterday's, idea again
swept through his head. But he shuddered not because this
idea swept through him. He really knew, he had a premoni-
tion, that it would unfailingly "sweep through," and had been
waiting for it. Indeed, this idea was not yesterday's at all. But
the difference was that a month ago, and even only yesterday,
it was only a dream, but now . . . now it appeared suddenly
not as a dream but in some sort of new, terrible, and to him
completely unfamiliar form, and he himself recognized this.

The punishment begins after the murder when Raskolnikov wakes up to find that the completion of the crime lies still ahead.

Raskolnikov may get around Razumikhin, who accepts actuality as it is, but he cannot get around the murder. He moves closer and closer to it from one level of intensity to another, descending into himself as Dante descended into Hell. As close as he comes to reaching that forgiveness which would obviate the necessity of crime is the dream of the horse which mankind killed because it could not pull mankind. The dream is an astounding analogy to actuality:

In a morbid state, dreams are often notable for their un-usual prominence, clarity, and extraordinary resemblance to actuality. Sometimes a monstrous picture is put together, but the setting and the whole process of the entire presentation are at the same time so probable and with such subtle, un-expected details, so artistically consistent with the complete-ness of the whole picture, that this very same dreamer could not have thought them up in his waking hours even if he were such an artist as Pushkin or Turgenev.

The book itself is the battleground between dream and actu-ality, between the art of life and the possibilities as well. Raskolnikov has a "terrible dream." He dreams himself back to his original innocence in a symbolic act of sympathy for the oppressed. The dream ends in the moment of symbolic fulfillment, the kiss—

With a shriek he rushes through the crowd toward the little grayish yellow mare, throws his arms around her dead, bloody head, and kisses it, kisses its eyes, its lips . . .

—a moment very much like the moment in which Christ kisses the Grand Inquisitor. This is that ultimate, dramatic moment in which good and evil are compounded in one gesture.

The vitality of the idea of murder is a product of the chain of coincidence which Dostoevsky builds up. Emphasis on arbitrary events outside a man's control, which, nevertheless, determine him to act in a certain way, produces a feeling of inevitability ("fate"). Coincidence heightens his awareness of a secret self within him which he can neither overtake nor escape. It is the irony of the coincidences after the murder which defines Raskolnikov's isolation and forces himself on himself. Wandering aimlessly through St. Petersburg, along the Neva, revulsed by the sight of the people, the buildings, and the shapes around him, Raskolnikov suddenly finds himself right next to Razumikhin's house:

"How did it happen that I didn't come to Razumikhin's on my own at all! Again the same story as then, when . . . But it's very curious: did I myself come, or was I just going along and dropped in here? Doesn't matter. I said . . . two days ago . . . that I'd go see him the day after that. Well, so I will!"

Irony of ironies, out of context a sort of obscene joke, he finds Razumikhin finishing translating a pamphlet called *Is Woman a Human Being?*, work on which Razumikhin, in Boy Scout generosity, offers to share with Raskolnikov, and about to take up translating scandalous pieces from Rousseau's *Confessions*. Later, on the way home, Raskolnikov is whipped by a coachman and given a bit of money by a woman who pities him, thinking him a beggar. He throws the money in the Neva. The perverted woman question, the false confessions, the useless and contemptible money marking him a pariah, and, finally, the days of fever and delirium are detailed exhibits of Raskolnikov's mindlessness following the murder.

They are the separate and translatable equivalents of the elements of the crime, the means for redramatizing it, like that "graceless, white flower" on the "dirty, yellowed wallpaper." The crime itself, as Zosimov says of Razumikhin's "reconstruction," is "the cleverest damned thing," because "it all fits together so neatly . . . just as in the theater."

Raskolnikov pursues his crime to catch himself, to reenact the murder that he may possess himself. He uses family, friends, the police, the total environment, to act out in his mind what he has done partially but cannot have done completely until it is composed in his mind. The "real-life" details—the wallpaper, the sock, the tavern whores, the horse, the river, the girl on the street, the newspaper—function as symbols because of their importance in the tension with which Raskolnikov continues to play a role he knows is false. Like Hamlet's, it is the self-assumed role of the extraordinary man by which he makes his life valid, by which he intends to prevent the success of that incoherence, that decomposition, which he feels threatens his personality. When finally the idea of the murder has become so enormous that it overwhelms him, he has come to himself.

Porfiry Petrovich starts his "questioning" of Raskolnikov by acknowledging that communication "between two thinking men" is difficult; they cannot find for conversation the topic which society ladies easily do. Raskolnikov wonders what Porfiry wanted to say. And Porfiry moves in by picking up, from Raskolnikov's article and from what he has not said, their agreement about juridical institutions. Reenacting the crime, Porfiry is dramatizing its intellectual aspect. This, which is his work (and, therefore, also Raskolnikov's), is pure art:

"Oh, by the way, one word, you know, leads to another, one thought provokes another. Now, recently you mentioned some-

*thing about the form of it, in connection with investigation,
you remember. . . . Now, why go by form! Form, you know,
in many cases is nonsense. Sometimes you just have a friendly
talk, and it's more useful. Due form will never disappear, let
me reassure you of that; but what, actually, is due form? The
investigator must not be restricted by due form at every step.
The investigator's work, you know, is, so to speak, a free art
in its own way, or something like that."*

The idea of human perfectibility is a democratic idea. It is a
nineteenth-century characteristic, as constant a theme in the
aristocratic and autocratic Russian society of the 1800's as,
in its literature, is "the transformation of the hero as a result
of his clash with life," to quote F. I. Evnin. The intellectual
sets no a priori limits. He experiences an attitude of perpetual moral crisis, finding that the forces of life are incomprehensible to the very individual for whose benefit they are
invoked. Reason's best effort is to organize, for spiritual convenience, the dichotomous propositions easily deduced from
life: God is good and unreal; or, God is unjust and real. Life
is approached with anger and fear, and taken, as found, as a
matrix of experience and emotion, circling each particular ego.
"If God exists," says Kirillov in *The Devils*, "all is His will,
and from His will I can't escape. If not, it's all my will, and
I am bound to show self-will." In the book, Kirillov can be
offered as a solution to the dilemma; he is. In life, there can
be no answer. Just as the judge of the book is not in the book,
so the judge of this life is not in this life—and if we ourselves
have access to another world, we cannot know it. Death
stands, as Melville images it in "Bartleby, the Scrivener," a
blank wall before us—inscrutable, devastating, and real. Porfiry Petrovich is Raskolnikov's reasoning self, the part of Raskolnikov which wrote the article and invented the crime in
the first place. He is the master thinker, the agent of plot

who knows all about the murder and can encompass George Lewes's *Physiology of Common Life* (1859), with its theory of "the functional indifference of the nerves," as well as comic structure and form in Gogol's writings. But he is a man of no faith and, therefore, beyond morality. He cannot complete the crime, but he narrows the game and points to the end. He forces Raskolnikov in on Sonya, and with her the climactic confession occurs.

The vividness of Dostoevsky's philosophic ideas derives not from any originality in philosophy but from a literary skill which puts every idea under tension and, assigning its plausible extremes to two contrary figures, stretches it like a rubber band. The banal is made to reveal love as the essence of life (*Poor People*; "A Weak Heart"); the incredible is made to show the significance of what underlies even the most ordinary life ("A Bean," "The Crocodile"). Dostoevsky always *tells* us, the readers, what he is doing—and then dislocates that into further meaning. In the beginning of "A Weak Heart," he says that he begins his story with action. He says he is doing it merely to be different from other authors. But we soon find that his "argument" with them is, rather, a principle of sophisticated literary construction which not only takes us into the story but also characterizes his prose in general. Actors appear before they are described or before their background is given (compare the opening passages of *Fathers and Children* and *Crime and Punishment*). One set of labels (the "goodness" of Razumikhin, for example) is shown to be inadequate to a different set of problems—for example, Raskolnikov's idea or Sonya's humiliation. Set phrases recur. Images form patterns: flowers, gardens, eyes (and the fear of eyes), bugs, water, light, steps, beats and knocks, the notion of games and of playing, and so on. One actor frequently misunderstands another, that is, misinterprets him: for example, Natasya says "it's the blood," referring to Raskolnikov's fever in delirium, but Raskolnikov thinks she is referring to bloodstains on his clothes. Throughout the novel an air of mystery is created by unfinished sentences, vague remarks, sententious looks: from one intense look on the stairs Razumikhin grasps with terror that Raskolnikov has killed the old pawnbroker. The idea of freedom—of "America" for Svidrigailov, for example, of marriage to someone *else* for Dunya —lures all the actors on. The shifting point of view increases suspense, multiplies interpretations, adduces other levels of story. Sometimes the viewpoint is the omniscient author's; sometimes, Raskolnikov's; sometimes, the other actors'; sometimes it seems to be the reader's own. In the opening scene it shifts from author to protagonist to spectators (minor characters often serve as a kind of prior audience)—and, in Raskolnikov's moments of greatest tension, we identify so closely with him that we regard his struggle with his guilt as our own.

Images of the garden present by analogy the "other world," the condition of freedom, the positive goal, denied in this here-and-now life, in which all men (except suicides) believe. The moral problem of "making a man" is the substance of the book. And this is hung together chiefly by images of seeing. Raskolnikov is not sure but that he is "only seeing" everything that is happening. After the murder, he tries not to be seen by the two men who come to the door. He sees the "devil" and re-views his crime—and the old woman laughs at him from under the ax blows. The sharpest and most significant visions are those of the dead. Svidrigailov has seen his dead wife three times; he asks Raskolnikov if he does not believe in "apparitions." Sonya sees her dead father on the street. Raskolnikov sees the little dead mare he kissed. Shortly before he confesses his crime to Sonya he experiences his greatest vision, the raising of Lazarus.

Dostoevsky gives Sonya the lines most relevant to his story, emphasizing "I am the resurrection and the life," the *four* days in the tomb, and the numerous conversions after the miracle. Sonya shivers and weeps as she reads. Again, Dostoevsky's context imparts fresh meanings to the old. Lazarus for Jesus, like Raskolnikov for Sonya, is: "he whom thou lovest is sick." Jesus replied, as Sonya does and will do—and will repeat in Siberia: "this sickness is not unto death, but for the glory of God." Raskolnikov proposes that he and Sonya, who also "has transgressed . . . who could transgress," both have only one road, together, ahead. She declines. He reminds her of the little children, of her little sister, and he puts together two contexts from the Gospels. Matthew, XVIII, 4–5 cites Jesus as identifying the humility of purity with eternal life: "Whoso shall receive one such little child in my name receiveth me." Matthew, V, 3 and 10 contain the line Raskolnikov cites: "Blessed are the poor in spirit: for theirs is the kingdom of heaven. . . . Blessed are they which are persecuted for righteousness' sake: for theirs is the kingdom of heaven."

This is the beginning of the peripeteia. Raskolnikov does not reverse himself, does not know himself, does not believe himself. The next day he even says that what is ridiculous about the crime is that Napoleon would have done it and thought no more about it. But the accomplishment of the reversal, like that of the recognition scene in the old Greek plays, depends on identifying the lost hero, the "stranger," the maker of plot who does not seem to belong. In the novel, the machinery of recognition proceeds, as in the original plan, by confession, an excellent device to reconstruct a chron-

ological sequence pointing up the different arrangement of
the dramatic sequence. The confession is deliberately partial.
It involves an eyewitness whose story we tend to believe and
who tends to deal almost exclusively with what is immediately before him, what is flying past (the illusion of the speed
of events). It combines two levels of story, remembered and
current, together against an imagined alternative, and it builds
drama by the conflict within the confessor among motive, act,
and judgment, and between the confessor and all other con-
sciousnesses, those he acted with and those he is confessing to.
In "White Nights" the dreamer, analyzed by the author as a
literary type, exposes a dream which establishes a chronology
and simultaneously alters the substance of the events of the
dream; what is subtitled "a sentimental novel" by parody becomes touching, perhaps tragic. The penitent's greatest fear
is not that he will humiliate himself but that he will not be
believed: that he will be laughed at. Raskolnikov is not satisfied to look like a man; he must be one. The process of the
book is, through its multiple stories and inversions, through
its parodying of philosophy (especially of Chernyshevsky and
of the English utilitarians) and of faith (Raskolnikov's crusade turns into a hideous joke), also a moral progress—the
making of a hero, of a complete man.

*He entered the courtyard rather briskly. He had to go up
to the third floor. "I've still the time going up," he thought.
In general, it seemed to him that the fatal minute was still
remote, that a lot of time still remained, that he could still
reconsider a lot of things.*

*Again the same litter, the same shells on the spiral stairs,
again the doors of the apartments wide open, again the very
same kitchens with their stink and fumes. Raskolnikov had not
been here since that time. His legs were becoming numb and*

buckling under him, but still went on. He stopped for a moment to catch his breath, to pull himself together, to enter as a man.

Raskolnikov tried to assert life by taking it. At the end of the book, he takes his own old one, by turning away from the paradox he put himself in.

The novel takes place in a setting of normality. The characters around Raskolnikov are not so much characters as positions. Even their exaggerations or eccentricities are stereotyped rather than significant idiosyncrasies—for example, the posturing of Luzhin, Raskolnikov's mother's devotion. The characters are points or moments of a circle around Raskolnikov's idea of himself. Like the hand of a clock passing through the hours, he moves through them to return to himself. There are many comic situations in the novel, as in all of Dostoevsky's work—mechanical repetitions, jerkiness, fractured gestures and incongruities, puns and fooling (names like Pseldonimov, Mlekopitaeva, Luzhin; jokes like "A Romance in Nine Letters"; slapstick inappropriateness, such as two men under one lady's bed or Nikolai's confession of the murder) —but the substance is serious. Dostoevsky has very few comic characters. This is, indeed, because the basis of his literary parody of the absurd is the tragic in life.

Gogol followed the eighteenth-century attitude of manipulating stock characters through plots of intrigue. The values by which they are to be measured are introduced by the author's (chiefly lyrical) digressions. Dostoevsky takes the devices of this style and turns them back on life. He presents a surface on his prose as inelegant and confused as the surface of subconscious life. To avoid being commonplace, his characters assert that their assertions are commonplace. They reflect life through the distorting lens of their mind's eye. As if standing behind them, Dostoevsky watches and counts details as carefully as a coroner, putting the details against one another, not in their "natural," chronological sequence, but in his esthetic sequence. The drama that comes from the tension built up by repeated words like "moment" and "shuddered" and "fatal" is informed by the symbols which the details become under exactly that tension.

The great change which Dostoevsky's work represents can, perhaps, be suggested by reference to a specific difference from Gogol. In *The Idiot*, his Don Quixote novel, Dostoevsky discusses Gogol and Gogol's characters, arguing that the commonplace character cannot be left out of any story, because the commonplace character is the constant and essential link in the chain of real-life incidents. "A writer must try to seek out points of interest and instruction even in the characters of commonplace people." But he says that the quality of ordinariness is most striking in those who, try as they may, cannot help being ordinary. "To fill novels only with types or, simply for the reader's interest, with strange and fantastic figures, would be unlifelike and, probably, uninteresting." But, we notice, he cannot help making the ordinary character fantastic, for he sees characters in terms of their contradictions, as witnessed by the example he immediately cites of a rich, handsome nobleman with no talent and no ideas of his own. Indeed, given the inevitable social and physical inner contradictions of a man, nothing could be more dramatic and more ordinary than the history of a failure of a middle-class man—especially if he is also a murderer. Dostoevsky seems to have re-created vividly the whole world of the city of Petersburg and its officialdom, but there is no extensive place description in his work, or, where there is, it is less a description of place than of consciousness. But, after all, that is precisely the only place where we are alive.

Despite our habit of aligning Dostoevsky's characters by types (the "doubles," the "meek," and so on) and of exaggerating his scheme of contradictions (pride versus submission, freedom versus slavery) into a philosophic system, we still come back to the stories and novels mystified and filled with admiration. We are ecstatically shocked by *Crime and Punishment*: the first time we read it, by the audacity of the idea of crime; later, by what Pasternak called the presence of art in the book. The surface refractions yield suddenly to the bright illumination of insight when, for example, as in "A Gentle Creature," art is in every sense brought to life: the girl's climactic response to a love scene is to establish a parallel with a scene of false emotion and false judgment from *Gil Blas*. Dostoevsky did not borrow from other books. He used them to make his real. For him, the true story is supreme fiction.

In *Crime and Punishment* simultaneous development of the crime and of the punishment follows from the Christian concept that the actor can never complete his act (that the meaning of an act does not lie within the act) and from the reciprocal relations between Raskolnikov and the set of characters around him. The characters in conflict take on, in mutual delimitation and definition, contrasting intellectual positions. The closer these characters are brought together, the more disparate they appear. Dostoevsky focuses on those actual moments when the mind hangs between attracting contraries.

These moments are played off against other, analogous moments. They are made to seem typical by being given so much attention (the importance of detail) or by being defined (the "elemental" conflict, the rational superstructure of the novel), but their meaning lies within the dramatic network of their relationships. Both Sonya and Raskolnikov, for example, dislocated by perverse uses of love, work through each other toward accepting that renunciation of self which, like the idea of the crime, must, if it comes at all, come as if in spite of itself. It is the disparity of their positions that allows each to complete the other's; Raskolnikov to be the vehicle for Sonya's dedication, Sonya to be the prophet from whom Raskolnikov may learn to accept the prison of love. He respects life too much to accept it as it is; he must learn to accept, at least, the love.

Raskolnikov finally goes to confess as a man. God is still beyond him, still outside the book. The book cannot embrace the completion that is atonement because it is limited by actuality to social institutions, and there is no actual institution, Dostoevsky indicates, through which an individual can reach God. The individual must move, as Sonya suggests in the purity of her humiliation, by imitation, by esthetic principles. The individual himself creates his guilt: that is the crime. Its measure is faith, which, if deep enough, allows a man to transform himself through purgation of the self-engendered guilt. To live is to walk the knife-edge between imprisonment and freedom. Only by rebelling against the conditions of activity and by transforming the rebellion through the symbols of faith into an act of faith can a man, as if in imitation of Jesus, taking on himself all actual guilt, resume his original, extraordinary dignity. Because the transformation is outside any possible social structure, the contradictions within the rebellion remain, forcing it always to be ultimately self-consuming. Ivan Karamazov found no way out of his contradictions; he went mad. Raskolnikov found no way out; he went to Siberia. There is no way out of these contradictions except death.

At midnight on Christmas Eve, 1849, Dostoevsky said he put on fetters for the first time and was driven through the snow-covered Petersburg streets off to exile. A coincidence? yes; symbolic? it would seem so. In *Crime and Punishment*, written some fifteen years later, we leave the boulevards of Balzac's Paris with their apartments of love far behind. We see issues deeper than those Oliver Twist and Fagin showed us. We are with a new reading of *Don Quixote*, which Dostoevsky called the most "profound and powerful work in the world, . . . the greatest expression of human thought, . . . the bitterest irony which a man can possible express." And he wrote in his notebooks:

If Don Quixote and Pickwick, as virtuous characters, are sympathetic from the reader's viewpoint and are successful, that's because they are ridiculous. The hero of the novel [The Idiot], *the prince, if not ridiculous, has another sympathetic trait, he's innocent. . . . The prince, in his most extreme,* tragic *and personal moments, is concerned with resolution of public questions, too. . . . [His task is] to renew and resurrect man.*

Both the "elegant spirituality" and the world's "negative signification," the "satire" in purgatory which Dostoevsky wrote his brother about when he was seventeen, come to life —our life—in *Crime and Punishment*. We have come beyond lost wealth, lost opportunity, and lost faith, the terms of the sentimental, the romantic, and the naturalistic novels, to where, out of the noblest motives, despite great courage and intellectual skill, a man has lost himself.

The Cathedral
Clergy

Russia in the late 1860's was in the anomalous position of reading Shakespeare, Rousseau, Hegel, and Darwin at the same time that its theoretical science was advanced and its sociopolitical institutions were still parafeudalistic. The manumission of the serfs did not change the bureaucratic structure of the imperial government or substantially alter the economic—and, therefore, social—dependence of the serf on the landlord. Suggestions of economic prosperity, especially with the considerable increase in foreign trade after 1848 and the rapid development of a merchant class, were not accompanied by educational or financial reform. Industrial expansion of the sort experienced in western Europe in the first third of the nineteenth century occurred in Russia only in the last fifteen years of that century. The more deeply that Russian intellectuals penetrated Western theories the more urgently did they seek the application of those theories to their society and the more stridently did they urge theories of their own. Some men supported as rapid as possible a Westernization. Others believed that the existing differences expressed national and cultural qualities which nothing could change. Unlike the Westernizers of the 1840's, who, like Chaadaev, believed "that we have arrived later than the others so that we can do better than they," these men believed that Europe had failed, that, as Kireyevsky put it, "the result of this [European] development . . . has been an almost universal feeling of discontent and of deceived hope." "In the

205

West," said Konstantin Aksakov, "*the soul shrinks* and is being replaced by improvements in government; conscience is being replaced by law; inner impulse, by regulations; and even philanthropy has become a mechanical business." Life was being made overly rational, these men believed, and the individual, his religious self split from his reasoning self, was losing his ties to the community. According to Khomyakov, an individual could not be an organ of cognition, for the vital capacities of higher intellect, as opposed to the self-centered activity of lower (the rational) intellect, could prosper only in the collective thought of free, wise, social love. Whether or not they wished to, these "Slavophiles" supported the status quo. Politically, they were apologists arguing that the writer's function was to clarify the conflicts that existed without changing any terms or any social structure.

The radicals, on the other hand, wanted to change not only the social structure but also the writer's function. They wished for radical change. They talked about making art mirror life, for they held life to be superior to art. They wanted to make life into art—free and perfect. They asserted the possibility of realizing here in this life those transcendentalized values of freedom and meaning to which art had long aspired. They believed that the free man was he who, in enlightened self-interest, offered himself in service to the welfare of mankind. Their literary heroes were men committed by sympathy and reason to the future of humanity, every moment of their lives illuminating the creed by which they moved.

Chernyshevsky said that beauty was life because, I suppose, he believed it a consequence of the definitions which he set up as his goals. He knew very well that life was not beautiful. He also knew that freedom, though a positive value, will bear only a negative definition—that freedom, posited as a value in contradistinction to the fact of pain, is absence of

pain, restraint, or want. By social revolution, he believed, freedom could be installed as love, a rational love for mankind.
Rakhmetov, the hero of his novel *What's to Be Done?*, "consciously and firmly . . . decided to renounce all the advan-
tages and honors which he might have demanded of life in
order to work for the benefit of others, finding his own greatest interests in the pleasure of that kind of work." But Chernyshevsky was well aware of the partiality of his argument and
of the antirational force in a man that was as responsible for
a man's fate as the effort to achieve desired aims. In a letter
to Nekrasov, he wrote:

*I myself know from experience that convictions are not every-
thing in life—the demands of the heart exist, and in the life
of the heart there is genuine joy and genuine sorrow for us all.
This I know from experience; I know it better than others.
Convictions occupy our mind only when the heart rests from
its joy or sorrow. I'll even say that, for me, personally, my
private affairs are more significant than any world problem—
men don't drown themselves or shoot themselves or become
drunkards because of world problems—I've experienced this,
and I know that the poetry of the heart has the same rights as
the poetry of the mind. . . . I have taken the liberty of being
so candid not just to tell you that I read poetry by no means
exclusively from a political point of view. On the contrary,
only by force does politics dig its way into my heart, which
does not by any means live by it, or, at least, would rather not
live by it.*

Chernyshevsky's "new man" was to instruct the nation
and to direct the strength of the peasants. He was to weld
the forces of revolution and of right. He was to be, rather than
an alienated, passive superfluity like the heroes before him, a
dauntless optimist, a convincing savior. A part of the life of

the people, he was the guardian of their grievances and the guarantor of their privileges. He was, it was declared, reintegrated with life. What he meant was what he did. Of course, he never existed. He was too much more than a man. He was an act of the rational imagination. He was a work of art.

His appearance in the 1860's followed from two main trends, which came together with exceptional impact: belief, supported by an ever greater body of examples, that the individual characteristics of a man were essentially moral, not physical or social; and a pronounced politicalization of the kind of theme to which a writer was expected to address himself. The 1860's had to answer the questions put by the 1840's. The difficulty of having to answer well is exposed in all of Leskov's work. Like a judgment, it fell on the careers of such writers as Grigorovich and Pomyalovsky.

After studying at the Engineering Institute, Dostoevsky moved into rooms with one of his classmates, D. V. Grigorovich, at one time an art student, by then a young, promising writer. Grigorovich's long story "The Petersburg Organ-grinders," with descriptions of city figures and city scenes much like those in Nekrasov's and Dostoevsky's prose of the 1840's, appeared in 1843. "The Next-door Neighbor" came out in 1844, a story of two men trying to sleep with another man's mistress, suggesting Dostoevsky's later story "Another Man's Wife." Grigorovich was the first to recognize Dostoevsky's talent and to promote Dostoevsky's work with editors and critics, whom he himself was just beginning to know. On his first visit to Belinsky, Grigorovich talked about Dostoevsky's recently completed translation of *Eugénie Grandet*:

But I had barely managed to mention the fact that the man with whom I shared an apartment—whose name at that time was totally unknown—had translated Eugénie Grandet, *when Belinsky started raging against our common idol with the cruelest abuse, called him a petty-bourgeois writer, said that if he just got his hands on that* Eugénie Grandet *he would lay out all the cheapness on every page. . . . I was completely confused and went away feeling scalded.*

A year later Grigorovich took the manuscript of *Poor People* to Nekrasov and at four o'clock in the morning brought an elated Nekrasov back to congratulate Dostoevsky. Dostoevsky soon met Belinsky, and, *Eugénie Grandet* forgotten, his career was started.

Grigorovich's own career moved more evenly but more slowly than Dostoevsky's. His work indicates, perhaps better than that of any other writer, the level on which successful and eminent prose was expected to be written, just as it indicates predominant interest in the countryside, where, Grigorovich said, he himself felt more at ease than in the city. In 1846 he published a long story *The Village*, a tale of an orphan girl, Akulina, beaten by her foster mother, "hounded, hunted and frightened," finally married to Grigory because the landowner's wife "wanted to see a village wedding" before returning to town. Akulina gives birth to a little girl but soon dies of consumption. Dying, she puts her hand on the baby and begs her husband not to beat it. The story emphasizes peasant habits, customs, superstitiousness; the wedding is described in naturalistic detail; dialect is frequently used in giving peasant speech, particularly in the matchmaking scene; a reader feels that Grigorovich has combined a story about suffering and vitality with the biography of a peasant against a background of sociological examination of the structure and attitudes in a peasant village. Belinsky reviewed the book, saying that Grigorovich had no talent for storytelling but was good at character description, "physiological sketching." Although he continued to write such sketches throughout his life, by the mid-1850's Grigorovich had come to believe that such sketches were not what the times required. His short novel *Anton the Unlucky* (1847), very favorably reviewed, had shown him the importance of focusing on the moral issues involved—in this tale, in which a goodhearted man ends imprisoned, on the dichotomy between peasant values and the laws of government institutions. "Its success," said V. I. Dal, "is explained by the fact that the story goes much more deeply into the bitter position of the peasant under the yoke of serfdom." "Has the Younger Generation in Fact Outstripped the Older?" was one of the chapter headings in Grigorovich's novel *Country Roads* (1850). In "Honorable People Burdened with a Large Family," he declared that he had no interest in doing "a likeness," a physical portrait; you could find that in a man's passport: "We must have the preciseness not of the physical portrait but of the moral."

Coupled with his estimate of the political issues of the 1860's, this led him to debunk radical ideas of social change, to try to demonstrate the imperturbability of values traditionally associated with the landowning class (*The School of Hospitality*, 1855), and to study patterns of urban and rural behavior and their "moral" consequences ("The Air of the Capital, a Sketch of Petersburg Manners and Morals," "The Fishermen, a Novel of the Life of the Common People," or the long tale forthrightly called *City and Country*). In his memoirs, he wrote:

The literary men of the forties had, by the way, full opportunity to write slowly and to groom their work; most of them were men of more or less independent means. . . . Conditions of life then were different; there was markedly less effort to make oneself comfortable, to get conveniences, despite the fact that from childhood on home environment and education fostered fondness of them. . . . Gradually there developed a broad class of men in literature for whom literature was their only means of existence; whether one wished to or not, one had to yield to the new demands and get used to rapid work.

Not political change itself so much as changed political perspectives changes the nature of literary work. In the winter 1861–62, there developed the "great schism" in literature. One group, the "gradualists," contributed to Kraevsky's *Notes of the Fatherland* and were much influenced by the magazine's coeditor, S. S. Dudyshkin, an apolitical literary critic best known for studies of French novels. The other group, around Nekrasov and Chernyshevsky on *The Contemporary*, impatient for real reform, were for "doing it now." The crucial problems of the day led not to philosophical truth, as in the forties, but to political action. They concerned broad but everyday issues such as: the position of the working class, the hiring of labor, the eradication of drunkenness, crime, police protection, the quality of medical treatment, the development of commerce and employment in business and trade, widespread local questions about military recruitment, taxation, *zemstvo* representation, land arbitration, changes in agricultural and husbandry methods. Whether radical or conservative of any degree, a writer was expected to discuss these issues not as a representative of vested (or nonvested) interests, but as a critic evaluating programs for the common welfare. For Leskov, said R. I. Sementkovsky, "writing was a solemn activity; it meant sacrificing everything to the general good. . . . There was not a single important question arising during his whole literary career which he did not attempt to cast some light on from his own point of view."

There arose a literature of exposé, *oblichitelnaya literatura*. In the 1840's and 1850's Gogol's Akaky Akakievich, much imitated as a type before the manumission, was taken as representative of the "underdog," the unknown man, standing to the 1840's as Chaplin's *Tramp* stood to the 1920's. But just

as the generation of the 1930's interpreted the facts of social
life in terms of political institutions and conflicts (*Down and
Out in Paris and London,* "Spain 1937," *In Dubious Battle*),
so the next generation in Russia, the writers of the 1860's,
set forth in sociopolitical terms the inconsistencies and the
corruptions which they believed either resulted from institutions (the radicals) or would result from proposed reform (the
conservatives). As N. G. Pomyalovsky, one of the young
writers, wrote to Chernyshevsky in 1862: "I much admire you,
indeed I am your pupil. Reading *The Contemporary,* I worked
out a view of the world for myself." Pomyalovsky's short life
—he died in 1863 at the age of twenty-eight of the DT's and
gangrene—fell between the two camps and illustrates well two
aspects of Leskov's work: a publicistic tendency and a concern with spiritual values in a definitely religious context.

Pomyalovsky's single work, *Seminary Sketches,* published
posthumously in 1865, consists of five parts, of which two
appeared in Dostoevsky's *Time* in 1862 and three in *The Contemporary* in 1863. Although he considered Chernyshevsky his
guide in political philosophy, Pomyalovsky associated with
the leading literary men of the time—Polonsky, Nekrasov,
Panaev, Danilevsky, Pypin, Turgenev, Saltykov-Shchedrin—
and felt himself a protégé of Dostoevsky's, at least until the
autumn of 1862, when he split with Dostoevsky and his
brother. "Seminary Types" appeared in *Time* in September; a
whole series of sketches was projected. But the May, 1862 fires
in St. Petersburg, which brought Leskov much trouble when
he asked for an investigation into their causes, led to arrests
and to government closure of the "Sunday schools," the public reading rooms, the Chess Club, and, for eight months,
The Contemporary—in short, led to excessive governmental
reaction. In the September issue of *Time,* along with Pomyalovsky's fictionalized essay, Dostoevsky printed an advertise-

ment for the following year indicating the magazine's support of the government and saying about the radicals, especially those on *The Contemporary* and *Russian Word,* that "they build not on solid ground but in the air." That winter Pomyalovsky was one of a small group of writers, including Leskov, who wished to set up, on a guild basis, an editorially independent magazine, *The Age.* Symptomatically, the group dissolved because of political dissension when the "editor" Eliseyev declined to accept a left-oriented article from one of the members.

Seminary Sketches is not autobiography but it is based on Pomyalovsky's life. It is not a chronicle, not a diary, not an essay, not a tractate, not a sociological survey, though it has elements of all these in it. The best "definition" we can make of it is as a novel exposing the violation of the individual's search for knowledge and the violation of theological values of Christianity by an institution, the religious training school. The book takes a boy, Karas, through school from matriculation on, pitting the society of the students against the society of the church:

But thievery, gossip, ruining others' things, and all kinds of dirty tricks were not considered vices only in so far as the seminary authorities were concerned; among the students themselves it was all honesty and fairness.

Bigger boys beat up smaller boys, just as the authorities beat the bigger boys. There is a strict hierarchy ranked by physical force and described ironically by Pomyalovsky through inversion of churchly language:

After a few minutes Karas was summoned to the supervisor's office and, in fact, on his first day of baptism into the seminary faith, he got an anointing of five strokes with a birch rod.

Filled with descriptions of boarding-school life and student slang, the book comes back again and again to the hypocritical dichotomy between what the institution preaches and what it practices. Pomyalovsky emphasizes the harm and the loss which the individual must endure because he is impotent to rebel or, alone, to effect reform: ·

After all, a pupil knows he ought to spit in his teacher's face, but instead of that has to smile politely; he feels rotten inside, and the smile that comes out is strange.

The various sections of the book were published under the tsarist government with extensive disfigurations by the censor. Indeed, it seems that the last two sections might not have been passed at all, even censored, had not Goncharov, the chief literary censor, been asked for an opinion. Ironically, his opinion, which accompanied his approval, may also stand as a judgment on the book, though certainly we would have made a different political interpretation. In July, 1863 he said:

The aim of all such stories is always the same: to expose the outrageousness of the cruel treatment of children and the uselessness of dead and outmoded instructional methods.

Pomyalovsky asked for more than attention to social extravagances ("When the Plain Dealer writ he lashed those crimes / Which then infected most the modish Times"). He was not so much a satirist, like Saltykov-Shchedrin, as a religious writer, like Leskov, whose faith was wobbly and whose experience contradicted what he wanted to believe. We may say of him as one writer said of Leskov, "Where Saltykov's work ends, Leskov's begins."

For Leskov, life, not literature, was the central concern, and he believed from childhood that life needed "good men," Christian in spirit if not in fact, willing and able to help fellow men. Pomyalovsky left among his papers plans for a novel to be called *The Vacation, or Civil Marriage,* an attack on atheistic radicals: "These sham avant-garde people have used the name of progress merely to conceal only a dirty cynicism." In the preface to his collection of sketches called *Righteous Men,* Leskov says:

Isn't there anything in any Russian soul except rubbish? Is everything good and fine which the artistic eye of other writers noticed once upon a time only made-up nonsense after all? . . . And so I set out to look for righteous men, . . . if only to find no more than three.

In "The Musk Ox" (1863), one of his first published stories, he expresses skepticism of all abstract theories and, typical of a liberal reformist (as distinguished from both radicals and conservatives) of the 1860's, has a religious tone dedicated not to mysticism but to practical affairs, to "acting and influencing men in real life."

Chernyshevsky once said about Belinsky that "in England this man would have been a parliamentary orator; in the Germany of the time, a philosopher; in France, a publicist; in Russia he became the author of articles on Pushkin." And Herzen, in his book *My Past and Thoughts,* said that for Belinsky "a line like 'such are our close relations' from *Eugene Onegin* was enough for calling family life to trial and for a penetrating analysis of the concept of blood relationship." The radical critics were less interested in the art work of a work of art than in the "reality" it exemplified. A book was considered a social contribution and, as such, measurable. These critics carried weight because, regardless of social programs, they were the most talented. Except for Apollon Grigorev, the conservative group had no essayist or critic with the power of insight and mordant style to match the radicals.

Not only were the radicals working in the direction of history —all the nineteenth century moved from revolution to revolution—but they supported the significant social accomplishments of their time. So that when Leskov, in an article in *The Northern Bee* on May 30, 1862, asked for investigation of the rumor that the extensive Petersburg fires of mid-May had been set by university students and revolutionaries, all the radical newspapers jumped on him, although he meant only that he thought the rumor should be dispelled one way or the other: "Is there any truth at all to the rumors circulating in the capital about the fires and who started them?" S. A. Reiser has shown that Leskov's ideas, as given in his previous polemical newspaper articles, reflected the reformist spirit of the beginning of the decade. Suvorin, editor of *The New Time*, said of his 1861–62 meetings with Leskov, that "Leskov burned with liberalism and inducted me into the mysteries of Petersburg journalism. He even suggested that we together study Fourier and Proudhon." But after the May article the radicals accused him of inciting the town against the students and of informing to the tsarist police. They boycotted him. And Leskov stopped reporting stories and started writing them.

His first short story, published in 1863, was followed a year later by his first novel, *No Way Out*. It was a book written about contemporaneous political dilemmas by a man who had been influenced in childhood by a Quaker friend of the family and who basically wanted to keep clear of political hassles. The radicals were disaffected by what they considered unflattering pictures of certain revolutionaries in the characters of Reiner and Liza, the young nihilists, and vilified Leskov as a politically weak, slanderous reactionary and spy. Their attack was so strong that even most conservative magazines wished to avoid publishing his work. In 1870–71 he published another extreme political novel, *At Swords' Point*, and, perhaps with malice, cursed the radicals as nihilists, scoundrels, and bastards. By this awkward act, through a talentless novel, he achieved with much effort what most writers accomplish with almost none: he alienated himself from all the critics. Grigorev had died in 1864. The radical critics, deeply committed to their vision of society's future and to the stature of the new man, could not tolerate a seemingly splenetic, conservative, middle-class novelist. Who liked him was the public.

In fact, Leskov did not wish to be alienated, and in terms of his beliefs he did not feel hostile to the radicals. In a review of Chernyshevsky's *What's to Be Done?* he praised Chernyshevsky for having advanced "good men" as the characters:

Mr. Chernyshevsky's people have, above all, a desire to extend prosperity to as many people as possible. . . . All one needs for doing this is good people, such as those Mr. Chernyshevsky has portrayed.

But, under the pressure of the nihilists' political advance, democratic ideas, revolutionary proclamations, the rise of populism and the beginnings of terrorist activity, Leskov turned to politically safe positions, for which he was further attacked. In the 1870's he was attacked by the conservatives, in turn, for religious frankness, his own attacks on abuses by the clergy being connected with his dismissal from government service in 1883. Perhaps he could have avoided dismissal, but he preferred to accept it and to devote himself to writing. In 1874 he broke with Katkov, the conservative publisher, following one of the several moral crises in his life, a kind of self-reexamination, a taking stock of one's values once more.

As a young man, Leskov had not only lived in the countryside but had spent several years traveling all through it as agent for his uncle, manager of two vast estates, a religious man who wanted to educate the peasantry in new methods and new aspirations. Leskov's fiction is characterized not only by exceptional variety of genre, theme, and treatment but also by a consistent "affection" for the peasant and a sense of style given in dialectal turns of speech. The six or seven years he spent traveling for his uncle, he said, "were the best time of my life, when I saw much and lived easily." From these years came most of his material for his prose. Leskov himself insisted that (very unlike Gogol) all that he knew about the peasantry he had learned from the peasants themselves:

The popular, vulgar, and bizarre language in which many of my things are written was not invented by me but overheard from peasants, semi-intellectuals, windbags, God's fools, and sanctimonious idiots. For many years I kept collecting it in phrases, sayings, separate expressions, caught quickly in a crowd, on barges, in recruiting offices and monasteries. For many years I carefully listened to the pronunciation and inflections of Russians in many different social levels.

He studied Russian history, especially of the sixteenth through eighteenth centuries, later talked of the "invisible spirit of the people" in *War and Peace*, admired folk fairy tales "with their ingenious inventiveness and patterned style, their wealth of adventures and the folk clarity of their images."

Leskov's prose is based on unconscious awareness of the conventions by which we get ourselves from one moment of intensity to another, an unconsciousness extracted to consciousness from the seemingly trivial moments of ordinary life. He assigns nothing to a tale which one of the people in it would not ordinarily think belonged. As author, Leskov stands at a subtly but carefully defined remove, moving his characters like puppets from moment to moment of consciousness through incidents acted out unconsciously in their lives. Character comes out only in incident; Leskov uses incident in the form of anecdote to expose character.

A story by Leskov is a narration, often told by the protagonist himself within Leskov's "story," of a particular action or series of actions forming a closed incident, told in such a way that the revelation of character parallels the exposition of incident. We proceed through the prose as if taking apart a *matreshka*, a nest of wooden dolls. Each actor must fit his acts. What Leskov is writing about has to be the same as what his hero wants to tell, which has to fit with what Leskov wants to tell about the hero, all of which has to support our interest. It is a stylized, artful device, disarming in its simple pretensions, literarily involuted. Leskov has a novel, *The Enchanted Wanderer* (1873), which is, in picaresque manner, a compilation of these "characteristic incidents" narrated by the hero to a group of travelers—"We were crossing Lake Ladoga"— and ending at the same time on the same moral level that Leskov ends "his" narrative: "I really want to go die for the people."

Leskov's very popular story "The Man on Watch" (1887) begins:

The event of which a narrative is here below put before the reader's attention, is touching and terrible in its meaning for the protagonist of the piece, and the outcome of the business so original that a thing like this could hardly have occurred any place except Russia.

It is partly a court and partly an historical anecdote, characterizing rather well the morals and the atmosphere of the very interesting but extremely neglected period of the thirties of the nineteenth century now coming to a close.

There is absolutely no invention in the tale that now begins.

The reader is informed, enticed, asked for sympathy and understanding. His snobbishness is catered to. His social lascivi-

ousness is appeased. His nationalism is encouraged. His fund
of knowledge is to be increased. He is promised, at last, a
meaningful picture of the real world. The "story" then begins
(Chapter II), and begins from the place which most people
begin from when they need a place to begin—the weather:

> *In the winter of 1839, around Epiphany, there was a great*
> *thaw in Petersburg.*

The mundaneness of the statement is transcended by its information: we want to know, why Epiphany? Still more important is the way Leskov declares his attitude to history and
shapes ours. The description of the thaw in the rest of the
paragraph seems told by an ordinary middle-class man of little
perceptiveness, describing what he sees and measuring the
change of weather in an anesthetized way:

> *It had become so slushy that it seemed absolutely as if it were*
> *going to be spring: the snow was melting; during the day water*
> *dripped from the roofs, and the ice on the rivers was turning*
> *dark blue and being covered with water. On the Neva, right*
> *in front of the Winter Palace, there were deep patches of*
> *water in the middle of the ice. A warm, but very strong, west*
> *wind was blowing: the water was being driven in from the bay*
> *and the signal guns were booming.*

Every perception is just slightly more organized than an average man ordinarily makes. The view is seen in just a slightly
broader than normal perspective. For example, we would not
think "*during the day* water dripped" but simply "water
dripped" and disregard it during the night. Our ordinary insignificance is implied in the perception of the noise of the
guns which some powerful authorities fire as the law they
made commands. The guns are remote from us, like the bay,
but are being fired near it; so, we associate the two, an ordi-

nary perception. The guns end the last sentence of the paragraph. The first sentence of the next paragraph begins by describing the kind of men who fire them. We move from the
man who hears them to the men who shoot them: "A company of the Izmailovsky Regiment was on guard at the Palace. . . ."

The "hero" of the story is a sentry named Postnikov,
"Guardsman," an Everyman—honest, devoted, insignificant.
On duty one night he hears a man cry for help from the
nearby water. To leave his post in front of the tsar's palace,
even to rescue a man drowning in the Neva, might mean, he
knows, the firing squad. He debates with himself. Finally, being sensitive to the pleas of others, he goes and rescues the
drowning man. Just as he has pulled him out, a frivolous and
impudent officer comes along. Postnikov flees back to his post.
The officer deposes to a sleepy police clerk that he rescued the
man, but the police begin to inquire because the officer came
out with dry clothes. Postnikov, anyway, is in the guardhouse
for having deserted his station. The police inspector gets two
reports and finally assembles them: one, that the officer rescued the man and, the other, that Postnikov had deserted his
station and rescued the man. He lets the officer's deposition
stand and, with an irony appropriate to persons in high places,
awards the officer the medal. Svinin, the commander of Postnikov's battalion, then sentences Postnikov to a lighter than
usual sentence, a beating, which only puts Postnikov in the
hospital for a while. The feat passes into rumor, Postnikov's
name is lost, and the episode finally comes to the ears of, as
Leskov puts it, "an ecclesiastical dignitary." This astute gentleman is aware that the rumors hold internal self-contradictions,
and when he happens to be visited one evening by Svinin, he
brings the subject up.

Each of the actors has presented his story of the episode.

Leskov's story is the one that is shaped by the disparities and differences among the other points of view. In the end Leskov, didactic and, at this time in his life, anticlerical, involves himself with the reader in a kind of complicity. His Eminence the astute ecclesiastic is treated ironically, then sarcastically, and then with contempt and hatred, caricatured by the phrase "again the rosary, again silence, and finally the gently rippling speech," or variations on it. The ecclesiastic's summation, against the background of the whole tale, is sufficient revelation of his own character:

It is perhaps much more useful for a warrior to suffer humiliation and wounds for an heroic deed than to be distinguished by a decoration. But the very most important thing in all this is that the whole matter be treated with discretion, and that there never be mention under any condition of what at any time was told anybody.

That last sentence is Leskov's trick in art. It reinforces the game, set out at the beginning, that "there is absolutely no invention" in the tale. Because the story is "real," the authorities fear it; that is, they must preempt it for themselves, so that the inadequacy of their institutions is not exposed. Reality is terrifying for the revelations it implies. The point of an event is the meaning of character it discovers.

The story was written at a time in Leskov's life when he had moved away from the Orthodox Church and, championing the meek, virtuous, Christian man, had come to regard religion in the manner of Tolstoy. In a letter to Tolstoy a few years later, in May, 1894, he wrote:

I do not wish to and cannot write anything like The Cathedral Clergy *and* The Sealed Angel, *but I would with pleasure write* Notes of an Unfrocked Priest, *taking as the hero a young,*

*openhearted, and honest young man who had become a priest
in order to do* what he could ad majorem Dei gloriam, *and had
found out that* there was nothing there *that could be done for
the glory of* God. *But it's a thing which in our country you
couldn't get published.*

Leskov, close to Tolstoy in the early 1880's, soon split with
him also, finding Tolstoy's religious views and those of his
supporters as ineffective and inappropriate in the eighties as
he had found the radicals' views in the sixties. In his story
"A Winter Day," published near the end of his life, he
satirized Tolstoyans as the new "new men," the "nonresistors
who are always planning to do something" but never do it.
Or what they do do is "completely pointless."

Leskov changed less than the world around him. He
wanted his idiosyncratic religious faith not to set up a cult but
to lead to moral improvement, to have, by example, practical
results. This attitude is partly written into Postnikov's story
and partly tacked on in the last chapter as a sort of epilogue.
As a composition, the story is deliberately symmetrically made,
like the Slavic Revival architecture then in vogue. Leskov
sums up his fable:

> *If I had the daring of Heaven's happy elect, to whom, ac-
> cording to their great faith, it is given to penetrate the mys-
> teries of God's plan, I should, perhaps, dare allow myself the
> suggestion that probably God Himself, also, was pleased with
> the conduct of His humble creature Postnikov. But my faith is
> small; it does not give my reason the power to view such lofty
> things: I hold to things earthly and mundane. I think of those
> mortals who love goodness simply for its own sake and expect
> no rewards for it anywhere at all. These upright and stead-
> fast people, too, I think, should be completely satisfied with*

*the holy outburst of love and the no less holy patience of the
humble hero of my accurate and ingenuous story.*

The hopeless modesty of the middle-class man is confounded
with the pious modesty of the virtuous Christian. Those who
expect no reward for good acts are not Christians but philosophers; Christians expect, at the least, to get into Heaven.
Postnikov is an example to us. He himself, according to the
story, understood nothing. He is even pleased with what happened to him because, with a chickenlike sense of fatality, he
thought he would be shot, and he is only beaten. Furthermore,
his punishment arrived irrespective of his actions. The fact
that he was beaten and not shot had nothing to do with him,
or with man. It was blind social behavior. It was mere chance
—assuming, of course, that the social command is not "Love
thy neighbor as thyself" but, as the astute ecclesiastic phrased
it, "One must never fail to perform one's official duty." Doing
one's duty, said Shaw, is the small man's excuse for cowardice.

One of the devices by which extremes of credibility in
fiction are stretched is the revelation of personal history, the
diary. Lermontov, Turgenev, Gogol, Dostoevsky—almost all
the fiction writers at some time or other used this trick. Leskov
uses it in his novel *The Cathedral Clergy* as a log of life's trivia,
which become meaningful by the exaggeration and symbolization which the diarist's mind puts them through. In the over-
all pattern of the novel, the diary is one way the author brings
out from concealment as many different facets as possible of
one man's ordinary existence and sets them against the movement of the novel. The character, like each incident which
takes its being from him and lends being to him, stands independent of the author's social program or even moral purpose.
The Cathedral Clergy is a concatenation of perceptions of in-
dependences. The first part lacks a story (it may not interest

you), and in the other parts the story is chopped up almost beyond recognition. The sequence of the book is not built on a series of causal nexi but on the development of events in the course of time according to the nature of life as we, ordinary men, ordinarily experience it. Motives, desires, ambitions, all shape the conflict among men but never chiefly. The single, all-consuming, glorifying passion that animates Anna Karenina and gives meaning to her unhappy life would be incredible in the petty world of this book. The intellectual power and pride of Ivan Karamazov would seem artificial, abstract, unreal. The single-mindedness of Chichikov would seem humanly impossible if not in fact inconsistent. "Perhaps, standing inside this [Tuberozov's] house," Leskov writes, "we will find means to glance into its owner's soul, as one gazes into a glass beehive, where the bees are building their wonderful honeycomb, with its wax for illuminating the face of God and honey for the delectation of man." Leskov wants to look every way at once, to see everything instantaneously in its abundance and labor, physically, esthetically, and morally. "We will go off into a realm," he writes, "unknown and invisible to all who gaze on the face either close at hand or from afar."

Sections of the first edition of the novel appeared in 1867–68, including a fond memoir of the orchards of Orel Province of Leskov's childhood. In 1872 the novel was published as a book, a fresh theme in Russian literature—the first portrait of the daily life, typical characteristics, and spiritual concerns of the ordinary Orthodox clergy. The characters are a mélange of types and sorts, a distinguishing feature of all of Leskov's work. The central three are: Savely Tuberozov, archpriest, an inspired orator, independent thinker, and opponent both of the narrow-minded regulations of higher officials, governmental and consistorial, and of atheistic reformers such as Prepotensky and Termosesov; his assistant, the meek priest Zakharia Benefaktov; deacon Akhilla Desnitsyn, one of Leskov's "righteous men," a massive, deep-voiced fighter of "terrifying strength" and "many Cossack virtues." Tuberozov was "the result of my imagination," Leskov wrote in 1890. Akhilla, he said, "is still living. That's my familiar deacon-*bogatyr*. . . . He's even now a threat to the inhabitants." Once these three characters are introduced, their houses described, the "strife" among them identified (Zakharia locked up Akhilla's staff on the grounds that the rank of deacon did not merit one), and the conflict between the churchmen and the townsmen suggested (Prepotensky, the schoolteacher, was arguing with Akhilla about the truthfulness of such signs and symbols in the Bible as Aaron's rod and the writing on the wall), the story of the life of the men in the church begins inside the story of its meaning.

Chapter IV opens:

A summer evening over Stargorod. The sun has set long ago. The part of town on the hill, where the sharp spire of the cathedral rises, shines in the pale light of the moon. . . .

and an old man is calling to a small boy. The first reference to Archpriest Tuberozov, the man into whose soul we are to lunge, is his wife's question: where is he? But the answer does not reveal much of that "unknown and invisible realm" we were promised: "He is playing checkers at the police chief's."

Finally, we get there—in the next chapter. We get into Tuberozov's diary, where for thirty years he has jotted down his private reflections. And the first entry we get, anxious with excitement for the revelation at hand, reads: "At my ordination to the priesthood, on February 4, 1831, by the Right Reverend Gavriil, I received from him this book as a gift for my satisfactory completion of seminary studies and for good conduct." If we are shown anything, we are shown ordinariness, that is, precisely what cannot be revealed because there is nothing revelatory about it. To be known, what is real must be revealed. Yet, on the basis of "real life" pretending that it cannot be, Leskov sets out to confute his own pretense.

Leskov uses but does not emphasize class distinctions. His book is not based on psychological analysis or economic explanation of social stratification. He does not depend on class differences for developing conflicts within the novel. Contrary to the word often attached to his work, it is not an example of "plebeianism." Leskov takes the obvious contrasts and similarities he observes—consciously, all his work is cast in terms of what he can hear, see, touch, smell—and lets them incriminate themselves, just as we, in our common behavior, let the fool, the conceited ass, the coward, and the saint expose themselves against the background of our normal understanding. Everyday experience is measured, by us in our simplicity and by Leskov in the sophistication of his talent and the perspective of his artistic remove, against our social tradition, everything of our total history which we actually possess. For example, in *The Enchanted Wanderer*, written shortly after *The Cathedral Clergy*, the hero, a typical, distinctive but undistinguished man representing all contemporary men, is measured in art against art's invention of the glorious hero, the Achilles-like *bogatyr*, who, in his time, was the paragon of his society:

By looks you could have said that this new fellow traveler of ours, who later turned out to be an extraordinarily interesting man, was just a few years over fifty; but he was in the full sense of the word a bogatyr, *and moreover a typical, open-hearted, good Russian* bogatyr *reminiscent of old Ilya Muromets in Vereshchagin's beautiful painting and in Count A. K. Tolstoy's poem.*

Art, for Leskov, means more than a mirror of life or a midwife to society. It is a glorification of the typical, and this typicality not only gives art its viability but also its meaning. Nothing is more than what it *is*. It is itself, divorced as essence from its contextual commitments and definitions, revealed in its ultimate nature so far as the terms of daily life are concerned.

The immediate concern of art, Leskov stresses, is life as it is lived by normal people. This is the substance of the human world and the matter of his art. It is apprehended directly by observation that attends experience. There is nothing definite or definable, in analogous terms, beyond this, except a faith, represented often as conjecture or dream, that the source of morality is divine. That faith is not significant in ordinary life except as men share attitudes toward it. Of itself, it does not ordinarily signify. Men's attitudes do. Leskov's charm and success derive from this simple but difficult discovery.

In *The Enchanted Wanderer*, Ivan Flyagin, the wanderer, tells a story within his story, indicating at the same time by his reproduction of dialogue that the pleasure of telling a story exceeds any sadness told about:

[*The Most Reverend*] *took a look at him and sees that in fact this little priest is a real drinker, and came to the conclusion that he shouldn't have a church. The little priest was very hurt and even stopped drinking, and starts wasting away with grief and crying: "What," he thinks to himself, "have I brought myself to, and what else is there for me to do now but lay hands on myself? This is all," he says, "that's left for me: then, at least, the Most Reverend will take pity on my unhappy family and will find a groom for my daughter so he can take my place and feed my family."*

The priest is not at the bottom, as Marmeladov is, nor is he a symbol of such a man. He is simply a regular man victimized, by conventional standards, by his self-indulgence, but, being such an ordinary victim, unimportant. No principle is or can be involved:

Well, all right: so he decided to finish himself off for good and set the day for it, but being as he was a man of good intentions, so he thought to himself: "All right, now: I'm to die, well, let's suppose I die, but of course I'm not cattle; I'm not without a soul—then where will my soul go?" And from that hour on he started being even more mournful.

The story ends with the priest praying for the souls of suicides.

If the little priest can be said to stand for anything, he is, I think, an unobtrusive illustration of Flaubert's request: "Let's go in for sadness in art, for that is the aspect of things we feel best, but let's have gaiety in our lives." The priest's use of liquor is not unlike our use of the story: efforts to escape the disasters and oppressions of our condition are only diversions in sadness. The real man is in tune with life because he sees, through the veneer of mirth and triviality, the profound sorrow of life. Leskov calls Flyagin's story of his wanderings a "dramo-comedy." In *The Cathedral Clergy,* Tuberozov, who reads not only Dashkova's memoirs and Bunyan's *Pilgrim's Progress* but also Herzen's paper and the novels of "very witty Pastor Sterne," says that "licensed nihilism is dying out and

shandyism is coming in, . . . a particular mental condition which in Sterne's definition "dissolves the heart and lungs and makes the complex wheel of life spin rapidly." And what makes me still more convinced that Russia has entered the shandyism phase is what Shandy himself said: "If I, like Sancho Panza, could choose a government for myself, I would pick not a commercial and not a rich one, but one in which people would laugh without stopping both in jest and in ear-

nest." *In faith, I fear this jesting Panza understood us poor wretches, for all that applies to us perfectly, neither rich nor generous but a great deal more full of laughter.*

In his diary, Tuberozov admits that the clergy is too poor to buy *The Imitation of Christ*, a truly priestly book, but also admits that he cannot tell the bishop this. An item, it reminds us of the disparity between what we would do or think we could do and what, in fact, we do do. A page later, Tuberozov asks: "Am I to preach—when there is no one to preach to; am I to teach—when no one listens?" How can he be priest without parishioners? How can we be ourselves unless others define us?

The diary in the book is used to penetrate a view from one corner (the hero's corner) of the life of Stargorod, or Old Town, which itself stands for all Russian towns. The diary, Chapter V of Part I, gives the background of its author and of the cathedral and recapitulates the history which precedes the novel. Where it ends the novel carries on. The diary presents a series of anecdotes and commentaries by Tuberozov. Later in the book, certain events in it are recast and narrated by the author from a series of new positions. Always the point of view from which the narration is told is biased in favor of what we are persuaded to call the human virtues and foibles of all the people in the town. No one person excels. No one character takes on a life or a development independent of the others. This is due partly to the mannered nature of the book and partly to the author's attitude:

I am extremely curious to know what you would do, you composers of fables and ballads and novels and romances, without looking at the threads of life which surround you and are worthy of being plaited together into a fable entertaining to a reader? Or you, you reformers of men's morals, who really have no concern for the actual life men live and merely want pretexts for vain rantings? Do you know what sort of life is led by the Russian priest, that "useless man"? . . . Do you know that the miserable life of that priest is not scanty but full of misfortune and adventures?

Art, for Leskov, is a composed reality: composed in the sense that it is a symmetrizing of natural experiences and in the sense that it assigns meaning and brings tranquillity to men's usual anxiety. This book does not end merely conveniently with the deaths of its three cathedral clergymen. Leskov says that we, the readers, must expect these deaths, and that when they have come, as he describes them, everything will be finished only because everything will have been ultimately composed.

"I have begun to compose a novel," Tuberozov writes in his diary for August 9, 1842, "from my ecclesiastical experience." Although he does not know it we do know that he has already begun doing that, that he has been composing a novel as long as the book in which we read about him has been going on, as long, in fact, as he himself has been "living." The transitions from the novel in Tuberozov's mind, the novel-in-fiction, to the diary, the novel-in-history, to his life, the novel-in-experience, are made without awkwardness. They do not violate the credibility we have assigned the book; they establish it. "From a personal confession based on a single, individual drama, Leskov reaches out across the broad canvas of a turbulent and stormy age," said L. P. Grossman in his book on Leskov. "This radically alters the basic compositional principle: against an independent novelistic structure with centrality of purpose he has set an uninterrupted and unceasing succession of events."

In collecting actuality, Leskov uses the idiosyncrasies of

speech which we often fall into and which reveal our thoughts. Leskov uses various sorts of "errors": the obvious pun, *po ves*, by weight, turns into *povesa*, featherhead; the word which means "pet corn" is mispronounced and means "bully" in the phrase, "Ouch, you've stepped on my bully," and we quickly perceive that the man *means* "Ouch, you bully!" Akhilla and Prepotensky, beaten up, switch initial letters around: "My spead is hlitting"; "I fecognize your race, but where I have remembered you I do not see." This is all normal. The use of this "erroneous" associative pattern seems unusual in the normality of this book because it draws attention to what we ordinarily do not perceive or try to hurry over in embarrassment. It is, also, humorous. It binds the characters together and us to them. It expresses what happens to us between desires and deeds under the pressure that other people present. It is analogous to the kind of implausible, sometimes incredible judgment we are often led to in order to clarify, just for ourselves against others' opposition, our own tenuous positions. After he cries out about his "bully," Prepotensky makes this sort of judgment: "Have you read Turgenev? *Smoke*. He's a gentleman writer, and in his work he proves that everything in Russia is smoke." A few moments later Prepotensky concludes the argument with "I'll be against the nobles, anyway, and for natural right." In all this, Leskov seems to be saying, we pretend we rationally develop opinions and judgments, but indeed we do not. They form themselves and, every time they are expressed, reveal our nakedness.

We also express ourselves on other than the conventional channels. The communication that undercuts conventions is of greater power. It speaks of so real a relationhip that we are always frightened by it:

Then suddenly Termosesov said in an entirely different voice, with the softest possible intonation, "Well, it is yes, isn't it?

Yes?" This yes was uttered in such a tone that something gave a thump in Madam Bizyukina's heart. She understood that an answer was required not at all to the question which had been asked but to one the tacitly understood meaning of which actually frightened her by its realism, and, therefore, Bizyukina remained silent.

Tuberozov says at one point in his diary that, not being used to boldness, he cannot adopt the daring and stylish speech of Herzen in *The Bell*. This same level of reality in political and social life is reflected in the episode in which Bizyukina pays little boys to come to her house to school. A caricature of the "new woman," she feels herself more intelligent because of this "school," as most people feel after their dog has learned a new trick. And the "young political lady," who had never done this before, was "extremely pleased with herself—her visitors [later] found her, as they say, *in full toilet.*" This is Leskov's measure of political life at the level of the individuals who would service the great machine called the state:

"Why didn't you offer yourself in Petersburg as a spy?" Bornovolokov asked Termosesov.

"I did go, indeed," replied Termosesov brazenly, "but with our present realism all the profitable openings in that line were filled."

Like *No Way Out* and *At Swords' Point*, this novel is political.

The story takes on dramatic and tragic qualities as it moves closer and closer to Tuberozov's anguish. "I was thirty-three," Leskov wrote in 1891, "when I tried doing a novel *with no love story, The Cathedral Clergy.* It's quite possible, and not at all without general interest." (In our day, Solzhenitsyn may say the same—and mean even more—about *One Day in the Life of Ivan Denisovich.*) The novel moves from Tuberozov's early appeal to God to help mankind's unbelief—"otherwise there is danger that we will arrive at the condition of a nomadic horde"—to his own transcendentally beautiful forgiveness of those who in their ignorance and bureaucratic responses seriously harmed him. The author, always conscious of plaiting the fable and of the story's obligations to its characters and to its readers, shifts the tone from caustic laughter to, at least in places, lyrical identification with the fates of men. Instead of the comic picture of people fighting to be reconciled and being reconciled to fight again and nothing disturbing the peace, we get images of nature and "the elastic leaves of the young oaks." The book, in which all action has previously been set forth in fractured scenes, in a series of inner movements or chronological consequences, now takes on, from the vantage of Tuberozov's suffering and liberation, an ingenuous, pathetic quality, which is one of the aspects of drama.

In the beginning of one of the closing chapters, there is a beautiful description of the coming of spring and of the arrival in town of the peasant boatmen, as visual and bright as a painting. (Grossman suggests that the thunderstorm in Chapter XVIII of Part III is like a painting by Nesterov.) The tone is straightforward in terms of nature, but ironical in terms of men, for, says Leskov, it is man who has so confused nature that those who plant the grain have to raft to distant regions what they lack at home. More peasants come than can be hired, but nobody bothers about these superfluous men. Similarly, Leskov implies, society does not bother about its superfluous men. Society is out of harmony with its environment. Men lack functions. Their lives move from day to day without meaning. Any specific remedy, however, falls into the same delusion by which society operates. There is nothing to do but everything to be aware of.

Leskov remains an independent talent revulsed by the radicalism of his day and, equally, by the cruelty and inhumanity of autocratic power. He advocated a kind of anarchic religion based primarily on an ideal of active charity and a scorn of spiritual pride. He argued for humility as a virtue: so, in some of his stories, whores possess real love, that is, those who have sinned are closer to sanctification. But even in his stories of Byzantine life, what he wants, like Flaubert in *Salammbô*, is a complete picture of life in its beauty and power. He would, I think, have sadly agreed with Delacroix that "one has to spoil a picture a little in order to finish it." For him, literature means ethics, edification, but, above all, beauty. Whatever commands commands because it has the necessary force of charm, because it has the power to be. One need not worry about the future of society: one can do very little, actually, about it.

"But do you know that freedom is not given, but is seized?" [*the ridiculed schoolteacher asks in* The Cathedral Clergy].
"Well, sir!"
"But who will seize it, if the new men are bad?"
"It will come about in the natural course of things."

Art neither preaches nor predicts; it simply perseveres in what is.

Anna
Karenina

¶ "In art," said Thomas Gilby, "the emphasis is on the thing to be done, not, as in the moral virtues, on our personal disposition in doing it." Tolstoy told A. D. Obolensky, talking about Levin's confession to the priest in *Anna Karenina*, that "I've noticed that anything, any story, makes an impression only when the reader can't make out whose side the author is on. And that's how it all had to be written, so that that couldn't be felt." Despite his lifelong scorn of journalism and of the behind-the-scenes politics of the literary magazines, despite his repeated withdrawals from the activity of the two capitals, Tolstoy responded to the most provocative questions of his time and regularly took positions which embroiled him in polemics. For he was against even the questions themselves, or, as he wrote in the epilogue to *War and Peace*, apropos of Natasha and the feminist movement, "Talk and argument about women's rights, about conjugal relations, about their liberty and rights, although not then called, as now, *problems*, were then just the same thing as now." In a letter to M. P. Pogodin in 1868, he angrily joked about founding a journal to be called *The Noncontemporary* from which he would exclude "99 per cent . . . of the cheap and rotten stuff" found in existing journals. Again and again, in his life and his prose, he responded to issues with nostrums which simultaneously denied the general assumptions behind the conflict of issues themselves. His response to the Crimean War was *Sevastopol Stories*, denigrating military glory and power. His response to the conflict between "fathers and sons" in the consciously democratizing period after the death of Nicholas I was "Two Hussars," a story in which Tolstoy showed preference for the father over the son for qualities associated with old aristocracy (he later admitted that the son was "portrayed lovelessly"). His response to the populist movement, *narodnichestvo*, was to turn teacher of peasants, to compile an *A B C* called "antediluvian" by educators, and to involve himself in a bitter and stupid public hassle with the Moscow Literacy Committee. His response to the feminist movement, to the changing status of the nobility, to the new relations between landlord and peasant and between the peasant and the land was *Anna Karenina*. Because he believed, with many, that the nobility had begun to lose authority (authority in the 1870's being rapidly assumed by the merchant class and the bureaucracy) ever since the centralization of government imposed by Peter the Great, he first planned a novel about the people of Peter's time but abandoned it as necessarily too historical: "The people are so unlike us." He turned then to the story of the "internal development of passion" and ended up forced by his own strange opposition to the great issues of his time to set a subjective story in an objective world. From a positive viewpoint, Tolstoy meant what he had Levin say:

I'm not at all convinced [that I haven't the right to hold the land]. On the contrary, I feel that I haven't the right to give it away, that I have obligations both to the land and to my family. . . . The most important thing for me is to feel that I'm not to blame.

From a negative viewpoint, Tolstoy deprecated the intellectual luxuries of Western civilization, insisting that the only source of forward social movement was the peasantry itself and that the only competent judge of men was God. On the basis of his "discovery" of Schopenhauer, he insisted on the propriety of moral purgatives and on the beauty of family virtue. Not only does Tolstoy thereby show his difference from the men of the forties sophisticated in Western culture—Turgenev derided him, and Botkin said that the next step was for Tolstoy to claim to have discovered the Mediterranean—but he exposed himself to the fair charge that he was plain ignorant. B. N. Chicherin said that Tolstoy "had no idea what philosophy was. He himself admitted to me that he had tried to read Hegel but that it was Chinese to him. Schopenhauer, recommended to him by Fet [who was translating Schopenhauer into Russian], was his only nourishment."

All his life Tolstoy experienced a discrepancy between his necessary ideals and society's unchanging values. He felt that he did not "fit," yet felt that he had to. This was the source of his moral anguish and, projected, of the constant drama between the accomplishments he believed himself capable of and the experiences he underwent. He was obsessed with himself. Every person, of course, has a sense of individuality; Tolstoy was pursued by his, compelled to turn his experience into literature. In this sense, Tolstoy is one of the most autobiographical writers. Time and again, the central character, episode, feeling, or attitude in one of his stories, or whole parts of his novels, essays and plays, is a faithful, imaginative, evangelical, astonishing transformation of what was going on inside him. Olenin in *The Cossacks* (1863) is Tolstoy, who went to the Caucasus to find "life," found it, and found that he did not fit in. Levin in *Anna Karenina*, especially the Levin of the last third of the novel, is Tolstoy, who married for family happiness, found it, and found that "still there will be the wall between the holiest-of-holies of my soul and others, even my wife."

Tolstoy's entire life is characterized by a conflict between standards of hedonism and of puritanism, which made any situation he was in unbearable—or, at least, unsatisfactory—and which was resolved, in the sense of comprehended, only in his creative writing. As he wrote in French from Tiflis in 1852, he felt pursued by a demon of failure:

I swear that in most of these reversals I'm complaining about I have myself to blame as much as fortune, but it's true, nevertheless, that a little demon exists which is continually busy making me . . . fail in all I do.

In June, 1847 he jotted down a feeling which illustrates the idealistic side of his moral character:

Will I ever get to the point of being independent of all external circumstances? In my opinion, this is a great achievement, for in the man who is independent of all external influence, the spirit necessarily, by its own requirements, overcomes matter, and the man will then achieve what he is cut out for.

The precepts and injunctions on himself which he continually listed in his diary seemed at times ineffective. In June, 1850 he made an entry which illustrates not only the sensual side of his life but also the rugged honesty with which he went after himself:

I spent the winter before last in M[oscow], lived a very irregular life, without a job in the service, without anything to do, without a goal; and I lived like that not because, as many say and write, everybody in Moscow lives like that, but simply because I liked that sort of life.

Desire satisfied, he regarded pleasure as turpitude. He used his diary as a confessional and as penance. In July, 1851 he wrote:

I went to Chervlennaya, got drunk there, slept with a woman; all this is very bad and torments me deeply. So far I haven't once spent more than two months well. . . . Abomination! but I write this as punishment for myself.

Women, said Tolstoy, "in this immoral, vicious age are worse than us [men]." He wanted to become immersed in the untrammeled, strong, beautiful life of the men of nature—first, the life of the Cossacks; later, as with Levin, the life of the peasants. He meant it when he said in his diary in July, 1850 that he would always say

that consciousness is the greatest moral evil, which only man can comprehend. It's painful, very painful, to know ahead of time that an hour from now I'll still be the same person, the same images will still be in my memory, but my outlook will have changed independently of myself, and consciously at that.

He wanted to become as pure, brave, and noble as he imagined the "natural man" to be, but he could not live without the furniture of culture, could not help writing, and could not escape the constant gnawings of remorse for what he always felt, after the fact, was weak and morally reprehensible profligacy.

All his life Tolstoy felt, despite his money and his aristocratic position, that he was outside society in a way he could neither avoid nor overcome. As he noted in his diary in March, 1852, "There's something in me that forces me to believe I wasn't born to be the same as all the rest." But what the source of this feeling was he did not know. He wrote willingly, he said, but, once he had written something, he loathed it, loathed himself and even the public who would read it. Half-way through *Anna Karenina* he stopped work on it, disgusted, and called the novel *gadky*, cheap and filthy. Tolstoy was, in-deed, looking for something—for truth, for God, for happiness —but he had no conviction that he would find it. His diary entry for August 24, 1862, runs, in part:

Afterwards I was as sad as I haven't been in a long time. I have no friends—none! I'm alone. I had friends when I served Mammon, and none now I'm serving truth.

The entry for August 28 begins: "I'm thirty-four. I got up with the habitual feeling of sadness. . . ." A man's actions in the present invalidate an aspect of his future, Tolstoy believed; to some extent we all sink ourselves. Anna Karenina is an un-fortunate but unexceptionable extreme of what he felt about himself.

In 1903, asked by his friend P. I. Biryukov to supply some autobiographical information for the first edition of a book on himself, Tolstoy cited the tone of moral crisis which he felt had pervaded his life, and listed four periods into which, he said, his life divided:

Remembering my life, i.e., thinking back on it from the point of view of the good and evil I did, I saw that my life falls into four periods:

That wonderful, especially in comparison to what followed, innocent, joyful, poetic period of childhood up to fourteen.

Then the second—a terrible twenty years or period of vulgar licentiousness, of ambition-serving, vainglory, and, chiefly, lust.

Then the third, an eighteen-year period from my marriage to my spiritual birth, a period which from the world's point of view may be called moral, i.e., during these eighteen years I lived a proper, honest, family life, not yielding to any of the vices castigated by public opinion, a period during which all my interests were limited to egoistic concern for my family, for augmenting my wealth, for achieving literary success, and to pleasures of all sorts.

And, finally, a fourth, twenty-year period, in which I am now and in which I hope to die, from the viewpoint of which I see the whole significance of my past life and which I would not wish to alter in the slightest, except in those evil habits acquired by me in previous periods. . . .

I think that, despite great inadequacies, such an autobiography would be more useful for people than all that literary chatter which fills the twelve volumes of my works and to which people nowadays attach undue importance.

Though the reverse is true—the actual importance of Tolstoy's literary work has required that attention be paid to all aspects of his biography—Tolstoy's life itself is a rare and edifying example of aristocracy. In "Two Hussars" the genuine count is the one who has the courage of his passions, the skills of a long memory, and a consciousness of vitality that encompasses in one night a ball at the marshal of nobility's and wild gypsy dances. The first Count Turbin extends the privileges of class to affirmation of life: he controls others by sympathy and devotion, asserting his will on them to their satisfaction. He unmasks the fraudulent, risks his own life to emphasize its realness, and pretends to no standards he cannot exemplify by his self-control. A count, he is an aristocrat by birth. His largeness of spirit, his daring, his sophistication, his integrity and love (he goes back to kiss sleeping Anna Fedorovna good-bye), his irreverence for the dead and the effete (he appears at the Gypsy debauche in Anna Fedorovna's dead husband's overcoat; he deliberately insults the cavalry-man for an attempt at specious friendship), his *manner* and the sympathies it expresses, define both himself and the sort of aristocracy for which inherited privilege is entirely natural. The count's son is a travesty of the father. We are kept in suspense to the end of the story doubting that the integrity with which the father seized life can actually be subverted by the son's manner.

At the beginning of the story, the discrepancy between the past and the present is given by a catalogue of socioeco-nomic changes which visibly measure changes of manner (de-portment). It is recapitulated at the beginning of the second part of the story (Chapter IX). The change is considered his-torically—from 1825 to 1848, from the spirit of the Decem-brists to the tone of the period leading up to the Crimean War —and marked by births, death, and the usual chronology of our social world. The story as a whole may be read, then, as a study in the meanings of manner.

The periods into which Tolstoy divided his own life may be considered equivalent to the catalogue of changes given in the story. Consciousness of life in all its details—which Tolstoy called his own highest quality—and sympathy for life in terms of an understanding of a harmonizing eternal and nonmaterial principle, or God, are analogous to the interlacing of details of manner and to the pattern of life which this story is about. In the story, as in life, the relations are neither infinite nor nonmaterial, which Tolstoy's *theory* about their spiritual source suggests they must be. In his notebook for July, 1908, however, among passages celebrating virtue and exhorting all men to live in God, he notes laconically: "Can't feel sorry for flies—there's a limit." It is the "fly" quality in the cavalryman for which the first Turbin slaps him down. It is this improper claim to possession which Tolstoy feels required by his own nature to hound down and expose and which forms a central thread in all his work, from the idealistic Caucasian romance of *The Cossacks*, begun in 1852, to the final and ironic Caucasian adventure story *Hadzhi-murat*, finished in 1904.

Tolstoy's continual examination of his own morality, starting as early as his first diary in 1847 with its prescriptions for moral and physical health, never, not even in his last years, precluded his responding to life with extraordinary consciousness. No matter what standards he subsequently applied to what he had done, he never withdrew from life. And even when he had withdrawn from the life of the literary world and declined copyrights and royalties, wishing to attach fresh and nonliterary meaning to his literary manner, he did not quit literature and he did not deny the significance of the physical details which, by one turn or another, make writing alive. Most of his work presents a haunting search for "truth"—a psychological keeness in the context of habitual lives in an upper-class world: even Kholstomer, though an "ugly duckling," is an upper-class horse. Tolstoy's ethical studies were analyses of the obligations of the individual to necessary and to possible social functions, but we understand the substance of his scholarship only through his transformation of it into fiction.

"Family Happiness" and *War and Peace* are combined in *Anna Karenina*. The story of a woman's search for herself in marriage and the story of an upper-class family's acting out of their national obligations are brought together in the story of the consequences of a woman's passion for which existing social institutions are inadequate. *Anna Karenina* is not just the history of a romantic failure; it is almost a textbook summary of the main philosophic and sociopolitical issues of the 1870's. But the issues are central to the story, for they concern precisely the institutions—marriage, government service, the army, education, the status and offices of the nobility versus the bureaucracy, landownership, provincial politics, economic reform, reorganization of the distribution of labor —which support the way of life into which Anna was born and bred but which do not answer the requirements she by her nature puts on them. In *Eugene Onegin* the institutions remain intact; the individuals lose. In *Anna Karenina*, the individuals lose, and the institutions are transcended: Levin attaches himself not to his class but to the earth.

Tolstoy's own notes and letters certify that the "source" for "Family Happiness" was his affection for and near engagement to Valeriya Arseneva, a girl eight years younger than he. The relationship was finally terminated (whether before or during his work on "Family Happiness," 1857?–59, is not accurately known) but the available biographical facts contradict the substance of the experience given in the story. Valeriya Arseneva was, apparently, not clever or imaginative or resourceful; after having broken off with her, Tolstoy was left with a certain indifference, even dislike. In the story, of course, the marriage is repaired as the romance ends. The moving force behind the "plot" is Masha's energy and passion, her desire to possess herself. Young and naïve, she has to proceed through the social school Sergei Mikhailovich has already passed in order to be aware of the limits she may claim to that self which she would be master of and to that position in the world which she asserts she has a just right to. If there be weakness in the story it is, I think, that the authority by which she proffers her claims is obscure. We grasp this by comparing the resolution of "Family Happiness" with the end of *Anna Karenina*. In both, an older husband and a lovely bride move onto an unexpected plane of understanding through affection for their infant children, symbols of their status and of the future, and through awareness of mutual support of one set of values. The title "Family Happiness" is fitted ironically to the narrative, as its only use indicates. Sergei Mikhailovich, arguing with Masha (Chapter VII), says:

You're sacrificing (he stressed that word especially) and I'm sacrificing; what could be better. A struggle in magnanimity. What other family happiness is there?

In "Family Happiness" husband and wife end in the tranquillity of sure affection, each possessing the other in marriage more than they at first desired. Carnal attraction and self-assertion have changed into a stable condition in which each partner is gratefully held in peace by the other. *Anna Karenina* begins by exploding the generalization with which that story ends.

All happy families seem alike; each unhappy family is unhappy in its own way.

B. M. Eikhenbaum, in *Lev Tolstoy. The Seventies*, has shown that Tolstoy took the epigraph for the novel not directly from the Bible but from Schopenhauer. In Book IV of *The World as Will and Idea*, Schopenhauer discusses the difference between punishment, which is also prevention, and revenge, which in human hands is only amoral retribution. The state may punish, but God alone has the authority to avenge.

But *Anna Karenina* is a study of the deviations from what is posited both as standard and as ideal. It is not just a French-type "family novel" about marital infidelity. Nor is it an allegory of the wages of sin. The whole world is bound in the gestures of an unhappy woman. "Vengeance is mine, I will repay" comes (through Schopenhauer) from Romans, XII, 19:

Beloved, never avenge yourselves, but leave it to the wrath of God; for it is written, "Vengeance is mine, I will repay, says the Lord."

In Deuteronomy, XXXII, 35 Moses says that those against whom the Lord reserves vengeance will act it out themselves:

To me belongs vengeance and recompense; their foot shall slide in due time: for the day of their calamity is at hand, and the things that shall come upon them make haste.

Tolstoy's scorn for the corruptions of social pretense and his faith in divine justice, buttressed by what he distortedly extracted from Schopenhauer (more than most writers, Tolstoy interpreted others only in terms of what was useful to him), are seen much more clearly in *The New English Bible* version of the passage from Romans:

My dear friends, do not seek revenge, but leave a place for divine retribution; for there is a text which reads, 'Justice is mine, says the Lord, I will repay.'

The passage continues, as if anticipating Tolstoy's own later and passionate credo:

Do not let evil conquer you, but use good to defeat evil.

In the context of the novel, there is double vengeance. Anna's revenge on Vronsky is equally society's revenge on her.

At first Tolstoy thought of an adultress, pitiable but not to blame. Later, influenced, Eikhenbaum says, by Dumas–*fils's* polemical novel about infidelity, *L'homme-femme* (1872), he described her as being at fault, a woman who did not need to be punished, for she would ruin herself. Still later, Tolstoy used the epigraph as the working title for a story subsequently called "The Candle" (1885), in which he lectured on the spiritual corruption of replying to violence with violence or to evil with evil. In *Anna Karenina*, Tolstoy makes clear that, although society cannot tolerate Anna's behavior and her abrogation of her pledge to support its institutions, society is not her judge. The world that calls Anna depraved is wrong. Anna knows this. Betsy Tverskaya, she says to Dolly in French, is "the most depraved woman alive."

With no means for escaping from the egoism of her passion, unable to relate it to a pattern of meaning beyond social conventions, she falls victim, not to her love—which, satisfied and then unrequited, is changed into longing, self-pity, self-hatred, and then revenge—but to her glorious vision of life. Her emotion is imperfectly communicated even to Vronsky. He is only part of it, anyway. Because her passion is self-fulfilling, it cannot be universally legislative. Too individualistic and too noble to accept the restrictions of conventional (and Tolstoy would say hypocritical, unethical) behavior, she reaches beyond life to self-glorification, to the realm of the jealous God of Herodotus and the Old Testament, who stands as the upper limit of human ethical perfectibility. She measures by her failure something of which her brother, in all his petty successes with governesses and ballet dancers, has no idea. She discovers that the illusion of freedom is the source both of human vitality and of evil in failure. Anna and Levin, like Tatyana and Eugene Onegin, cross. Anna finds her vital self outside of marriage and loses; Levin denies his self, then finds it in marriage. Anna's intensity wears her life out; Levin diminishes his intensity until it becomes a faith and then, as Blackmur says, diminishes faith into the momentum required by human life. But he and Anna are very near to the same point, are directed equally to life or death—it is hard to say which. A few pages before Anna tells Vronsky that her dream of the peasant portends her death in childbirth, Levin, who is not far from a new life, tells Kitty's cousin that "it's time for me to die."

A moralistic reading of *Anna Karenina* treats the double

plot as an allegory of good and evil: Levin rises through labor and sincerity to an affirmation of life, to a "sense of the good" which "he has the power to put into it"; Anna wears herself out by her corrupt love and properly commits suicide. In this view, the book is not so beautiful as it is politically (or religiously) potent, an extended essay on the ethical nature of man.

All power has an element of mystery. This book is a study of the power of the substance of life—of love, of death, and of human institutions. In the change from life to art, the mystery represented by power is transformed into the mystery represented by religion. The change is from the experience of history to the sense of tragedy. Against the background of a pageant of politics and catastrophe, this book, like *Antony and Cleopatra*, is a story about the tragedy of man.

Historians rely on the externals of behavior. They cannot alter sequences of action to form another pattern. Tolstoy, a novelist, must uncover the hidden life, must make his figures seem real by making them seem complete, must make the pattern of meaning in his book coincide with the intentions of the particular individuals who compose it. He must abjure the inconstancy of actuality. He must make all human moves and motives permanent by making them total, by fixing the substance of his theme in the future of our lives. He must make all emotions intense—and any intense emotion has the illusion of permanency. The measure of art is intensity. *Anna Karenina*, began in March, 1873 and finished in the summer of 1877, remains the example in prose of the greatest excellence in that intense drama between what is determined and what we dream may ultimately be free.

At first delighted by "Family Happiness," Tolstoy turned sharply against it, even considered publishing it under a pseudonym not to sully his reputation. In a letter to Botkin on May 3, 1859, having received the proofs of the second part, he wrote that

I saw what shameful crap, what a blotch, not just as writing but as morality, this foul composition is. . . . I'm now buried both as a writer and as a man. This is for certain. Especially since the 1st part is even worse.

To his relative A. A. Tolstaya he wrote that, on rereading, the story "appeared such shameful filth that I can't pull myself together from shame and, I think, I'll never write again."

Of course, he did go on writing. The more he wrote, the more he tried to establish a literature based on national history, specifically, during the last thirty years of his life, on "folk" epic. But the shift is apparent even in changes made in *War and Peace:* in the 1873 edition, Tolstoy not only removed most of the anti-historicist argumentation to an appendix but also translated nearly all the French.

The interpenetration of the story by digressions into historical analysis is not purposeless. The digressions retard the narrative, increasing suspense, and supply another viewpoint from which to bring the reader back to the narrative. They give the author narrative time, that is, they allow him scope in manipulating chronological time without forcing a distortion of chronology. Because they are, in fact, evaluations of persons and events in the story, they expand the entire frame of reference of the book, making it seem to include long years of judgment and thousands of miles of space. They establish the basic organization of the book—among the parts within it and between each part and the whole. In *War and Peace* first, as later in *Anna Karenina*, each chapter is autonomous, as if it were a small and independent story which only by juxtaposition contributes to understanding of the next. The unity of the separate parts is constructed and magnified by the continual interruption of the sequential plot by digressions which create a surprising and important new kind of narrative order. The device of establishing narrative coherence by digression with a central theme (which Tolstoy learned from Sterne, also from Pushkin), which occurs in *War and Peace* as historical analysis, in *Anna Karenina* is even more successful. The digressions there proceed from images encased in the characters' actions and, by repetition, establish symbolic and thematic values that lie outside the actions themselves (for example, the treatment of free will in *War and Peace* compared to the motif of the train and all the images that attach themselves to it in *Anna Karenina*).

Under these conditions, a detail can be isolated and, under the attention we give isolated things (nothing in nature is alone), made to assume the importance of typicality. At times it functions as synecdoche: the cold, alabastrine magnificence of Helene's shoulders stands for Helene; the white puffy hands of Napoleon stand for Napoleon. A particular of experience comes into immediate relation with history and assumes meaning as a universal of history, much as we interpret "if a = b and b = c, then a = c": if Napoleon's hands stand for Napoleon and Napoleon stands for empery, then the white puffy hands, with a certain irony, come to stand for all absolute power in history.

The technique has been called "behavioristic." A person is translated into understandability through observation of the minutiae of actions and habits, clothes and conversations, translated as a complete image. Although observations are reported as matters of experience, in the book as in life, what we, the readers, make of them is greater than all of them together. The novelist interpolates himself into his book by using only his experience as understood through fractioned images and refrains (except in digression) from explicit comment or from drawing attention to some other aspect of presentation. The drama comes from his own—and, therefore, our—involvement in his observations. We like Tolstoy's characters, and we think of them as friends, usually referring to them by first names. Tolstoy exhibits the faculty of being able to imagine himself in other people's positions and, equally, of being able to imagine other people in situations in which he has been. He can translate experience from person to person, so that each of the 559 characters in *War and Peace* (somebody counted them) maintains a private independence or, Spinoza would say, perseveres in his own existence.

Natasha in *War and Peace* is a vital but separate figure to whom we readily assent because every feature of her is quickly recognizable—the old comfortable dress, the narcissistic fascination with one's body and gestures, as if one were someone else and doubly lovable for that. The finality with which she is captured in art lends her imaged being a poignancy that increases what we think her natural charm. We love her because she is so artfully made. No matter what we do to her or want to do, she remains as perfect as before, a bright symbol of life and of our longing:

Having had tea, she went into the reception room, which she especially loved for its powerful resonance, and began singing her solfeggios (singing exercises). Having finished the first lesson, she stopped in the middle of the room and repeated one musical phrase especially pleasing to her. She listened delightedly to that (as if for her unexpected) charm with which these sounds, flowing out, were filling all the emptiness of the reception room and slowly died away, and she suddenly became gay. "There's much to think about, and that's good," she said to herself and began walking back and forth across the room, taking not ordinary steps along the ringing hard-

wood floor, but at each step shifting from her high heel (she
had on her favorite new shoes) to her toe, and listening, just
as delightedly as to the sounds of her own voice, to this meas-
ured pattering of her high heel and to the scraping of her toe.
Passing the mirror, she glanced into it. "That she is me!" the
expression on her face at the sight of herself seemed to say.
"Well, and all right. And I don't need anybody."

Tolstoy fastens labels to his characters so that we may
think we are seeing them really. We move with him to comprehend the patterns which the characters make up beyond
themselves. In *Anna Karenina*, Stepan Arkadich, for example, is red-faced; Dolly has thinning hair, lined features;
Kitty, pretty legs; Levin, heavy shoulders; Anna, white arms,
a white neck, a white body; Aleksei Aleksandrovich, big ears.
Stepan Arkadich smokes regularly; Levin, never. Levin eats
heartily, knows little about food; Stepan Arkadich is proud of
being a gourmet.

Kitty wants very much to go to the first ball to be seen
and to see Vronsky. She urges Anna to go, says she thinks
Anna will probably wear a lavender dress. At the ball, Kitty
is in pink with pink slippers and a medallion on a black velvet
necklet. Looking over the guests for Anna, she finds her, finds
what, for her, is a "completely new and unexpected" Anna:

Anna was not in lavender, as Kitty had certainly wished, but
in a black, low-cut velvet dress, setting off her finely shaped,
like old ivory, full shoulders and bosom and rounded arms
with their thin, little wrists. The whole dress was trimmed
with Venetian guipure. On her head, in her black hair, her
own black hair, was a little garland of pansies, and there was
also one on a black ribbon round her waist between white
lace. Her hair-do was unostentatious. Noticeable only, mak-
ing her lovely, were these willful little ringlets of curly hair,

always coming loose on the back of her head and at her temples. On her finely shaped, firm neck was a string of pearls.

For Kitty, the dress is "only a frame" for Anna. All Kitty sees is Anna herself, "simple, natural, elegant, and at the same time gay and lively." Through Kitty's sense of defeat in elegance by the older, married woman and through the alluring and deeply sensual portrait of Anna (the dramatic chiaroscuro of romanticism, whether Lermontov's or Tolstoy's), we are wholly prepared for Anna's taking Vronsky from Kitty. Indeed, as we look back on it, we say it happened in this moment in this image.

The world against which Anna protests and in which her love affair takes place is delimited by the Oblonskys, especially by Stepan Arkadich, whose world is defined by an image combining, as if in metaphor, two otherwise disparate gestures. Just before Stepan Arkadich goes into Dolly's room to beg her forgiveness, he puts his cigarette out in a mother-of-pearl ash tray:

"However, it has to be done sometime; it obviously can't go on like this," he said [to himself], trying to work up his courage. He threw back his shoulders, took out a cigarette, lit it, took a couple of puffs, threw it into a mother-of-pearl shell ash tray, hurriedly crossed the dark living room and opened the other door into his wife's bedroom.

Not much later, sitting with Levin in a private dining room in the English Club, he orders oysters to start off what he knows will be a sumptuous dinner:

And the waiter ran off, his coattails flying, and five minutes later flew in with a platter of oysters opened on their mother-of-pearl shells and with a bottle between his fingers.

There is so much talk about oysters that they become a symbol of that style to which Oblonsky has schooled himself and in which he seems attractive and likable. They are equally that ash tray in which he crushed out his cigarette before he went into his wife's room, that "other side" of Oblonsky in which, for a frightening moment (he was annoyed he had been caught), the manners threaten to break down. They are an example of Tolstoy's method of defining a character by a detail or by a gesture, which is then repeated in other scenes, sometimes as defining other characters, to set up understanding of the context in which all the scenes occur. Always in careful, lucid, simple prose, the artful distortion produces a deep awareness of life.

Tolstoy's rewriting of historical description also illustrates how he constructs a dramatic situation by focusing the conflict in images of action. As V. B. Shklovsky pointed out, the historical source for *War and Peace* at one point reads:

Night came on, clouds covered the sky. The weather was dry, but the earth was moist, so that the troops moved without noise, and even the artillery was not audible.

but in the novel the passage runs:

It was an autumn night with dark lilac-colored storm clouds but without rain. The earth was moist, but there was no mud, and the troops moved without noise; only the strumming of artillery was weakly audible in the distance.

The situation is made dramatic by giving form (color) and substance to the landscape and setting it off against the men in it, against the imagined individual who is imagining it. The storm clouds are a threat; the artillery is waiting with destruction for the soldiers marching toward it. The sound of the artillery is suggested by the onomatopoetic *brenchanie* (strumming), the sound of plucking a bass viol. The musical con-notation of the image is an even sharper contrast to actuality.

Tolstoy makes a moment, a character, a gesture seem actual because he exploits his own point of view in such a way that we think it ours. He shifts his point of view (which Percy Lubbock says is the governing principle of "the whole intricate question of method in the craft of fiction") with ours. Except in digressions, of which there are few in *Anna Karenina*—one might even say none, except the first sentence—there is no difference between what Tolstoy sees and what we see. Unbeknownst to us, symbolic gestures define the purpose behind everything that happens. Art is the mediator between event and meaning. Here, it is the successful mediator which offers each in terms of the other simultaneously. Abstracted, Levin's "philosophy" is simplistic to the point of gentility. It is meaningful only in the process which compiled it, just as Anna's identity has meaning only by the indentations and scratches which she has made on the blank wall of history—her son, her husband, her lover, her friends. Since, to each character with views even more partial than ours, purpose is often obscure and self-realization seems discouragingly elusive, each moment threatens more than it promises. The more hopeful a man is, the more terribly does he dread death.

The individual is always, really, alone, waiting for death. The more alive he is, the closer he is to it. As Tolstoy said,

If a man has learned to think, no matter what he may think about, he is always thinking of his own death. . . . And what truths can there be if there is death?

The loneliness of man—in this book, especially of Nikolai Levin and of Anna—is summed up in dying and in all the approximations to it. A man's involvement in life is marked by the success of his loves and by the history of the battles in his war with society, each next battle of which he is always afraid of losing (Anna's disastrous night of defiance at the opera) and which he must finally know he cannot win (Anna's ultimate vengeance; Levin's awareness, at the end, of the incommunicability, of the mystery, of his sense of what is real).

In between, there is a world of regulations, habits, conventions, manners—the means we use to deal with others and to move closer to ourselves. Every self-fulfillment is, also, violation of someone else, and in our most intense moments of private experience we cling most stubbornly to habit, as Anna does during the birth of her little girl, as Aleksei Aleksandrovich does to the point of absurdity, basing his whole social position on the revelations of a fraudulent medium who pretends to have direct access to the ethical basis of life. The gravest question of personal happiness depends, finally, on some fool's whim.

Anna Karenina is a study of manners, in all the senses of that word: of ways of acting, of modes of procedure, of characteristics and behavior, of customs and morals, of deportment and fashion, of guises, and of style. Through them it studies man in his social functions and the value of the excellence (or viciousness) of his performance. Pushkin's *Eugene Onegin* was the first Russian novel to include as part of its excellence a significant analysis of an entire society through the prism of the family, to assign the novel a social function. Although Pushkin was relatively ignored in the 1870's, Tolstoy returned to him in admiration for "the simplicity and clarity of portrait and line," kept rereading *Belkin's Tales* as he worked on *Anna Karenina*, studied Pushkin's critical articles, and said that he was learning much from Pushkin, "he's my father." *Anna Karenina* is the last great "classic" in which society is presented as basically unified not through political allegiance but through family life. Saltykov-Shchedrin said that the mid-nineteenth-century novel had been based on the family structure but had changed into a social novel (*Smoke, The Devils*) because of the changes in family life. Tolstoy proceeds in a manner contrary to Dostoevsky, extracting politics from what he considers the basic, nonpolitical social institution and, indeed, arguing that society through its institutions can transcend class and convention to very near realization of ultimate values of freedom (the marriage of Kitty and Levin and their way of life).

His book comes to this obliquely. It begins by focusing on the opposite: the particular unhappinesses of an unhappy family mired in frustration and ignominious scandal. Relevance to our own experience leads us immediately into this novel of the failure of a woman's love affair. The generalization is particularized at once: "All was in confusion in the Oblonskys' house." That sentence itself, Eikenbaum said, is an adaptation of a sentence from Tolstoy's doggedly outlined but then abandoned novel on the age of Peter the Great: "All was in confusion in the Tsar's family." It links the personal and the historical, setting what Eikenbaum refers to as Tolstoy's "node of life," the family, against a background of historical significance. At the same time that *Anna Karenina* combines the themes of "Family Happiness" and *War and Peace*, it reverses them: we have a story of family *un*happiness leading to the woman's dying and the man's going off to war.

The pattern of relations among the characters depends on the fact that all the characters, no matter how much they misunderstand one another, assume that they are working within fixed rules. Actually, they are not. Vronsky and Anna fall in love at, so to speak, first sight in the Moscow Railroad Station. Vronsky's mother then talks about Anna's charm and elegance on the ride from St. Petersburg and starts talking to her son about love, complimenting him on his courtship of Kitty Shcherbatskaya. The irony, based on his new, real love, is what we see. At the Oblonskys', Dolly is reported as having felt something false in the Karenins' "high style"—her relationship to Anna can be only partial—and Anna is revealed by the children's affection and by Kitty's thoughts about her, that a woman of such station and beauty can be so intimate. The codes by which these people have agreed to move are always inadequate in any urgent moment. The manners of love break them down. The misanthropic idealist Nikolai Levin abandons his class and lives openly and gratefully with a luckless, unhappy whore.

A series of couples are played off against one another. The only value judgment passed on them is what each by its nature, by its interpretation of the experience contained in the opening generalization, must pass on the others in order to preserve its righteousness and its happiness. Confident in his marriage, Karenin supports divorce in the name of humaneness. His confidence destroyed, Karenin supports marriage and denies divorce in the name of holiness. He judges the rest of the world from his own position in regard to the institution from which he claims support. All the characters do this. Anna herself supports her enchantment with Vronsky in the name of love and her rejection of her old way of life in the name of her right to assert individual freedom. Unfortunately for her, the cause of independence is greater than any individual. The closer the individual gets, through love, to manifestation of the force of life, the closer he is, also, to death. In his approximations, his happiness depends on someone else's unhappiness. At least, this is true at times for even such a person as Anna, whose initial passion with Vronsky is intensified by its secretive character. It is almost always true for such people as Stepan Arkadich and Aleksei Aleksandrovich, who do not understand the force that moves life and who are always prepared to regulate their lives according to the most convenient conventions. They even compromise themselves to maintain the conventions, the false manners, as Stepan Arkadich does to try to get a better job, and as Aleksei Aleksandrovich does to try to take care of his relations with his wife:

Stepan Arkadich chose neither trends nor opinions, but these trends and opinions came to him themselves, in exactly the same way that he did not pick out the shape of his hat or coat but took those that were being worn. To have opinions was for him, who moved in upper-class society, with its requirement of a certain activity of mind developing usually in the years of maturity, just as essential as having a hat.

The conventions are fitted to life. The manners are a serious style. For example, the particularization of the opening sentence is a portrait of convention from inside an experience of an actual family. The adultery of which Stepan Arkadich is guilty is a corollary in convention to his wife's indignation and misery and to the servants' timorous sympathy. The convention is so clear and its "problem" so actual that the old nurse, Matrena Filimonovna, can aptly tell Stepan Arkadich to "make up," once again to complete the convention by completing his part. She knows that the rest will follow, that Dolly has no place to go, that Anna will persuade her to forgive, and that life in the Oblonsky house will go on afterwards exactly as before.

"You go in, sir, say you're wrong, again. Maybe God'll be good. She's suffering terribly, it's pitiful to look at her, and everything in the house is turned upside down. . . ."

"But she probably won't accept. . . ."

"But you do your part. God is merciful, pray to God, sir, you pray to God."

This is actual, yet the life led inside such a pattern, with its elaborate dining, sleeping with actresses, shooting game, and maintaining face comes, finally, not to God, not to any transcendence or liberation, not to any sort of independence, but to ceaseless harassment (Dolly's continual displeasure at being in debt to the shopkeepers) and to dependence on the false convention of money:

"No doubt about it, I can tell him [Karenin said], but why do you personally want to have this job?"
"The salary is good, [Oblonsky said], up to nine thousand, and my means . . ."

The depersonalization to which Oblonsky comes or to which Karenin is reduced (his career comes to a stop without his knowing it and without anyone's knowing why) lies within the conventions against which both Anna and Levin, in their opposite ways, have rebelled. Anna's most terrible moment comes when she is reduced to asking Dolly who she is:

"But I wanted to ask you directly, what do you think of me, of my life?"

She is not guilty, she says. No one is. What, even, does being guilty mean? But she knows that she has almost lost Vronsky and, in any event, has lost her rebellion. The beautiful intensity of love toward which she boldly and consciously offered her life (once she found that she was honestly involved) was a force more powerful than any combination of manners of response. She gave herself up to the integrity of her passion, in the name of which she violated all the rules of behavior sanctioned by her society and by its religion, and for which she left her society for a while. But even abroad in Italy, wholly at leisure, she and especially Vronsky

had to be busy with something sixteen hours of the day, for they were living abroad in complete freedom, outside that circle of social conventions which had taken up their time in Petersburg.

They are, for a while, so nearly free that they hardly know what to do to be happy. Even as her love fails, the world that ignores her out of fear and self-righteousness can be, Anna knows, seduced. Almost vindictively, she charms Levin. And she knows that she is on the bottom. As she tells Dolly,

"What wife, a slave, can be a slave to such a degree as I am in my position?"

She cannot bring her past and her future together. She cannot find any manner by which she can have both Serezha and Vronsky. These are the images of the limits of conventions, and she, if she is to go on living, must bind these limits together and obliterate them. She cannot do this. She knows that she cannot, but she does not understand why—why the force released by her love is greater than herself.

"The Death of Ivan Ilyich," first published in the 1886 edition of Tolstoy's works, focuses less on a summary moral (though, to be sure, one may read the ending as announcement of Ivan Ilyich's identification with the love that moves the world) and more on the psychological responses a man makes to, and in, his functions in the world. As a story about what Jung called "the terrible ambiguity of an immediate experience," about responding to the force of life, it comments on the individual ethics of *Anna Karenina*. As life is, literally, an approach to death, so a man's social performance is an ever more nearly apt definition of his value. At the end of the

story, of course, the terms are altered: the values behind
social performance are defined as contradictory to eternal human values. Ivan Ilyich Golovin has possessed many *things*;
he slowly shucks them all, with the support of gentle Gerasim's
ministrations, until, in a sort of epiphany, he finds himself
literally self-possessed. Encircled by an indifferent world—the
image early in the story of the mourners around the coffin,
each occupied with a separate duty—he reaches a mystic vision
("Instead of death, there was light") in which he experiences
charity toward his family and finds that he has transcended
pain. The power and loneliness of his discovery are emphasized
by its inaccessibility: "For those present, his agony lasted another two hours." The story is framed by third-person response, which, of course, is our point of view. Ivan Ilyich is
made so skillfully to respond to it that we, in turn, are con-
verted to Ivan Ilyich's point of view. The deepest understanding of death is affirmation of the highest vitality of life. This
esthetic formulation is comparable to the strongest philosophic analysis; only, its instruction is presented as experience
and, therefore, much closer to us.

The closeness of the experience is enforced above all by
the literalness of detail. The eighteenth century conveyed its
understanding of a man by his "humor"; Tolstoy presents a
man in any given moment as equal to a detail. Each of the
characters in the opening scene, for example, is fitted to a
pattern composed of all the separate details put together. We
are taken into the dead man's room by the eyes and reflections
of Petr Ivanovich, who is worried about the proper manner:
"One thing he did know, that crossing yourself at times like
this never hurt." The phrase "like all dead men" is repeated
several times, each time modified by a detail: how the stiff
limbs have sunk into the bedding of the coffin, how the waxy
yellow forehead and nose stick up, how the face seems more

important than in life. The motifs of death are threaded
through with the motifs of dead, that is, unconscious, life,
symbolized by the game of vint. The details of Ivan Ilyich's
disease are presented so literally that, according to N. F.
Golubov,

*the actual facts in the description [of the disease] are so clear
that not only a doctor but even any third-year medical student
could make an almost exactly accurate diagnosis. . . . Having
read Tolstoy's story, one may say with nearly certain conviction that Ivan Ilyich died from cancer of the abdomen, somewhere in the region of the caecum or the right kidney. The
cause of the disease (the contusion), its picture, development
—and even the necessity of [the patient's] lying with his leg
raised—everything confirms it.*

The description of the disease parallels the description
of Ivan Ilyich's life. That is, selected details are presented in
an ever-increasing intensity leading to a central, or final,
apotheosis by which the process of selection is explained and
justified. We see the "progress" of Ivan Ilyich's life, the progress of his disease, and the progress of his philosophic speculation which follows from the two. Throughout the story, we
are aware of a purpose toward which the whole terse narrative
is moving. The last detail—the *fact* of the ultimate vision—is
something we can never confirm, but, here, it is something we
must assent to as both the source and the consequence of that
progress of life, Ivan Ilyich's and our own, to which we are
addicted, body and soul.

The story is characteristic of much of Tolstoy's later
work: the language moves with economy and severity to a
denouement that is simultaneously a moral lesson. Yet the
terms of that morality are not reducible to precepts or commandments. Of course, Tolstoy also preached. Often, we tend

to confuse his homilies with his fiction. The reordering of chronology itself (the story moves from the dead man, as a fact, back through his life to his death as meaning) reminds us how Tolstoy has reordered life that we may *see* it forever. "Errors" in time help keep us in the story: for example, both children are about five years older at the end of the story than they should be if their dates of birth in the story are remembered. The story is, literally, foreshortened.

In "real life" Ivan Ilyich was not Golovin but Menchikov, brother of the well-known scientist Ilya Ilyich and lawyer in Tula, prosecutor for the district court. Tolstoy's wife's sister remembers that "during Menchikov's stay at Yasnaya Polyana, Lev Nikolaevich became extremely fond of him, having realized with artistic flair that he was an outstanding man." She adds that afterwards Menchikov's wife "told me his last thought and conversation on the futility of the life he had led, which I passed on to Lev Nikolaevich." Menchikov died of cancer, forty-five years old, on July 2, 1881. Tolstoy immediately thought of a story, "The Death of a Judge," a "description of the simple death of a plain man." Turgenev's very painful death in 1883 and Urusov's in 1885—both men were at that time close to Tolstoy—undoubtedly pushed him on to finish the story left in outline form since 1881. Ivan Ilyich Golovin, born in Petersburg in 1837, dies February 4, 1882, not long after Sarah Bernhardt and her troupe visited Moscow and Petersburg, as referred to in the story.

Historical accuracy is incidental. These footnotes are only the symptoms of literary provocation. Like *Anna Karenina*, the story is about consciousness of the force of life. In the world of civilized society—that "rational, egotistical human association which . . . destroys and opposes the needs of instinctive and loving human association" ("Lucerne," 1857), "one of the greatest forcibly imposed evils to which a part of mankind is subjected"—in that world the individual lives not by acts but in consciousness. What he does not understand does hurt him. In so far as he is alone in the midst of society, he is pathetic. In so far as he is alienated, he is potentially tragic. When destroyed by his own effort to join society, he is tragic. Ivan Ilyich is physically wasted by disease, as Anna is wasted by lovelessness, but both are destroyed by their failure to apprehend the nature of the force of life. This is the force which destroys both Eugene Onegin and Yury Zhivago, but which both Pushkin and Pasternak comprehend in their poetry. The raw force of life, for Tolstoy, is death. It is the backdrop to life, also the ever-threatening next moment in the drama. Aristotle assumed the good to be that at which all things aim; Tolstoy assumes death to be the goal and consummation of the ethical substance of life. He has his characters mime not private or even national chronologies (as in A. K. Tolstoy's historical dramas) but central moral experiences. Ivan Ilyich comes to a kind of beatific vision. Anna sees the same light before she dies. But the more complicated tale and the crossed plot make the imitation of morality (the acting out of *praxis* in consciousness) in *Anna Karenina* more nearly adequate to all the facts.

Most importantly, Anna is filled with life. The black dress, the pearls, the little ringlets of black hair, her grace and elegance at the first ball, establish her immediate, feminine vitality. Her love for what is, her compassion for those who need love, is presented in the desperate scene in which she surreptitiously goes to see Serezha, wakes him up and kisses him and talks to him, stares coldly at her husband as she quickly walks out—and forgets to leave the birthday presents she had carefully bought the day before. She was overcome, for a while, by her love for the boy. His simple faith that his mother was not dead, as they had told him, and that she would love him still according to his need, confirms the existence of that great love which Anna found in the middle of life. The irony of her commitment to it is Aleksei Aleksandrovich's adoption of her daughter Ani after her death, in an effort to atone for his guilt, as Vronsky atones by leading a detachment off to the Turkish War in Serbia, as we all are guilty, seek atonement, and continually, desperately, hope to become the real and living concretization of our dreams of ourselves.

Anna moves from favorite aunt at the Oblonskys' and most exquisite lady of her world to a disillusioned failure, a woman of enormous pride and self-determination who has been driven literally mad by the irreconcilable contradictions between what the world promised her and what it allowed her. She exhausts life, destroys its possibilities, and makes it intolerable. In her frustration, the life force is driven back against itself. She may want to punish Vronsky, but society is punishing her. Vronsky the landowner, the hospital-builder, the *zemstvo* politician, returns to society, to the "manner" to which he was "born." The catastrophe which Anna is facing is summarized in the gesture of her sitting thinking how her death will erase her husband's and her son's shame, her own terrible shame, and will make Vronsky repent, feel love for her, and suffer for her. She sits "pulling off and on the rings on her left hand, vividly imagining from different points of view his feelings after her death." Told a little later by Anna's maid that Anna has a headache, Vronsky honors the convention and leaves her alone. This breaks her. This is betrayal. Reversing the roles, as she has all her life, she then goes to him and looks lovingly and hopelessly at him as he lies sleeping. But even at the end, even as she is about to throw herself under the train, the little red bag—the last, the littlest convention—gets in her way.

The arrival and departure of Anna are framed by the trains, by the death of the watchman, and by her own death. At one point, Vronsky dreams of a little dirty peasant gillie, who had played an important role in the bear hunt, associating the peasant with Anna. He awakes and recalls the dream:

"The peasant gillie, seemingly small, dirty, with a tousled beard, was doing something hunched over and suddenly said some strange words in French. . . . Now why was that so terrible? . . ." Fear ran in a shiver down his spine.

Late, he hurries to Anna, finds her sick and miserable. They talk unhappily for a while, then Anna says, "I'm going to die. I had a dream." Symbolically, she, too, dreamed of the symbolic peasant. Remembering it, "fear was on her face":

"He is pottering about and saying something in French, very rapidly, and, you know, making French r's: 'Il faut le battre le fer, le broyer, le pétrir . . .' And I started asking myself what it meant. And Korney says to me: 'Childbirth, you'll die in childbirth, childbirth. . . .' "

The nearly simultaneous dreams dramatize the lovers' separate consciousness of the failure of their love even in the moment of physical evidence of its consummation. Romantic devotion has become little more than a sordid sexual affair. But, above all, the dreams, being one, present the symbol of the continuity of life against the losses to death, that moral reality which Anna knows about but to which she has no access.

All life occurs against the background of death. Those who carry life on, who labor and produce—in this book, the peasants—do not grieve over it. They know it is coming, and they have faith in the virtue of their collective labor. All they can wish, as the old woman says, is to die peacefully with the last rites.

They are people who have unconsciously organized themselves to life, the people in whose regularity and self-abnegation the goodness of life is to be found. Levin's affection for the newborn calf, his hours of reading Mill and books on agriculture and social systems, his unsuccessful efforts to write a book of his own (Anna Karenina, in contrast, did write a "very good" children's book), his mowing with the peasants and his redistribution of the produce and labor on his estate, his wish to marry a woman and have a family (actually, to have a family and, therefore, necessarily to marry someone) —all this is his attempt to belong to "the people," to be identified with the source of the momentum of life. His excellences in manner are sharply restricted: ice-skating, bird-shooting, and knowledge of practical affairs useful for running an estate. His philosophic and religious abilities, as given in his conversations with his brother and half-brother and Sviyazhsky, are small indeed. After his first failure with Kitty, he moves farther and farther from passionate intensity toward faith in the goodness of his land and his way of life. Kitty does, also, after her "training" abroad. Their unexpected, temporary excitement with each other and, after their marriage, their common experience of Nikolai's death, lead them toward that mutual awareness of the inevitable continuum of life and of what they feel is the sheer goodness, as we say, of being alive. Kitty's discovery of her pregnancy the day Nikolai dies, like Vronsky's breaking the horse's back, is one of those implausibly coincident and patently symbolic moments which Tolstoy uses to establish a pattern of meaning separate from the confused and imperfect understanding that follows from the pattern of the characters' actions.

Tolstoy's philosophy of history opposed the prevailing post-Hegelian thought, which viewed the meaning of social movement as inextricably part of a vast historical process and posited, in Russia, the *proklyatye voprosy*, those crucial, human, moral questions which every intellectual had to answer and by his answers be judged by his society. Tolstoy's philosophy of history was an extension of his search for reality. The natural and plebeian world had been unexpectedly uncovered, and everyone was rummaging around in it for goodness and eternal fortune. In their search men accumulated, like rags in the attic, ill-understood and uncorrelated facts. Tolstoy stood like a rock against this compilation. "History," he said, "will never reveal to us what connections there are." History, in his view, will never show causes. If events had indeed occurred as historians say they wish, Tolstoy argued, historians would have nothing to do. "History," he remarked a year or two before he died, "would be an excellent thing if only it were true." He regarded life as spontaneous activity involving personal consciousness of free will and of the actuality of moral choice, dependent on the margin of error which faith can tolerate but which reason wipes out. He believed that the man who knows life knows that he cannot understand it.

Levin comes to life when he acknowledges its mystery. He does not understand it, and he does not control it, but he adores it. So acutely aware of his own inadequacies that he at one moment thought of suicide ("But Levin did not shoot himself and did not hang himself and kept on living"), he surrenders to life as if to a faith. Not exactly as to a faith, for he does not presume any other essence except what he experiences. He quits his passion. He turns in on himself for his manner. He yields to his idea. He follows the movement of life as it is. He follows precisely what Anna denies is meaningful, for he asserts that love for the things of this world is the source of its own symmetry (its own manner). He stands as the best example of what, for Anna, is the real failure of the world: the abrogation of the independence of the individual.

Levin is not "right," and Anna is not "wrong." Levin makes an adjustment to life which Anna cannot, so he continues to live. In terms of the desirability of living, Levin's way is the practical, or "right," way; in terms of the necessity of self-affirmation, Anna's way is the only way, the "right" way. Both ways are also equally wrong. Anna's passion does not fit this life, and Levin's acquiescence denies the freedom of human dignity.

The symbolic moments in the novel point to a didactic pattern of meaning, which supports the pattern built up by other moments. The analogies are built less by the broken-backed horses than by the mother-of-pearl shells, by the dreams, by the slightly dislocated repetition of husband-and-wife (or lover-and-lover) experiences, by the unobtrusive bit of information which leads backward as well as forward: "Levin was about the same age as Oblonsky and on 'thou' terms with him not just by champagne alone." Aleksei Aleksandrovich's background is given only toward the end, at the end of the divorce attempt, when it is brought to bear as a determinant in his decision. The Anna and Levin plots weave in and out through each other: for example, the Karenin plot is taken up in Part III, Chapter XIII at the very point it was dropped in Part II, Chapter XXIX. There are repeated parallels of theme—Petritsky and Baroness Shilton discuss the problem of a woman's getting divorced; of style—Anna on the train reads an English novel of love, which she wishes to put to the life; and of manner—each chapter of *Anna Karenina* an almost integral section narrated mainly from the viewpoint of a chief character, stands in contrast to the point of view of surrounding chapters. An example of this is the slight shift in tone but pronounced change in viewpoint between Chapters XXIX and XXX in Part I. The description of Anna's trip from Moscow home carries over from XXIX to XXX. Through the seemingly impersonal description, our response as readers is, in fact, highly committed to Anna's. Details take on life as she sees it. The technically omniscient author moves continually back to her and away, as if weaving a web among the pillars and trains and lights and people. Anna remains the center of interest, almost the physical center, in a carefully arranged photograph supercharged with the meaning of dramatic tension. The tension comes from the effort against the storm and from the contrast between her position and the movements of other people. Only she is doing nothing, just enjoying, filled with the memory of her recent meeting with Vronsky. The crooked shadow of a man first appears at her feet, a symbol of the looming shadow that will cut her off from the light (when she died "the candle . . . went out forever"). The ordinary affairs of ordinary people outline her loneliness and her devotion. The incident, revealing another aspect of her character, stands as a premonition of her failure, of her death, and of the complex of social, human relationships which she has wanted to reform. The image of the train (the idea of adventure, of escape), the image of the snowstorm (she left Moscow in a snowstorm), connect with the thoughts in her head. The event connects her first meeting with Vronsky to her own suicide, when she remembers that first meeting and when she stands on the platform wondering what to do and watching the ordinary people, remembering the dead watchman killed by the train, and studying the wheels and getting ready to take revenge.

In all these parallels, the details seem innocent. They seem to be there as if they actually were. The unimportant figures that pass back and forth are related to one another only by our understanding of the character central to the scene. For example, in the scene of Anna's suicide, Anna misses the moment she first planned because of the interference of her red bag. The red bag in itself is not significant, but the interference in our lives—here, in her death—without special significance, of impersonal trivialities is a regular and literal experience. The detail itself (unlike a detail in a Dostoevsky novel, which is turned into consciousness by the character) contributes nothing. It is something to be overcome, as Anna overcomes her handbag, as Oblonsky gets out "the right answer," as Levin knows that he will patch up any quarrel with Kitty.

This tragedy of love is equally the story of life. The most skillful and beautiful lady loses herself in an impossible love, and the most ethical (and, therefore, most practical) man, who loses himself, finds the skill to live. For living is essentially a manner, a style, or a performance in which what is and what may be are married. Anna's brave invocation of potential becomes her loss of herself. Levin, also, loses himself: he finally celebrates the bare force of what is. In *Anna Karenina*, to quote Eikenbaum, Tolstoy, swayed by the suggestiveness of Tyutchev's and, especially, Fet's poetry, "orients himself on a method of philosophical lyricism, adopting its impressionism and sets of symbols. . . . This influence of poetry on prose prepared the future transition from realism to symbolism."

The only world in which both Anna and Levin are "right" is their book, in which the necessity of this world and the values of transcendent freedom lie together in the same images. Anna, the most passionate and promising dreamer of all, is the greatest realist, the warmest woman, and the most ineffable corpse.

Three
Years

¶ In his notebooks, Chekhov puns on the Russian word for man. A male human, he says, *muzhchina*, consists of a man, *muzh*, and a title, *chin*. In story after story he sets one against the other, self-consciousness against public recognition, promises against tabulations, creative self-will against conformist dependency. Most of his stories and plays, particularly those of the last fifteen years of his life, turn around a hollow core of consciousness in a central figure who plays two roles at once: he is straight man to the other characters' vanities and jokes, exposing pretentiousness; measured by them, who are successful, he is an incarnation of failure. He does not collapse; he waits. He is always waiting. (In *Three Years*, all the pivotal scenes begin with or lead to somebody's waiting.) The central figure holds a view of himself which the facts of his life deny. He proposes to others that he is guilty, but actually supposes himself superior to them because he feels different. The short stories focus on an episode in which the feeling of being special causes the hero to assert himself in a way that provokes others unconsciously to block him, to dismay him. Almost all the stories are about love, that possible positive condition in which the hope for successful self-willing most sharply contradicts consciousness of failure. Chekhov called *Three Years* a "short story," but it has the properties and some of the proportions of a novel. It does not focus on an episode but on a way of life. It is not about one man but about a society. It is Chekhov's novel about "family happiness."

In the skit "After the Theater" (1892), sixteen-year-old Nadya, who with her mother has just come home from seeing *Eugene Onegin*, wants to emulate Tatyana. An officer and a student have told her they love her, but for her

Onegin is interesting because he does not love at all, but Tatyana is enchanting because she loves a lot, and if they loved each other equally and were happy, why they would probably be dull.

So, she begins a letter: "I love you . . . but you don't love me, you don't!" She cannot decide which man to send the letter to, remembers them both, throws the letter out, thinks ahead to the summer of being courted by both men, and turns to the icon over her bed in anguished rapture. We see her between two frames: the play, which she wants to imitate, fancying herself in her surprisingly desired femininity as passionate and self-willing, as catastrophic as Tatyana, and, on the other hand, the world of her mother, croquet, light chatter, and ordinary social conventions. Chekhov deleted from the skit several paragraphs referring to Nadya's inability to understand social ideas in works of art; they were not necessary. We see very clearly that Nadya's great joy is a pointless delusion. It is as close as she can get to real emotion. The point of the story follows from our perception of that gap, of her failure. She knows that she is not Tatyana, but all she has to use for saying who she is are the conventions appropriate to her "title" of sixteen-year-old middle-class girl.

In "The Bishop" (1903), the bishop is out of ordinary people's reach, beyond even his closest relative, because of his position. Because he cannot communicate to others the content of his emotions, he feels that others are inaccessible and that his life is meaningless. His emotions are part of his official function, his professional profile, his social role. They engender emotional responses in those who honor him, using him as an officer in their appreciation of God. But these responses take the bishop even farther from what he surmises is his center of being. Toward the end of his life he becomes aware—he feels guilty—that his life's work has not been willed. He has, he thinks, committed an offense against his proper self, yet he cannot distinguish what or who he is, because his image of himself is masked, marred by the success he has achieved and by the reverence that isolates him from his admirers. He finds, unexpectedly and perhaps suddenly, that he has lost himself to others when all the time he intended exactly the opposite.

And he, who never allowed himself in his sermons to speak ill of people, never reproached them, since their lives were pitiable, got out of patience with petitioners, became angry, and threw their requests on the floor. During the whole time he had been here, not one person had spoken sincerely to him, spoken simply, candidly, as man to man; even his old mother, it seemed, was not herself, not herself at all. And why, he asked himself, did she talk to Sisa openly and laugh a great deal, but with him, with her son, was serious, usually silent, shy, which wasn't at all like her? The only single person who acted normally in his presence and said exactly what he wanted to was the old monk Sisa, who had spent his whole life around bishops and had outlived eleven of them.

The past presses against the future (as in most of Chekhov's stories and all of his full-length plays) in such a way that one is indistinguishable from the other and both are the present. Everything the bishop was—everything that he has done—is what he is; neither more nor less, externally. Internally, of course, he is oppressed by his awareness of his inability ever to consummate his desires. He is not "a sinner." Simply, he *is* what he has not done, what he never can do, what he now sees as incomprehensible and overwhelming. He is caught, tormented, punished, in the sense of drama, by his own incompleteness. If you call Paolo and Francesca's a sin of commission, then the bishop's is a sin of omission. When he weeps, he weeps for his self, although he cannot discover or define it. He believes it exists, though even in his memory he cannot find it:

. . . and now the past seemed alive, beautiful, gay, something that, for sure, it had never been. And perhaps in the next world, in the next life, we will recall the remote past, our life here, with the same emotion. Who knows! The Right Reverend was sitting by the altar; it was dark here. Tears poured down his face. He thought how he had achieved everything that was possible for a man in his position to achieve, how he really believed, but that, all the same, everything was still unclear; there was still something missing; and he would like not to die. It seemed that still he did not have the most important thing which sometime or other he had vaguely dreamed about, and now in the present he was still made anxious by that same hope for the future which he had had in his childhood, at the academy, and abroad.

Unimportant in itself, death is not some extraneous threat, some melodramatic device to wrap up a plot. It is an interruption, perhaps, an unprepared and unconditional change which precludes all chance of further change. The bishop does not want to die because he does not know what is dying. He, yes; but who is *he*? He even thinks, or suggests he thinks, that he is already dead. Death is delivery. The terror is not in dying; rather, it is, under such conditions, in living longer, in living forever. Taking the bishop as hero and example, we may say that Chekhov described the individual not merely as alienated from society by his function but actually as alienated from himself. The bishop's necessary ("predetermined") life of compromises turns out to be an unnecessary life. The compromises have been overextended. Rather than enhancing his activity by adjusting it to patterns of social behavior, his efforts at compromise have betrayed himself. He does not remain even as a promise. Freedom is *not* comprehension of necessity. Freedom is a value of which we are conscious, but it is untranslatable and unrealizable. It is a beautiful illusion, sometimes ennobling and grand. The closest human approach to it is the transcendence of self-consciousness by work. In *Three Years* Laptev, like the black dog, is kept from "leaving the yard" and going out "into the fields and forest where it would be free and joyful" by "the habit of necessity, the condition of slavery"—what we may call the unalterable program of existence.

Ultimately, all recognition and record of the bishop vanish, just as if he had never been. There is one exception: the story remains. In the world of art, like Paolo and Francesca in the eternal hell of their sin, which they have become, he is given being. The intangible center around which all actions move is there fixed. The actions assume a pattern. The intent of the man's life becomes meaningful. But this is beyond the story, in the story *as* story. As far as events are concerned, nothing is left:

A month later a new bishop was appointed, and no one remembered the Right Reverend Petr. And then they completely forgot him. Only an old woman, the mother of the deceased, who lives now with her son-in-law, a deacon, in a remote little district town, when toward evening she would go fetch her

cow and would meet the other women near the common pas-
ture, would begin to talk about her children, about her grand-
children, about how she had had a son who was a bishop, and
she would talk about it humbly, afraid that she wasn't be-
lieved. And, in fact, not everybody did believe her.

"In actual life," Tolstoy said to Gorky, "what people
say is silly and incoherent, and at first you can't make out
what a peasant wants to say. That's deliberate! Under the
silliness of their words there always lurks the desire of allowing the other person to show what's in his mind." What we
see is objective only if we see it in terms of a general purpose,
only if we can relate all parts. To see everything at once is to
see nothing. Tolstoy wrote:

A man with a beard, in a blue or a black long coat, comes
along driving a horse and sitting alone on the box—you just
have to look whether the horse is sleek, whether the man is
well-fed himself, how he's sitting, how the horse is harnessed,
what the tires of the wheels are like, how the man is belted,
and you can see at once whether the man does business in
hundreds or in thousands.

The obverse of theory is fact; the obverse of ethics, daily
life. The novelist must bring the two sides into view simultaneously.

After the emancipation of the serfs, most novelists interpreted daily life as a series of illustrative examples for a
theory of social reform. By the turn of the century, the desire
for reform had taken definite political shape. Political parties
had arisen, each with specified sociopolitical goals and a program. And most of the novelists, unable to accept any one
program as adequate to all the facts, had abandoned hope for

"constitutional" reform. Either they were entertainers, in the sense that they emphasized "true" but socially useless themes, such as sex (Artsybashev's *Sanin*), or they detailed the complexities of prevailing injustice and the "need" for desirable, violent social change (Gorky's *Foma Gordeyev*, *Mother*). Whatever our fondness for them, we now regard such writers as romantics excessively involved in private notions of individual glory or pleasure. Chekhov, for one, stands against them, encompassing themes of both broadly social and narrowly psychological urgency, bringing together—however sadly —the state and the man, the ethical theory and the facts of daily life.

In the mid-1840's, Sergei Aksakov had begun to write and to publish a series of sketches and remembrances the like of which had not been met with before. Born in 1791, dead in 1859, he lived his life outside the ferment and revolutionary thought in Europe and Russia which followed the French Revolution and the rise of Napoleon and the bourgeoisie. He was an odd example of the kind of man against whom the rebels were rising.

In St. Petersburg in the 1840's, Aksakov became a friend of Gogol, nearly twenty years younger. Gogol persuaded Aksakov to assemble some of his material on country life, especially since stories and small collections of hunting tales had been enthusiastically reviewed, by Turgenev as well. Aksakov worked simultaneously on hunting sketches and reminiscences from childhood of family life in Bashkiria, publishing *Notes on Angling* in 1847, *Notes of a Game Hunter* in 1852, and a trilogy of memoirs, *Family Chronicle* (1846–56; book form 1856), *The Childhood Years of Bagrov's Grandson* (1858) and *Memoirs* (1856). Gogol encouraged Aksakov to open up the whole of life as a possibility for literature. Despite a Biblical outlook and conservative social views, Aksakov learned that the smallest and seemingly most trivial detail of actuality could be a clue to revelation of human nature.

He saw things. His books on fish and game, models for later field guides, show extraordinary ability to discern the distinguishing features of a bird or a fish, asserting in the description both the actuality of the example and the generality of its species. His characterizations of snipes, for example, are excellent preliminary studies for learning the structure of character descriptions not involving incident. The birds are "naturally" alive, chronicled down, like Old Testament figures, with skill, kindness, and a sharp, disinterested eye.

The snipe does not have a large body, about the size of a three-week-old chick, but has a very long bill and legs. Its back, wings, and short tail are covered with mottled feathers, the dark brown-grayish color of which is hard to discern. Its belly and part of its crop or breast are white; its eyes, dark, somewhat bulging, rather large and cheerful; its legs, darkish, nearly black; the three foretoes are very long and have sharp and rather long claws. . . . You can shoot only at the moment when the snipe is directly overhead. . . . Many shells have gone off vainly into the heavens, and the shot, coming back, has fallen, like light rain, around the hunter. . . .

The double snipe has feathers and a build so much like the snipe that you can't tell them apart right away if you don't pay attention to the difference in size. . . .

However, these feathers [of the hairy snipe] are not at all like hair but could rather be called braids, but the hairy snipe has no other name in Russian, and therefore has to be content with its German name, not entirely appropriate but familiar to everyone.

Gogol said to Aksakov, "Your birds and fishes are more alive than my men and women."

Aksakov's memoirs have almost no ethical content. As impersonally as possible, the author reports what, he says, he remembers he saw. He tries to remove himself as personality. Because memory is expansive, the picture of his world is not like a photograph, which establishes its contrasts by setting up a strict frame, nor is it like a film, a series of photographs offered in rapid succession giving an illusion of motion. It appears to be everything we see, feel, and think about, including also those thoughts and feelings which custom requires of us. But it always turns on or returns to the specificity of a moment, the actuality (whatever it may mean) of *this* gesture:

When everything was ready and everyone went in to bid final farewell to the deceased, a wailing started up in the room, echoing loudly throughout the house; I felt a profound uneasiness, though no longer from fear but from a mysterious understanding of the gravity of the event and pity for my poor grandfather, and sadness at never seeing him again. The doors of the house were all wide open; it was freezing cold everywhere; and my mother told Parasha not to take my sister in to bid farewell to grandfather, although she was crying and begging to. So, just the three of us were left in grandmother's cozy room. Suddenly the hollow echo and tramp of a multitude of feet started up in the hall, sobbing and weeping moving along with it; all this passed right by us—and soon I saw how, as if on the heads of the people, the wooden coffin went down off the porch; . . . many standing in the courtyard bowed to the ground. Moving slowly, the crowd went out onto the street, stretched out the length of it, and finally vanished from sight. Standing on a chair and looking out the window, I was crying from the bottom of my heart, filled with sincere love and grief for my grandfather, so much loved by everyone. For a moment I even wanted to see him once more and to kiss his emaciated hand.

Aksakov's style is the antithesis of Gogol's hyperbolic, metaphorical rhetoric and poetry. It is as clear as a map, but it is not a simplicistic style, the kind you find in old chapbooks or in letters from semiliterate people. It is not an epistolary style, not a classical style—the sentimental symmetry of Karamzin or Richardson. The author is trying to look back into time as he sees it in his mind in images and scenes and to recapitulate a lost life in the life of the present, as, indeed, Proust did. Proust, however, takes the life of the mind as also part of the whole life; Aksakov calls life only that which has occurred as an "event." He uses reflection to prepare the reader for looking at the event the way he remembers it or the way he feels he now wants to remember it. His style is transparent, wholly adequate to what it expresses. It is a self-effacing style. He leaves you looking at what you think is an objective portrait of life in all its placid, continuous, unimportant details: toothaches, deaths, meals, and rainy days. Out of a brief time spent among the Russian gentry colonizing Bashkiria, he wrote a chronicle of what happened around him, from children's suppers to peasants' murdering their landowner. He looked back with the eyes of a child but the mind of an old, trained man on the period when he, like any child, discovered the world. As he wrote to his son Ivan in 1849, "You won't ever straighten out this foul everyday world, thinking about it dispassionately; you'll just ruin your health; and I lose myself in reverie, going off into the eternally peaceful world of nature."

A passage from Chekhov's story "The House with the Balcony" (1896) recognizes man's complicity in nature and describes it from man's point of view. The story is subtitled, "An Artist's Story," but the art in the description is the removal of the artist's personality. His figure is the only animation in the world he walks through, which remains as vague and as unchangeable as an image in a dream. He does not need to call up his childhood; it itself haunts him.

Once, on my way home I accidentally wandered onto an unfamiliar estate. The sun was already going down, and the evening shadows were lengthening across the blossoming rye. Two rows of old, closely planted, very tall firs stood like two solid walls, forming a dark, beautiful alley. I easily climbed over the fence and went along the alley, slipping on the fir needles which here lay two inches thick on the ground. It was quiet, dark, and only somewhere high in the treetops a bright gold light was shimmering and falling like a rainbow on a spider's web. There was a strong, almost suffocating smell of fir cones. Then I turned into a long alley of lindens. And here, too, there was emptiness and oldness; last year's leaves rustled sadly underfoot, and shadows lurked in the twilight among the trees. To the right, in an old orchard, reluctantly, in a weak voice, an oriole was singing, surely also old. But then the lindens ended, too; I passed a white house with a terrace and a balcony, and suddenly before me a view opened up on a manor-house yard and a broad pond with a bathhouse, a mass of green willows, a village on the far side, and a tall, slender church tower on which a cross shone like fire, reflecting the setting sun. For an instant I was filled with enchantment with something kindred, very familiar, as if I had already seen precisely this whole scene sometime before in childhood.

The artist's personality is not exploited, as it is, for example, in Dostoevsky's description of Petersburg; it is removed. Some man stands here, unknown but concrete, the basic image and measure of the actualization of human values, bringing the past up to date.

We object to language aimed more at provoking affectation in us than at affecting us. Good poetry is the greatest possible extension of meanings with which words are invested by experience. Allen Tate has called this achievement of poetry "tension," "derived," he says, "from lopping the prefixes off the logical terms *extension* and *intension*." In a letter to Gorky, Chekhov illustrated the first step in building this tension by his comments on some stories Gorky had written:

The only inadequacy is that there is no discretion, no elegance. When for a specific action a man expends the least amount of movement, that is elegance. . . . Your frequent anthropomorphisms—when the sea sighs, the sky looks, the steppe basks, nature whispers, talks, languishes, and such things—all these metaphors make your description somewhat monotonous, sometimes saccharine, sometimes obscure; vividness and expressiveness in descriptions of nature come only through simplicity, through such simple phrases as "the sun set," "it grew dark," "it rained."

The direction of Chekhov's effort is even clearer in the revisions of the short novel *Three Years* between the time when it was first printed in January and February, 1895 in *Russian Thought* and when it was included in his *Collected Works* in 1901. Chekhov significantly reworked the story and shortened it. For example, in the following passage:

She sat down on the sofa, put her hands on her knees and became lost in thought. Laptev looked at her and envied those who know how to please, who are witty, resourceful, who can sing or talk charmingly. He knew that he was homely. . . .

Laptev's sentence is eliminated. The final version reads:

She sat down on the sofa, put her hands on her knees and became lost in thought. Laptev knew he was homely, and it seemed to him at this moment that he even felt his own unattractiveness all over his body.

Or, another example: an inchoate description—

In the house, he went to his sister's room. Nina Fedorovna seemed still strong and gave the impression of a well-put-to-gether, powerful woman, but a harsh paleness made her look like a dead person, especially when, as now, she lay on her back with her eyes closed. Beside her sat her older daughter, Sasha, ten years old, reading her something out of her school anthology.

"Alesha has come," the sick woman muttered quietly to herself.

is, in the revision, completed by an apt, dramatic gesture:

An unspoken agreement had long ago been reached between Sasha and her uncle: they spelled each other. Now Sasha shut her anthology and, without saying a word, quietly left the room. Laptev took an historical novel out of the chest of drawers and, having found the page where he had left off, sat down and began to read aloud.

The incident carries with it all its required meaning, insepara-ble from the intension. The repetition of the movements in the change of guard, the shutting and opening of the books—analogously characteristic books—carries out and away the simple phrase, "Alesha has come," and the futility of the dying woman's life. We know at once that she is dying, not because she is said to look like a dead person when her eyes are closed, but because of her unresponsiveness to the shutting and open-ing of books and to the vital change of people. The actions suggest everything necessary to their meaning. Extension and intension are the same. Since the man and the girl have similar attitudes to the dying woman, the same symbols, the same gestures, our attitude is delimited. She loses that mys-teriousness and unpredictability by which we distinguish the living.

The novel is narrated in the third person but always from

the point of view of the central character, Aleksei Fedorovich
Laptev, son of a wealthy wholesale haberdasher in Moscow.
At the beginning of the novel he is staying outside Moscow
with his older sister Nina, whose husband keeps another
"wife" and children openly in the same town. Nina is dying
of cancer. Laptev is in love with Yuliya, the daughter of the
old doctor who looks after Nina. When Laptev asks Yuliya to
marry him, she, anxious to live, at first rejects him but then,
afraid of spinsterhood, changes her mind and the next day
accepts. Just before Laptev's proposal, there occurs a series of
episodes around the symbol of a parasol. Yuliya came to see
Laptev's sister but left without her parasol. Nina asks Laptev
to have it returned the following day. Laptev takes it with
him and, upstairs in his room after supper, notices it, and, in
the first version—

*Once home, downstairs, he started walking through the
rooms, laughing at himself and calling himself mad. His hands
and legs were shaking and his head still felt the touch of the
soft feather. On a chair he caught sight of the parasol Yuliya
Sergeyevna had forgot, grabbed it, and passionately kissed it.
The parasol was silken, no longer new, held by an old elastic
band; the handle was white, though not bone but of some
composition. For a long time Laptev looked at it with a tender
feeling, then sat down and opened it up over himself. Now
he felt very fine, easy, free. Out of habit he consciously observed his own emotions, was surprised, and said to himself
that he never before had experienced such delight. It seemed
to him that there was even an odor of happiness all around
him.*

In the later version the parasol carries the incident, as the
incident carries the characters. The action is intense and in-
tensional:

Once home, on a chair he caught sight of the parasol Yuliya Sergeyevna had forgot, grabbed it, and passionately kissed it. The parasol was silken, no longer new, held by an old elastic band; the handle was of plain white bone, cheap. Laptev opened it up over himself, and it seemed to him that there was even an odor of happiness all around him.

The connections are "logical." The events move toward a fatal accidency. Their meaning follows from their consequential arrangement, paralleling the sequence of the words.

Chekhov sets up a series of contrasting positions—Moscow versus the provincial town; conversation on love, a "psychosis," versus the effects of being in love, of "not knowing what to say"; the older generation, the fathers, versus the younger, the doctor's daughter and the haberdasher's son; the past versus the present; health versus illness; here, this moment versus any place else later; distraction and boredom versus work and purposefulness; the many, the circle of family and friends around Laptev, versus the one, Laptev himself—and puts through these positions, as if through the questions of an examination, a set of normal characters each of whom is presented in a dominant, stereotyped trait. Laptev is indifferent: "Tomorrow the same thing all over again. What for? And when and how will it end?" His sister Nina is full of superstitious self-pity: she worships her unfaithful husband and blames her cancer of the breast on her own jealousy and crying. Yuliya is romantic, a typical ingenue: at one point she uses a deck of cards to try to tell her fortune. Her father, the doctor, manipulates real estate on the side and complains that nobody appreciates him, refers to himself as an ass, a beast of burden which everyone abuses. Panaurov, a roué and ruined landowner, Nina's husband, loves women and spends money on luxuries. Kish runs errands. Kostya, a young lawyer, dreams of being a novelist (rather than of writing well). Yartsev, a teacher, pretends that all knowledge is his province, but "when he talked about something in botany or zoology, he did it as an historian; when he discussed some historical problem, he did it as a natural scientist."

The plot of the novel is the love story between Laptev and Yuliya. Presented in the opening chapters as a simple boy-meets-girl tale in which the rich young man (not handsome) wins the beautiful young girl (full of doubt), the story is then complicated by the past being brought forward (up through the present and pressed against the future). Everyone in some sense fails. In their failures, Yuliya and Laptev unconsciously take on the characteristics and even the values of the other. Yuliya, who dreams of a thrilling life, unconsciously becomes bored by religion and concerned with money. Laptev, who despises his family's merchant manners but fails to understand art, finally takes over the family business with forthrightness and an almost disinterested sense of vocation, born of obligation to Yuliya. The future is imaged as everything that the past was not. "You know," says Yartsev, "every day I'm more convinced that we're living on the eve of the greatest triumph." An intellectual semifailure himself, he is example of another of Chekhov's devices—putting positive values or judgments just off center, attributing to only partial characters terms which are complete:

"But without a desire to die," said Yartsev quietly. "No philosophy can reconcile me with death, and I see it simply as ruin. I want to live."

The asymmetrical characterization is confirmed by the asymmetrical plot. Attention is put on moments of heightened emotion or reflection when choice seems significant and involvement in life is keenest, but these moments are then subverted by the facts of the plot, the machinery of the everyday world. For example, Yartsev and Kostya's emotional commitment to Moscow and their exhilarating night walk through the city are stopped short by a brief paragraph announcing the death of the Laptevs' baby and their return to town.

The action moves through common and appropriate moments. Description of details catches up Laptev's habit (our habit) of dispassionate observation and transforms it into intensive commitment. In the series of episodes around the parasol, Laptev makes a symbolic gesture which is particularly his, that is, a gesture defining him in his self-conscious state of loving. It is a private gesture wholly indicative of his emotion and impossible for anyone else, although it defines everyone else's sense of failure and hope of success. What Laptev wants to happen is what he, in this gesture, feels happens, in the same way that the limited, intense emotion of a child invests a toy with a greater, fantastic reality. When he returns the parasol, Yuliya Sergeyevna greets him:

"But Papa just went to your place," she added, glancing at the children [playing ball in the yard].

"I know, but I haven't come to see him, but you," said Laptev, charmed by her youth which he had not noticed before and which he seemed to have discovered in her only today. It seemed to him that now he saw her thin, white neck with the gold necklace for the first time. "I've come to see you," he repeated. "My sister has sent the parasol. Here. You forgot it yesterday."

She put her hand out to take the parasol, but he pressed it to his chest and muttered passionately, unrestrainedly, given over again to a sweet ecstasy such as he had experienced the night before, sitting under the parasol, "Please give it to me. I'll keep it in remembrance of you . . . of our acquaintance. It's so wonderful!"

*"Take it," she said and blushed. "But there's nothing won-
derful about it."*

Laptev's enchantment by the beauty of the girl's neck
completes for us, by accidence, his identification of her with
one of her things, a part of her property. (Unlike Sobakevich's
furniture, which is a caricatured attribute of Sobakevich in the
rational argument of *Dead Souls*, the symbolization of the
parasol is initially outside Yuliya's power.) Laptev's effort to
announce both the identification and the enchantment in a
conventional plea, imposing on the girl unpleasant obligations
of which he is unaware, confuses her and prevents her indifference. Marriageable Yuliya's involvement with Laptev is
seen in its necessary, stupid, forlorn, chance nature. We are
prevented from considering Laptev's request absurd (although
it is baldly sentimental) because of the self-consciousness of
Yuliya's reply. She is bewildered by the power of his personal
association of herself with the parasol. She can only see the
parasol, like herself, for what it does. She can only understand
his words for what they say. His discovery of apparent meaning baffles her. This little drama both presumes and predicts
its own reversal—when his ecstasy is gone, when he has lost
hope of being loved, when he can no longer make her love
him through such analogies as the parasol. After a short period
of marriage, Yuliya becomes disillusioned and tries to ignore
Laptev. Later, older, she begs him for comfort and companion-
ship, and again the parasol reappears as the symbol of their
special, common bondage. The emotion occurs as action and
engenders other actions, which affect our emotions and lead
to understanding.

The parasol returns at the end of the story. Laptev and
Yuliya have fallen away from each other, yet have discovered
something about themselves in this sorrow. Ironically, Yuliya

wants Laptev to go into the family business and Laptev wants to do almost anything else. Their positions have been reversed.

"Whatever may be, one must say good-bye to thoughts of happiness," he said, looking out on the street. "There is none. I've never had any, and, I suppose, there isn't any at all. But, once in my life, I was happy, one night when I sat under your parasol. Remember, you somehow forgot your parasol at my sister Nina's?" he asked, turning to his wife. "I was in love with you then, and, I remember, I sat under that parasol all night in a state of bliss."

In the study near the bookcases stood a mahogany chest of drawers with bronze handles in which Laptev kept various useless things, including the parasol. He got it and handed it to his wife.

"Here it is."

Yuliya looked at the parasol for a minute, recognized it, and smiled sadly.

"I remember," she said. "When you told me of your love for me, you held it in your hands." And, noticing that he was about to go out, she said, "If you can, please, come back a little earlier. I'm lonely without you."

And then she went into her room and for a long time looked at the parasol.

The reversal and imperfect recognition scene revolve around the parasol, dramatic symbol not only of the past but also of the future as extension of the past. He now gives it to her, and she, as he did once, takes it into her privacy in a disenchantment inversely analogous to his former enchantment. They have moved, like dancers, around the symbol of their desires.

The symbol cuts into the imagination, into those deeper passions which they, like us, do not dare exhibit. Here, at the end, each stands where the other began. What is bitter about their reversal within the reversals of action, the formal reversals, is that, since time moves only one way (only to its consumption), neither can recover himself. Laptev is disillusioned both out of his love for Yuliya and out of the possibility of her loving him. Yuliya, in turn, corrupting and corrupted by Laptev, has relinquished her vivacity. She doubts even the possibility of giving the affection of a faithful wife.

The discovery is ironic. What is discovered is what was thought to be possessed but was not understood and, therefore, was not possessed. The morality is as freshly mimetic as the dramatic form. Yuliya and Laptev become certain of what they had tried to avoid even perceiving. They lose the illusions which they at first had tried to guarantee. By the effort to make happiness secure and personal, both lost it. Very ironically, their positions at the end are, in terms of motivation, the same as at the beginning. Although they have moved behind appearance to a fragmentary self-revelation, what they have to work with is unchanged.

Nina's self-indulgent husband, Panaurov, represents those for whom change is irrelevant. He does not ask how his life can be significant. He only wishes to make it pleasant. And he has, despite his ignorance, enough confidence to support his theories about everything. As his wife lies dying, he explains to Laptev what cancer is. The first version reads:

He spoke slowly, gently, convincingly, and he pronounced the words "you can't imagine" with an imploring voice. He was already forty-eight but by old habit he now, as fifteen to twenty years ago, squinted, sighed, languidly shook his head and smiled graciously, in kingly fashion, and you felt in his every movement, in every glance, that he was satisfied with himself, that it seemed to him that by his presence and conversation he gave others great pleasure.

Laptev listened apathetically, not trying to understand, and thought only: "What a coquet!" He kept hearing—lymph, thorax, gall. Finally he had had enough, got up from his seat and said, "I'd like something to eat. . . ."

In the later version, Chekhov alters this so that the movements themselves are implied extension and the description takes on its intended irony:

He spoke slowly, gently, convincingly, and he pronounced the words "you can't imagine" with an imploring voice, squinted, sighed languidly and smiled graciously, like a king, and it was obvious that he was very pleased with himself and didn't think at all about the fact that he was already fifty.

"I'd like something to eat," said Laptev, "I'd very much like to eat a little salty something."

The transitions which we use to get from description to discourse or from discourse to chatter have been removed. Again, Laptev's request defines the preceding description as part of Laptev's consciousness. Similarly, looking at it from an external point of view, Laptev's phrase belongs to the description, that is, to the story, and is fixed there. The act and the meaning are simultaneous. Nothing can be changed.

With few exceptions, Chekhov tries to remove himself as interpreter of intentions, to let his language work through itself, to make the area of intensions (to use that other word again) as specific and as vast as possible. Each event in the story is a mimetic act. It occurs as an independent gesture which could be infinitely repeated. Only that which occurs in consciousness is an event. For example, Nina's dying is a series of events for the doctor, for Panaurov, for Yuliya, for Laptev, for her daughters (especially after she has died), for the servants—for all the people who experience it in their consciousness. The *fact* of her dying, unlike Nikolai Levin's, for example, is not important. It is not a dramatic action. The dramatic action is the older daughter's, Sasha's, interpretation of it and her desperate search for her father.

The novel builds up a tension in prose in which purpose, including the author's attitude toward his narrative and toward the characters' responses, is an impossible, rational, verbal extension of the sequence of actions. But in fact there is nothing except the events of the story as they "happen."

Chekhov stresses the relationship in consciousness between events and desires. He translates the discrepancy into a phrase of habitual discourse, a common generalization, when he has Yartsev say platitudinously, "In short, man is never satisfied with what he has." This statement is the limit in fact of what we have learned is the action in consciousness.

Chekhov deals with desire as intension and as event, and he measures it against the very story he is telling. For example, in the first version he characterizes Kostya's impossible ambition to become a novelist:

In his creative work there were chiefly noticeable two peculiarities: first, in his novels he described only the countryside and landowners' estates, although he saw the country only rarely, only when he was with acquaintances at their summer house; he had been on a landowners's estate only once in his life when he had gone to Volokolamsk on court business; and secondly, he always wrote only about current events; so, if for some reason some official position was not to his liking, he then wrote about an unsympathetic hero in that position.

In the revision, discussion of a literary style is replaced by fragments of that style, which is judged by the style of Chekhov's story (as in *The Sea Gull* Treplev's tragedy is forecast by the contradiction between his play and Chekhov's). What Chekhov is doing and what he means are made clearer and more important by narrative being reduced, like drama, to its ancient roots in mime.

In his novels he described only the countryside and landowners' estates, although he saw the country only rarely, only when with acquaintances at their summer house; he had been on a landowner's estate only once in his life when he had gone to Volokolamsk on court business. He avoided a love element, as if ashamed, described nature frequently and in these descriptions liked to use such expressions as "the intricate outline of the mountains," "the whimsical shapes of clouds," or "the oneness of secret harmonies." His novels were never published, and this he explained by the restrictions of censorship.

In a later speech in which Laptev curses himself and his merchant background—"Our grandfather beat our father; our father beat you and me. What did this distinguished species give us? What kind of nerves and what kind of blood did we inherit?"—words that imposed an argumentative definition were struck out. Words that cursed too strongly were replaced by words that suggest the desire of cursing strongly but an impotency to do so. Laptev's values are too ambivalent; the ambivalence is reasserted. For example, "in succeeding generations we will have only cowards, criminals, and madmen" becomes in the revision "Oh, if only God would grant that we were the end of this distinguished merchant species!" "Distinguished" carries all the irony Laptev is capable of. It shows brightly, as if through glass, the desperation of his understanding in this outburst of self-consciousness, failure, and guilt.

Not one of the characters has a proper understanding of himself and, in his grave *mis*understanding, clings ever more tightly to all the other characters. Each is in some way deluded about himself, just as everyone in Nina Fedorovna's house is deluded into thinking that she will get well by the fact that she walks into the living room one bright morning. Each inverts himself, as Nina Fedorovna, only thirty-nine, once was well but now is fatally ill, as she was called a Muscovite but dressed as a plain peasant. Each character exaggerates his inadequacies or his attributes: the doctor falsely imagines that he is a martyr; old Laptev worships himself and imagines he has a family and a warehouse full of loyal followers whom he has made happy; as for Laptev, everyone "preferred in him what he himself thought least of." The characters fancy that they mean to do good works—Laptev entertains the project of establishing a charitable flophouse; "without work," he says, "there can be no pure and joyful life"—but they only mimic themselves: not knowing whether or not Yuliya has rejected Laptev, the doctor begins a false, tear-jerking, self-mocking whimper of self-pity; Yuliya says she turned Laptev down; the doctor feels relieved, "but he was no longer able to stop himself and continued" his crocodile tears. Kostya has no idea that his speech to the jury indicates every reason why he will never succeed as a novelist. Dying Nina craves romantic historical fiction, but Kostya asserts that "fiction is significant only when it treats the idea of some serious social issue." "Life flowed on as usual," and, as if without good reason, merely out of habit, "in May the Laptevs moved to their summer house in Sokolniki. By then Yuliya was already pregnant." Against this background, Yartsev's reply seems almost out of place; he asks what would be the point of having in *Romeo and Juliet* not elaboration of the theme of love but "a discussion on, say, freedom of teaching or on prison sanitation." But the talk, in which Laptev and Yuliya take part, is not so relevant to any decision of the issues as it is to Chekhov's story. The irony is not lost on the reader, who, catching the reference to *Romeo and Juliet*, remembers that Laptev himself, many

months before, reading an historical romance to his sister
and reflecting bitterly that Yuliya did not love him but, like
many girls, was marrying for the sake of convenience, said
sarcastically and deprecatingly, "Romeo and Yuliya. . . . I'm
Romeo, Nina. You can congratulate me. I proposed to Yuliya
Belavina today."

The conflict between love and social usefulness has come
back against him triply hard. And he is powerless to reply.
Similarly, when Kish tells him that with his money he can
do much good, Laptev says that money did his dying sister
no good:

*"Yesterday you asked me to help some mathematician who
is looking for a job. . . . I can give him money, but that's
not what he wants. Once I asked a well-known musician for a
job for a poor violinist, and he said to me, 'You've come to me
precisely because you're not a musician.' "*

Unlike Nina, who believed in charity, and unlike Polina Ras-
sudina, a caricature of the emancipated woman, Laptev too
much respects men to assume their guardianship. He cannot
answer the question, "What for?"

The atmosphere of hopelessness is invented and then
enacted by the actors. It is the product of their self-consciousness, their "original thought"; it alone is the fact "which holds
good for all observers." Even in Moscow, where life, for Yuliya,
is at first the image of vivacity and worldly charm in contrast
to that of the provinces, enjoyment of art becomes, "because
of the lack of talented people and the same singers and reciters
being at all the parties," "a boring, monotonous obligation."
Turned from plausible accomplishment, the characters reflect
on themselves in soliloquies, provoked by the apparent freedom or happiness of the others to whom they have no access
and whom they misunderstand, as Laptev misunderstands his

wife's motive for urging that they move to the business. Near
the very end of the novel, Laptev is in a garden and hears steps
on the other side of the wall. He has just brought the firm's
accounts into order and, bemused, comes out into the city after
midnight. Bird-cherry is in flower all around him. He over-
hears two lovers in the next garden.

The whispering and the kisses behind the fence excited him.
He went out into the middle of the yard and, opening his
shirt, looked at the moon, and it seemed to him that he might
right now order the gate unlocked, might go out and never
more come back. His heart sweetly trembled from a forebod-
ing of freedom, he laughed joyfully and imagined how it might
be a wonderful, poetic, and perhaps even divine life.
But he still stood there and did not go out, and was asking
himself, "What keeps me here?"

Laptev presents himself, like the protagonists in Chekhov's plays, as he might have been in the very moment of
recognition of what he is. He applies reason to himself, turns
to his obligations, and obscures, further, his possibilities.
Work, he implies, is antithetical to happiness. At any rate,
life is not sufficiently elastic to include both. In this moment
of psychic intuition—this moment of focused action—real
change occurs. A man of conventional behavior moves from
desperately particular emotions through self-revelation to an
understanding of conventional behavior. He does not and can
not change externally. He changes internally—and in one moment, the climax of his life and of the story. Laptev is not
sorry for himself or sorry for the black dog that, out of habit,
Laptev says, sits near him in the garden and does not run
away to the forest. He is sorry for his inadequacy to honor his
discovery, to act according to his desire, to function meaningfully. He is freed of his personal need for irony but disap-

pointed that life can be only an approximation for anyone.

The next day he and Yartsev go to the summer house where Yuliya is. As the others go in to dine, Laptev sits alone on the terrace and watches

how quietly his wife went along the alley, heading for the house. She was thinking about something, and there was a sad, enchanting expression on her face, and tears shone in her eyes. This was not the former thin, frail, pale girl, but a mature, beautiful, strong woman. And Laptev noticed with what delight Yartsev watched her coming, how her new, beautiful expression was reflected in his face, also sad and elated. It seemed that he saw her for the first time in his life. And when they lunched on the terrace, Yartsev somehow delightedly and shyly smiled and all the time kept looking at Yuliya, at her beautiful neck. Laptev followed him with his eyes involuntarily and thought how, perhaps, he would live another thirteen, another thirty years. And what would he happen to experience in that time? What does the future hold for us?

And he thought:

"We'll live—we'll see."

Whatever revelation will come, being part of a later, extrinsic, rational framework, will lack the meaning of that one moment of self-consummation in self-discovery. Self-recognition has been completed. An epiphany, such as Ivan Ilyich's, would be unbelievable.

Chekhov has built up a central image of an ineffable reality by precise use of ordinary language, that is, by putting words into motion, so that adjectives like "beautiful" and nouns like "delight" and verbs like "to love" refer not to concepts or to rose-colored photographs in our minds but to figures in action. Even the moments of immobility in the story presume and predict a life of movement and labor. The words do not fabricate only a visual system, a countryside of natu-ralistic details. The images are always dramatic. The tension of the language is the same as the tension of perception. We are continually left not with a defined understanding of some-thing to which we may say "right" or "wrong," but with the desire to make a responsively appropriate gesture, some kind of gesture of knowledge of despair. If our gesture were adequate to the story, as, say, Oedipus's blinding is adequate to his, perhaps we could say that it was understanding, but, after having read Chekhov, we are never sure what the adequate gesture would be. He leaves us, like his characters, somewhere between the two parts of ourselves, the "man" and the "title." Living in a commercial and industrial society, with contra-dictory sets of values, without faith in progress, in doubt of the goodness of human nature, and skeptical of superior au-thority, we in our time do not know how to put the parts together again. Chekhov's life crossed into our century, and his work separates the classical novel from the modern. After Chekhov, Sholokhov's *Silent Don*, a vast, naturalistic romance, is an anachronism. For us, as for Laptev, the ironies of life can be encompassed only by the formal irony of comic tragedy.

The Petty
Demon

One of Chekhov's contemporaries was Fedor Sologub (pseudonym of Fedor Teternikov). His success came later than Chekhov's—early in the 1900's, not in the late 1880's—a result of different attitudes rather than of unequal talents. Chekhov worked apart from the symbolist movement, though he was highly conscious of it; Sologub worked more or less within it. Sologub's novel *The Petty Demon*, written between 1892 and 1902 and published in book form in 1907, brought him enormous celebrity. Mirsky's standard *History of Russian Literature* refers to it as "the most perfect Russian novel since the death of Dostoevsky" and says that its hero, Peredonov, is "the most famous and memorable character of Russian fiction since *The Brothers Karamazov*." Initially popular (seven editions in six years), the book subsequently was neglected.

As a tale, a story, it is chiefly weird: Peredonov, a schoolteacher, is obsessed with obtaining a promotion and haunted by a notion of his neighbors' incessant ill-will. He and the people around him live, or operate, in a kind of maniacal vulgarity until he himself, insane, kills his "best friend." His promotion depends, he thinks, on a princess's favor, which his mistress, Varvara, in order to get him to marry her, persuades him to believe is at hand by having a friend of hers send him forged letters. Peredonov hopes to transcend his friends and his mistress, but the letters convince him that, married, his chances are better. He spreads slander and blackmail among

302

his acquaintances and the parents of his pupils, aiming particularly at the young lovers Sasha and Lyudmila, whose beautiful bodies tempt them to flirt more with a certain sexual self-indulgence than with each other. Everyone lives in the same town, and the two "subplots" (Peredonov and the young lovers) are woven together by the characters' relative social positions, scandalmongering, and other forged letters.

The book has been read either as a libidinal nightmare or, in terms of another prejudice, as an instance of the absurd polarities of Sologub's symbolism. A step toward understanding it is to consider it in relation to the Russian symbolist movement (from about 1895 to 1910), whose adherents, much like the French symbolists earlier, considered art to be a total view of society, a dramatization of social and political "problems" and their solution by the "logic of imagination," the revitalization of language and artistic form.

Our acquaintance with history tells us that the moment in the mind and the moment in actuality are not identical; that society supplies an individual with forms to express his desires and his meaning and, by the same forms, exploits and restrains him. Art, as symbolic action, as Kenneth Burke has it, exists as encompassing solution to a situation which has not caused it. If then we take a book as "solution," we must look to the book for the "problem," also.

The impressive work of the Russian symbolists falls in the period between the turn of the century and the start of the First World War, when there was a special, strange, and profound feeling about the homogeneity of all intellectual activity. Theirs was a period that was intensely conscious of its own vitality in the midst of political decay. Allied to this was a pervading sense of the paradoxical shadow that always falls between the idea and the reality, between the motion and the act. "In this effort to combine the artistic devices of various cultures," said Bely in his book *Symbolism* (1910), "in this fit to create a new relationship to reality by means of reexamining a series of forgotten world views, lies the whole power of the new art."

Symbolism emphasizes the preeminence of creativity over knowledge, the possibility of transforming images of reality in creative writing; in this sense, symbolism emphasizes the meaning of the art form, in which the pathos of creativity is of and by itself reflected; symbolism therefore emphasizes the idea of culture in the study of style, rhythm, and use of language in poetry and prose, acknowledges the basic significance of the solution of problems of technique in music and art. A symbol is an image taken from nature and transformed by creativity; a symbol is an image uniting in itself the artist's experience and figures taken from nature. In this sense every work of art is essentially symbolic.

And therefore the present symbolist movement . . . must tie itself in with the more general problems of culture.

In prose fiction, because of the realistic façade of character and plot demanded by middle-class culture, the development of form must be also a moral development. If there were another form available to the novelist, he surely would take it, but, as the Philosophy Teacher tells Monsieur Jourdain in *Le Bourgeois Gentilhomme*, a man must choose prose or verse, "for the reason, Monsieur, that there is only prose or verse by which to express oneself."

The accessibility of prose in our modern world commends it as form, in the same way that the accessibility of dramatic verse in ancient and aristocratic Athens commended drama then. The Russian symbolists thought in terms of (and wrote) prose fiction when they meant to express by mimetic plot their moral judgment of a man. As Mikhail Kuzmin said in

The Wonderful Life of Iosif Balzamo, Count Kaliostro (1916):

What chiefly interests me are the many and varied ways of the spirit leading to one goal but sometimes not leading the traveler all the way to it, but letting him turn off into side alleys, where he always gets lost. . . . What is important to me is what place the various heroes occupy in the general evolution, in the general structure of God's world; and the external, variegated change of scenes and events is necessary only as an intriguing wrapping whose place can always be taken by imagination, the younger sister of clairvoyance.

He is not denying the reality of the wrapping; he is denying the validity of our substitution of it for what it wraps. He wants to go beyond the fragments of experience to discover the force that controls them.

"A man must be like a river or a mirror," Kuzmin said. "He must accept whatever is reflected in him." Kuzmin's novel *Wings* (1906) is about the *gimnazist* Vanya, who has to learn the morality not of civic piety but of anticonventional individualism. He has to study his cultural tradition in order to respond to experience spontaneously. The "story" takes place after the boy's mother's death. It is not a story in the nineteenth-century sense, like those novels of Prévost which the ladies in the novel read, but rather a "scheme" for a story. The first part describes the boy's life with relatives in Petersburg and a love affair in which his cousin, a girl, is involved with a man, Strupp, whom Vanya has met, though in a different connection. The affair ends—or begins, from the basic, moral point of view—with another girl's suicide. The second part describes Vanya's life in a summer house on the Volga. The third part describes his life in Italy, chiefly Florence, where he again meets Strupp and goes away with him, that is, accepts him. The supreme agent of plot and of morality, Strupp, and the young boy himself seem equal but different aspects of the author, the extremes of experience bound by a common mind and mutual, sexual attraction. The book itself is bound by the symbol of wings: the image of eternal freedom and the means to move toward it. Early in the book, Vanya sees Strupp and Ida Golberg in the Summer Garden:

She was walking along, limping and leaning on the arm of an elderly lady, and meanwhile Strupp, on the other side, was saying: "And people saw that all beauty, all love, comes from the gods, and became free and bold, and they grew wings."

At the very end of the book, when the boy's development has come to its crisis, Strupp tells him to send a note saying "yes" or "no," meaning that he, Strupp, should either get out of the boy's life or remain:

"Just one more effort, and you'll grow wings; I can already see them."
"Maybe, only they're very heavy when they do grow," said Vanya, grinning.

The intimacy of love, described by Mariya Dmitrievna at the beginning of the second part, and its violence (symbolized by Ida Golberg's suicide, by Fedor the servant's red, unbelted shirt) or violence and sensuality together (symbolized by Nata's story of the suicide told to the accompaniment of a choir's singing) do not fit usual moral measurement. Conventional, Christian morals with their emphasis on self-denial cannot comprehend them, just as Vanya's aunt cannot understand. Conventional morality judges all acts quantitatively: the doing is what's done. Kuzmin argues against this, saying, through Prokhor Nikitych, that "Sin is not in the doing but in the application, in how the doing is done." Otherwise, he says, freedom is impossible.

Irony, indifference, and personal energy are enough to make a man reject romanticism and asceticism, the terms of his time. They are not enough to complete preliminary education for receiving life, for uniting everything in oneself. To experience the past as if it were present is to build one side of the figure which a man must be. A man is the history of everything that has come before him that he has taken in. His history is the sum of the terms by which he makes his life. Nothing by itself is anything, for the source of its definition is the individual himself. "Of course, a fact or a bare essence is not important," said Kuzmin, "but what's important is your relation to them—even the most outrageous fact, the most improbable situation can be justified and made pure by your relation to it." Beyond the life of the world, but part of it, is the life of the idea:

The body itself, matter, will perish, and the works of art, Phidias, Mozart, Shakespeare, let's say, will perish, but the idea, the type of beauty bound in them, cannot perish, and this, perhaps, is what is uniquely valuable in the changing and transient motley of life.

Slowly, tentatively, courageously, the individual must work his way through experience back to himself. Frequently, he cannot be sure of the aptness of his act or of the validity of his direction, for experience comes disconnected and fragmented, and one's relation to it, one's understanding of oneself, may be illusory:

"It seemed we were at a funeral," Vanya remarked.
"There are people who seem to be at their own funeral every minute," said Strupp without looking at Vanya.

"When an artist dies, it's very sad."

"There are people who are artists of life; their loss is no less sad."

"And there are things which it's sometimes too late to do," Vanya added.

"Yes, there are things which it's sometimes too late to do," repeated Strupp.

What matters above all is the effort to build oneself one's space, to build with that "beautiful clarity" which Kuzmin said characterized the best prose.

In *The Petty Demon* we are given a society out-of-joint that has lost all value and all chance of communion, a society with an inadequate language. Prevailing social abuse of language occasions Sologub's exploitation of words to restore reality, an exploitation that, in a sense, leads Sologub away from the very society he is trying to circumscribe. The reader is taken as the norm of that society, an individual consumed by the confusion of his own subjectivity and the loss of significant communication with anyone on any level. Because the language lacks suppleness, refinement, and the precision of gesture—because there is no such thing as what Edmund Wilson has called "the ordinary language of literature"—and because the relations perceived are dynamic, Sologub is prevented from narrating or from allegorizing. He has to move from the world as he perceives it into his book. He must create in his book special situations which in themselves symbolize the intended meaning. He must invent his form as he goes along in order to bring back to his reader the compelling "logic" of a real perception. His book is a sign of how far away he has been taken, and he must fight through it back to the world he first perceived. When he says, in the preface to the second edition, that his novel is a scientifically accurate mirror and that "both the deformed and the beautiful are reflected in it equally exactly," he means not only that men are good and bad for the same reasons and in much the same ways, but also that the "duality" of man is finally judged or made real by the power and excellence of uncaused talent. The precision is within the book, not in the applicability of the book to life.

The book begins with life:

After the holiday Mass the members of the congregation scattered to their homes. Some stopped in the churchyard under the lindens and maples by the white stone walls and talked. . . . It seemed that people in this town lived peacefully and amicably. Even happily.

But it is not consequently accountable to life. It is neither an awkward poem nor a moral documentary. It makes its own life—it is symbolic action made—consciously out of inadequate words. When it is made, the words are, as in a library book, expired:

At last they became bold and entered. Peredonov was sitting dejectedly and mumbling something incoherent and meaningless.

Preoccupation with language is, of course, not particular to Sologub. Since the last part of the nineteenth century, serious writers have necessarily been, above all, concerned with constructing a voice to define oppositions in social forces which the ordinary language of conversation and politics cannot embrace. The language of politics excludes Turgenev's "born observer," the outsider who watches and means to judge. The outsider must exploit style as the reality—we talk of the "mandarin" style of James. James works to extract from verbal movement a source of life. The novelist's subject, like the painter's, consists, he said, in "the related state, to each other, of certain figures and things." In the first version of *The Portrait of a Lady*, Caspar's embrace of Isabel was described in one sentence:

His kiss was like a flash of lightning; when it was dark again she was free.

In the final version, James expanded the description to fix that related state:

His kiss was like white lightning, a flash that spread and spread again, and stayed; and it was extraordinary as if, while she took it, she felt each thing in his hard manhood that had least pleased her, each aggressive fact of his face, his figure, his presence, justified of its intense identity and made one with this act of possession. So had she heard of those wrecked and under water following a train of images before they sink. But when darkness returned she was free.

To those who might object that in that short novel he had not seen his heroine "to the end of her situation," James remarked in his notebooks:

The whole of anything is never told: you can only take what groups together. What I have done has that unity—it groups together. It is complete in itself—and the rest may be taken up or not, later.

The story is absorbed in embodying a perception of the regime, the discipline, of suffering, of the common bond of sin —that emotional identification of one man with another. Turgenev supported his belief, James says, that the important thing to start with was not an airtight plot, but rather a character or group of characters who are so alive that the main question becomes to "invent and select" the complication that such characters "would be most likely to produce and to feel."

"Really, universally, relations stop nowhere," he said in the preface to *Roderick Hudson*, "and the exquisite problem of the artist is eternally but to draw, by a geometry of his own, the circle within which they shall happily *appear* to do so."

James conceived form as the imposition of perfection, as standard and as agent, in a manufacture of words. Sologub's attitude is the same. Sologub complicates his architecture by overt symbolism—the figure of the *"nedotykomka,"* for example, a made-up figure and word—which lies like a mantle on the semicredible characters. Sologub moves expertly backward and forward between pictures of men and caricatures of men, just as in Bosch's "The Temptations of St. Anthony" the fish and beasts, symbols of obliquity, are kept alive and credible by being recognizably human and patterned in a dramatic relationship which describes what in that moment really is wanted and which carries, like a burden, a moral explication. In the book, as in the painting, the irony and the satire—the lyric horror—almost overcome tolerance of reality:

During supper they all got drunk, even the women. Volodin suggested that they dirty the walls some more. They all were delighted. . . . Afterward, they invented tearing strips off the wallpaper at random to see who could get the longest. At this game the Prepolovenskys won another ruble and a half.

Volodin lost. Because of this loss and his intoxication, he suddenly became sad and began to complain about his mother.

The depravity—the fascination with self-abuse and the meaningless defacing of what is an extension of someone else in a frenzy of self-affirmation—the seduction into self-righteous barbarity, as presented in the book, is the mark of the success of evil. Corruption that is respectable, like the Devil in *The Karamazov Brothers*, is real corruption. It is un-

definable and incorrigible. What is Anthony's advantage in
his picture is that the horrors come as symbols. Or, that is our
advantage as we look at the picture. They are frightening but
not invincible. Peredonov, however, has no anagogical or
moral ladder up which to escape from his vision of horror.

The first moment in the process of self-destruction is the
self-enforced delusion of superiority. One is not merely different in one's corruption; one is better. Peredonov is satisfied
by what he feeds on—himself—since he has excluded all other
possible relations. He is charmed by his turpitude and afraid
of usual people. In contradistinction to Don Quixote, that
moral visionary whose books were burned for him, Peredonov
—the "Don done over"—burns his books himself. And he
stops reading:

*Meanwhile in the living room Volodin soothed their host
by promising, for certain, to get the May issue of Russian
Thought and to read Mr. Chekhov's story. Peredonov listened
with an expression of obvious boredom. Finally he said:*

*"I haven't read it either. I don't read silly things. They
keep writing nonsense in their stories and novels."*

Nadezhda Vasilevna smiled politely and said:

*"You're very harsh on contemporary literature. But now-
adays, too, good books are written."*

*"I've read all the good books already," Peredonov declared.
"I'm not about to read what's being written now."*

He is afraid that he will be read out of his corrupt mediocrity.

The world given the reader is peopled with devils and
fools. The devils impose on the fools because the fools yield
to any attraction. (Evil in any form is at least initially attractive.) The devils enjoy success up to that point at which their
activity becomes wholly introverted and they absurdly and
pathetically avenge themselves on themselves. At that point,

all common value is lost—this is the given condition—and whatever has worked has generated its own validity. The signs, like empty words, reveal internal pauperism and barbarity:

The lull in the streets smelled of sadness, and it seemed that these pitiful buildings had risen up for nothing, these hopelessly decayed structures that timidly hinted at an impoverished and monotonous life lurking inside their walls. . . . Only children, eternal, untiring vessels of God's joy over Earth, were full of life and ran around and played—but already inertness lay even on them, and some sort of featureless, invisible monstrosity, nestling behind their shoulders, looked out now and then with eyes full of menace at their suddenly dulled faces.

The curse of insensibility—the noise of dumbness—threatens life. Words fascinate people, playing on the surface of consciousness as light and shadow play on water. But because the words are perverted or broken, they are tools of torture:

"No, I'm not lying, and I can prove it," Rutilov said gloatingly.

"Prove it," Peredonov demanded.

"Just wait. I will," Rutilov answered in the same tone of malicious joy.

They both stopped talking. Peredonov waited nervously, and his anger at Rutilov tormented him. Suddenly Rutilov asked:

"Ardalyon Borisych, have you got a pyatachok [*a five-kopek coin; a pig's snout*]?"

"Yes, but I won't give it to you," Peredonov replied maliciously.

Rutilov burst out laughing. "If you have a pyatachok, how can you not be a pig!" he shouted happily.

Peredonov in horror grasped his nose.

"You're lying! What pyatachok? I've got a man's mug," he mumbled.

These people, like barbarians, want language.

Words evaluate behavior, arrange celebrations, provoke fights, cast spells. The tacit power that works among men is imported into understanding by the ambivalent but precise turns of words. When Peredonov grasps his nose, he shows he is under the spell of the language. When, later, he talks of having been seduced by black magic and says, "Until I recited the countercharm, I was completely drugged," he understands that he got over the spell of words with words. The language, itself a possible response to fear, has made him afraid. And his demonic activity consists of practicing a kind of verbal duplicity or legerdemain: he wants the princess to write the words he needs—announcement of promotion—and he goes around talking deceptively to others to secure his own best advantage.

Each man's total, or mythic, view of reality impinges on the others' to force, somewhere, the inevitable disillusion of discovered self-deception. The reality which the symbols are intended to apprehend is, for each man, only the "reality" of one consciousness. The continual and necessary effort at judgment is ironic. The quest for power is both ridiculous and true. In this book, among these fragmentary characters, it is ultimately self-destruction. It is partly comic, since there is the common, systematic denominator of desire or power, and partly horrible, since it is, like the activity of Kafka's beetle, plausible.

The book as a whole stands against the characters: that is, the book comes to judgment. The "petty demon" is a symbol of a total understanding, a motionless figure of despair, in a mind outside the book.

Literally, the *nedotykomka* represents a deliberate symbolization by the author—retained from an earlier poem which begins with it as a dramatic persona—characterizing not so much Peredonov's state of mind (he clearly is a paranoiac) as his contact with another reality. The first stage in his withdrawal is marked by the introduction to the twelfth chapter:

Even in his calm state, Peredonov, like all coarse people, could not accurately appraise small incidents: either he did not notice them or else he exaggerated their importance. Now, agitated by expectations and fears, his perceptions served him even worse, and little by little all reality became clouded over before him by a thin haze of repulsive and evil illusions.

The hallucination which Peredonov suffers reflects the infectious autonomy of evil and the acute sense of individuality which accompanies it—its multiplicity of meanings.

The obfuscation is moral. Out of deference to custom, Peredonov has his new house blessed. At precisely that point at which he experiences religious ecstasy, he is visited by his devil. The *nedotykomka* appears, the invention in language to which Peredonov's vision is an analogously invented reality:

It chuckled and trembled and circled around Peredonov. When he stretched out his hand toward it, it swiftly slipped away, ran behind the door or under the cupboard, and appeared all over again a minute later, and trembled and mocked again—gray, featureless, nimble.

At last, when the praying was finished, Peredonov was suspicious and began to make hexes in a whisper. The nedotykomka hissed very, very quietly, shriveled into a little ball, and rolled behind the door. Peredonov sighed in relief.

Sologub assumes, like Aristotle, that essential conflict is individual and ethical, but, unlike Aristotle, that rational solutions or demonstrations of solutions are implausible because the intellect is neither virtuous nor vicious. Who asks for solution only discusses himself. The "problem" is the system of problems which people live by. The "solution" is the game of animating the problems—that is, of playing them off against each other so that one problem is both the impulse to and the resolution of the next. The whole is a huge ethical gesture which, because it is ineffable gesture, yields only to a series of particular dramatizations. In this sense, reality is a group of essentially moral scenes each moving away from and back into the others and pointing toward an ultimate vision, presented as reality contemporaneous with us, to which we must assent.

The vision as symbol has perhaps two directly analogous moments elsewhere in the book: the dreams and the murder of the bug. Lyudmila's first dream, for example, makes both her and us conscious of her reality. It functions in the book as an expression of the naturally secret, the private, in the only way we do express it. It is a particular, sexual dream, a sudden revelation to and of Lyudmila:

First she dreamed that she was lying in a stiflingly hot chamber, and the blanket was slipping from her and exposing her hot body—and suddenly a scaly, ringed snake had crept into her deathchamber and was climbing up, was crawling up the tree trunk, along the branches of her naked, beautiful legs.

It also serves, literally and allegorically, as an obvious symbol of physical and spiritual Eden in the book's general moral structure.

Peredonov's murder of the bug is an image given as dra-

matic action. It symbolizes the reality of individual consciousness moved against the pattern of consciousness:

> *"I've killed a bedbug," Peredonov explained sullenly.*
>
> *His eyes gleamed in wild triumph. Only, one thing wasn't
> right: it smelled foul. The spy, transfixed on a pin, rotted and
> stank behind the wallpaper. Horror and triumph shook Pere-
> donov—he had killed an enemy.*
>
> *His heart had been hardened right to the end of the murder.
> An imperfect murder—but for Peredonov it was murder per-
> fected.*

At the end of the book, when he kills a man, not a bug, he
effectually kills himself—he loses consciousness. He, like his
words, is used up. But when he kills the bug, he celebrates
the act. He takes his new sense of size from the fact of having
killed, of having accumulated enough power in evil to transcend mere defamation. This also leads to the irony of his
delusion:

> *Mindless horror had forged in him a readiness for crime—
> and the unconscious, dark image of future murder, lurking in
> the lower strata of spiritual life, the tormenting itch to mur-
> der, the condition of basic hostility, oppressed his depraved
> will. Still fettered—many generations lay on the ancient Cain
> —it found gratification in his breaking and spoiling things.
> . . . And the ancient demon, the spirit of prehistoric confu-
> sion, the decrepit chaos, rejoiced in the destruction of things,
> as at the same time the wild eyes of the mindless man revealed
> a horror like the horrors of monstrous death agonies.*

Self-gratification works against the self: because there is no
system in corruption, either, the delusion is like the obverse of
a two-sided mirror. As one tries to get to that invisible reality

in the middle, which does not move but is, one seems only to get smaller and smaller, that is, farther and farther away. Against the series of conflicts taken in Freudian terms, the book, as form, is the imposition of laws of meaning on the chimerical and passionate violence of all the devils.

The transformational powers are an aspect of art in its function, of the ability to construct meaning by using symbols which lie between actuality and reality, between an image and its idea. In one of Sologub's poems, for example, each object, put into its proper "related state," becomes something specifically more than its naturalistic self. The repeated moon image at the end of the poem, as if in refrain, defines the difference between the two hypostatized worlds.

> In anguish still, and still inflamed,
> The quiet day's not dead,
> And still the overtired dawn
> Has not yet fallen into shade.
> Just visible, the crescent moon
> Is already raised above the world;
> The silence, by its breathlike sound,
> Has bewitched the wastes of fields.
> All things themselves all things presage—
> What holy, happy wonders lie
> In the remote valley, the peaceful sky,
> The heartbeat of my anxious age.
> As a distant, silent sound,
> There comes the breathing of the things of calm;
> And the lonely crescent of the moon
> Hangs already raised above the ground.

The dichtomy between what seems to be and what seems to be able to be is terrifying and humiliating, like any perception of implausible contrast. The original esthetic impulse that

identified the moment or the thing as real has discovered that
that moment belongs in a system made intelligible by the life
of the symbol: " 'Not everything just seems,' Peredonov mumbled sadly. 'There's also truth in the world.' " But everything
except the symbols, being transient and outside a communicable system, lacks reality. Everything else turns against the
person who mistakes it as real.

Even Peredonov craved the truth in accordance with the com-
mon law of all conscious life, and this longing anguished him.
. . . He could not find truth for himself, and he was confused
and was perishing.

Since Peredonov lives off his delusion and depends, for
his life, on others taking his delusion at face value, he is sur-
rendered in all his subjectivity to the overwhelming and cha-
otic subjectivities of everybody else. He cannot see what they
want or think, and they cannot see him except as a madman.
Everyone is afraid of losing himself—his position. Nobody can
do anything to help anybody:

"How can I live if they don't give me the place?" he
thought.
He kept devising new plans of defense against his enemies.

Serious efforts at self-explanation are, consequently, bad jokes,
that sort of twisted irony which is barely instructive and very
painful. At one point, for example, Peredonov and Volodin
wear neckties as emblems expressing hidden feelings. The
preposterous fantasy of the situation quickly shatters illusions,
but, in this world of damned isolation, no one's attitude
toward himself is ever altered:

Peredonov put on a white stock; Volodin, a bright red tie
with green stripes. Peredonov argued this way:

"As I am to do the matchmaking, mine is a sober role. I must live up to it. So I must wear a white tie, and you, the lover, should show your flaming feelings."

With intense solemnity, Peredonov and Volodin seated themselves in the Adamenko's living room. Peredonov sat on a sofa, and Volodin in an armchair. Nadezhda looked at her visitors in astonishment.

In a different setting, the same sort of thing occurs in an episode between the young lovers, Sasha and Lyudmila. A pun on the word *rozochki* (little roses; birch rods) combines two assumptions into a third (the "real") context. We move subtly between the beautiful and the violent, both aspects of passion.

"Do you like roses?"

Sasha sighed, opened his eyes, smiled tenderly, and whispered: "Yes."

"Large roses?" asked Lyudmila.

"Yes, all sorts—large and small," replied Sasha quickly, and he gracefully slipped off her knees.

"And so you like rozochki?" asked Lyudmila gently, and her vibrant voice trembled with suppressed laughter.

"Yes, I like them," answered Sasha quickly.

Lyudmila began to laugh. "You stupid, you like rozochki! And there's no one to whip you," she exclaimed.

They both laughed and flushed.

Desires innocent for being aroused unavoidably were, for Lyudmila, the chief charm of their relation. They excited one, and yet they were far from coarse, repulsive attainment.

The young lovers' passion contrasts to the old lovers' depravity, but both couples are mad. The only applicable judgment is an ultimate paradox, a kind of symbolic action charged with as much tension and meaning as possible.

"Understand, stupid," she said in a quiet, persuasive voice, *"only in madness is there happiness and wisdom."*

"Well, sure!" said Sasha incredulously.

"You must forget, forget yourself, and then you'll understand everything," Lyudmila whispered.

Self-revelation to another person is also keeping oneself socially concealed. The alternative, rather mystical, even Christian, is equally real. Whichever way one moves one also simultaneously moves in the opposite way. One is always doubly exposed.

Peredonov deliberately, madly exposes himself. He attaches his delusions to (most charming symbol of all) the society of cards and blinds all the men and women there. Cards are not only a symbol of social games in the present but also, like the tarot pack, a means for revealing the mysteries of the future. They are mysterious in their self-sufficient competency, which all the more poignantly measures Peredonov's impotency.

The faces of the court cards did not please him—they were so oxeyed.

Recently, when playing, it seemed to him that the cards smirked like Varvara. Even an old six of spades had an impertinent look and wiggled obscenely.

He cannot tolerate their self-confidence. He cannot endure their authority. So he kills them. He arranges an *auto da fé* which turns on its inquisitor. His martyrs and victims mock and frighten him. The murder is a bitter joke.

[Peredonov] understood that the end was approaching, that the Princess was already here, close, quite close. Perhaps in this pack of cards.

Yes, undoubtedly she was the queen of spades or the queen

of hearts. Maybe she was hiding in another pack, or behind other cards—what she looked like nobody knew. The trouble was that Peredonov had never seen her. No point asking Varvara—she'd lie.

At last Peredonov got the idea of burning the whole pack. Let everyone burn. If they creep into the cards to spite him, then it's their own fault.

Peredonov seized a moment when Varvara was not home and the stove in the living room was going—he threw the cards, the whole deck, into the stove.

Crackling, the mysterious pale red flowers opened out— and burned, charring on the edges. Peredonov stared in horror at these flaming flowers.

The cards curled up, bent over, moved, just as if they wanted to jump out of the stove. Peredonov grabbed the poker and thrashed at the cards. Tiny bright sparks showered out everywhere—and suddenly in a brilliant and evil riot of sparks the Princess rose out of the fire, a little ash-gray woman bestrewn with dying flames. She wailed piercingly in a thin voice, hissed, and spit on the fire.

Peredonov fell on his back and howled in horror. The darkness embraced him, tickled him, and mocked him with cooing voices.

The symbols themselves become further, purer symbols through the alchemy of gesture, and we as readers are prepared to accept the mockery because of the sympathy which Sologub provokes. As we read, we soon become aware that even Peredonov's ambitions are only half credible. If they were wholly credible, the book would be a sort of humorous, medieval allegory of Hell. The structure of the book, however, makes all the personae plausible. They believe one another, and they love themselves.

As Peredonov moves through his comedy into his agony, as he tries to grasp his illusions, like Quixote at the beginning of his quest, we condone his acquisitiveness and destructiveness. But, because he, unlike Quixote, wholly fails, we are removed from him to an understanding of the book itself as symbol of an actual relation and an artistic perception. The closer we, like Peredonov, try to get to invisible reality in the center of the circle, the smaller we seem to become, the farther away we seem from ourselves. Outside the symbols there is no truth, for outside them there is nothing real. Finally, even Peredonov himself becomes a symbol. We understand the book as a symbol, and we reject the life within it. Our symbolic response is the real solution. We know that Sologub's analysis has been a device for convincing us:

Peredonov sensed in nature a reflection of his own dejection, his own fear at the mask of its hostility to him; of that inner life in all nature inaccessible to external definition, of the life which itself alone creates true, deep, and indubitable relations between man and nature—of this life he was unaware. . . . Blinded by delusions of personality and independent existence, he did not understand primordial Dionysian ecstasies exulting and screaming out in nature. He was blind and pitiful, like many of us.

Although perhaps no more sensitive to primordial Dionysian ecstasies or to an Eden of love than Peredonov, we know that he, like the book that encompasses the "problem" of his society, is not decadent. The author's disillusionment is not romantic. For him, society is a system of uncaused problems operating fortuitously without value or meaning. It cannot cause its own solution. Love, like hatred, is only a necessary invention for personal security. Usually, it amounts to less.

What life adds up to—short of the mystery which Sologub assumes lies beyond, at the center—is known only as a sum of obvious absurdities. What it means is the burden of his book's words.

Petersburg

¶ *Petersburg* can be read in many ways. It may be read as satire on a complacent, empty-headed autocracy; as a symbolic cityscape haunted by bigotry, stupidity, and the threat of violence; or as an imaginative rendering of the revolutionary currents in the Russia of 1905. It may be read as a great game of language, written to test the limits of expressibility by the play of utmost skill. It may be read as a kind of masque of consciousness behind the mask of mere event. It may be read, as the editor who first rejected it observed, as "a subversive book, very malicious and even skeptical."

In terms of Bely's directing image in *Petersburg*, the artist must try to work out the figures of his geometry—that science of properties and of relations of magnitude in space—so that the definitions in the mind and the definitions in the world fall together in a new meaning:

> *Caught in the form of limitation*
> *Between un-being and being.*

Just as in the Christian concept that no act can ever be complete in itself, so human gesture is completed only in its *story*. The result is the novel, where real-life designations are irrelevant and everything is true. Bely's accomplishment was to set up a story that completes the gestures of life by mocking them and, through the irony directed at life, more fully expresses its meaning. What is *said* about life, to contradict Wittgenstein, is finally also *shown*. When social unity is gone, when ordinary life seems to have no significant purpose, when we see nothing ahead but dull obligation, a novelist must find the truth by writing in contraries, by writing on that back side of beauty.

In Russia, the novelist's obligation to himself (his geometry, his pattern-building) was compounded with his own sense of obligation to society. His work had social importance and a social function. If the work was serious, it was taken seriously (and still is). On the elementary level, it had to be socially responsive: "The state, having become abstracted from the social forces which formed it," said Bely, "oppresses us with a brutal weight." "Capitalism," said Sergei Solovev, reflecting the Russian symbolists' general opposition to the existing political and social structure at the turn of the century, "is a manifestation of universal evil . . . [and is] no less hateful to the poet than to the socialist." The symbolists' manifestoes and programs of literary reform were aimed not only at reviving techniques of art and at restoring respect for poetry, but also at reordering men's intelligence that they might see the shapes and patterns of their world. "Symbolism, like realism," said Vyacheslav Ivanov, "wants the 'true reality.' "

The Russian symbolists wrote all *kinds* of literature and nonliterature—plays, poems, essays, book reviews, novels, short stories, fantasies, memoirs, letters, opera and ballet librettos, dissertations, and committee reports. Their prose fiction may be characterized as of three types. They wrote social fantasy satirizing existing political institutions and social organizations—for example, Valery Bryusov's *The Republic of the South Cross* (1905), a tale of the horrors of oppression in a modern, fantastic state laid out at the South Pole, in which all the streets run north along the longitudes from the frigid center. They wrote historical romance not merely to capture exciting adventure and to extend and glorify the mystic themes derived from the Middle Ages, but also to express a system of humanistic values which they felt lay behind their own disintegrating culture. For example, there were Bely's *Northern Symphony* (1903) and Bryusov's *The Fiery Angel* (1907), a supposedly eyewitness account of the relations among the Devil, a young German mercenary, and a girl tried as a witch. Set in the Germany of 1534–35, the story is remote, obscure, and titillating—but, like Blok's drama on medieval themes, *The Rose and the Cross* (1912), it had contemporary significance. Speaking about the narrator, Bryusov says: "The ideas derived from unsystematic reading mixed, in him, with traditions inculcated since childhood and created a world view completely self-contradictory." Indeed, as if in answer to the built-in contradictions in their own world view, the symbolists wrote another type of prose fiction: a story protesting the conditions under which they lived—for example, Merezhkovsky's *Alexander I* (1911–12). There is, above all, the story of a contemporary figure in a contemporary setting who must proceed by contrary or devious means to "find" himself, his place, even the values by which the author believes the world moves—for example, *Petersburg*.

Bely's novel is "about" the city in a year of revolution. Petersburg–Leningrad lies partly on the mainland and partly on some one hundred islands at the mouth of the Neva River. (They exist in fact and at the same time figure in Bely's dreamscape. "Personally," says the author, "we'd say, O Russian people . . . don't let the crowd of shadows off the islands; black and moist bridges are thrown across the waters of Lethe. They ought to be torn down. . . .") The Winter Palace, the Admiralty, the Senate and former Ministries are along the left bank of the Neva. On the opposite side are the Peter-and-Paul Fortress and Vasily Island where the university is and the stock exchange used to be. Further west were

—and still are—middle-class and working-class residential districts. "There, the many-thousand human swarm wanders every morning to the many-smoke-stacked factories," says Bely.

Petersburg is also about a surreal city projected in geometrical figures. The configurations of real things are transformed, in thought, into their geometric prototypes. One of the sections is titled, "Squares, Parallelopipeds, Cubes," of which this is a sample:

The carriage flew through to the Nevsky.

Apollon Apollonovich Ableukhov swayed on the satin cushions of the seat; four little perpendicular walls shielded him from the nasty throng in the street; in this way he was separated from the flowing crowds of people, from the wistful drenched red covers of the little magazines being sold over there on that corner.

The systematization and symmetry calmed the Senator's nerves, which had been agitated both by the lack of smoothness in his domestic life and by the helpless circling of our wheel of government.

His tastes were marked by harmonic simplicity.

Most of all he liked the rectilinear avenue; this avenue reminded him of the passage of time between two points in life; and of one other thing: all other cities were a wooden pile of little houses, but Petersburg was strikingly different from them all.

The geometric figures are the external, objective equivalents for the content of Apollon Apollonovich's mind. They are the laws and functions by which he apprehends the world around him. They are that world. It does not simply please him to drive along the great avenue but "inspiration would overcome the Senator's soul when the lacquered cube [of his carriage] would bisect the line of the Nevsky." And: "Next to a straight line, the figure of a square relaxed him most of all. . . . At the point of intersection stood a policeman." As for his work, "love for governmental plane geometry sustained him in the polyhedrality of a responsible post." The front hall of his home is black and white checkerboard; he wears a cylinder hat; he has designated all of the shelves in his house alphabetically and by the points of the compass (such as: Shelf B, N.E.). The city itself is both a point on the map and an infinite circle of consciousness:

There is infinity in the infinity of avenues running with infinity into the infinity of running, intersecting shadows. All Petersburg is the infinity of an avenue raised to the nth power. Beyond Petersburg, there is nothing.

This realm of transformations, where things are geometrical figures and geometry is reality, always seems to be expanding, swelling toward an annihilating zero. The young protagonist Nikolai Apollonovich as a child used to have the hallucination that an elastic ball "would often assume the appearance of a spherical fat gentleman; the fat gentleman, having become an oppressive sphere, would get rounder, rounder, rounder, and threaten to fall with all his weight: 'Pepp . . . Peppovich . . . Pepp . . .' And—he would burst into pieces." Nikolai would shout that "he, too, was growing round, that he was a zero." There are numerous references to circles and zeros and points, many associated with a bomb in a sardine can that lies in Nikolai's desk through most of the story. Finally, when it is about to explode in the house—Nikolai has lost track of it—he imagines from the sound of the ticking that some pointer, or hand, is moving round toward "the fatal point."

"Oh, oh: what's it mean, 'I am'?"
"Zero . . ."
"And zero?"
"A bomb . . ."
Nikolai Appolonovich understood that he was the bomb:
and, having burst, gave a bang.

Aleksandr Blok, a close friend of Bely's, has a poem about the lines and parallels of love, derived from an experience of following his fiancée along the streets of Vasily Island. In this poem the "lines" of reality are the figures the lovers traced in their promenade. In Bely's novel, the lines of the city are the "grid" of Senator Apollon Apollonovich Ableukhov's regularity and solidity. But this elaborate drawing of figures in the novel's space is neither merely a formal allegory nor a rigid system of "symbols." It is a pattern of the movements and of the consciousness of human beings, characters with whom Bely, as novelist, is involved but never identified. The supremacy of the pattern is that it is his invention.

This old Senator Ableukhov, a governmental department head until his son's doings became scandalous, is a reactionary bureaucrat of considerable power. Although Bely treats him as a serious and sometimes even pathetic figure, he also satirizes him with zest. Ableukhov feuds with Count Dubleve, head of the Ninth Department. When Ableukhov was appointed to the headship of his own department, he succeeded in completely immobilizing the rival one by hounding it with memoranda and "where necessary, with speeches promoting the importation into Russia of American binders and files. (The Ninth Department was against the importation.)"

His son is an emotional, unstable young man who is described as having, especially in moments of contemplation, enormous eyes and a forehead traced with little throbbing veins. He has flaxen-white hair. He is a student, and he has certain advanced ideas, which have led him to flirt with the revolutionary movement. At the same time as he plays this game, he also plays a teasing game with Sofiya Likhutina, the arty and bohemian wife of an army officer. One of his acquaintances, a terrorist named Dudkin, hands over to him a bomb, "a little sardine can with terrible contents," for safe-keeping. Nikolai draws the attention of the newspapers—and the police—to himself by masquerading in a red domino, a device meant to allure Sofiya. But, at a real masquerade party where Nikolai appears again in the domino, Sofiya passes on to him a note commanding him to use the bomb to kill his father and to "carry out the Party's will." The impact of this message seems to turn the world into a dream, the fantastic dream of a red domino, and Nikolai passes through several stages of a nightmare experience in which he wishes to throw the bomb into the Neva while at the same time being trapped in a fantasy of indecision. Before he can retrieve the can, his father finds it and unthinkingly carries it into his own study. At this point Nikolai's mother, who had deserted her family some time before, returns for a reconciliation and the three Ableukhovs sit down for a family dinner with the infernal machine ticking away somewhere in the house. At last—in the night—it does blow up, sets fire to the house, but kills no one.

Andrei Bely, whose real name was Boris Nikolaevich Bugaev, was born in Moscow in 1880 (he died in 1934), the son of an eminent mathematician, dean of the faculty of science of the University of Moscow. Close to Sergei Solovev and to Blok, encouraged by Bryusov and the Merezhkovskys, he quickly became well known among those sympathetic to symbolism, but, with few and later exceptions, was never widely known outside it. His literary work is voluminous and important: several volumes of memoirs, many lectures and essays and books on symbolist theory and on prosody in general, plays, poems, and novels, most of it striking, highly inventive, facile, mercurial, truculent, dynamic, extraordinary, magical. He read omnivorously, had opinions on everything. He wrote appreciative essays on Baudelaire, Tolstoy, Chekhov; revered Vladimir Solovev, Nietzsche, Wagner, Schopenhauer; used Humboldt, Rickert, Wundt; framed a book of poems, *The Star* (1922), with poems to his anthroposophic friend and disciple of Nietzsche, Christian Morgenstern; first opened the way to formal analysis of verse forms (especially, his study of Pushkin's "The Bronze Horseman," a poem and theme which recur as central images in *Petersburg*); and wrote a brilliant book on Gogol, whom he identified as the Russian "source" for symbolist prose, as Tyutchev was the Russian source for symbolist poetry. He closely associated his own work with Gogol's, especially *Petersburg* with "The Overcoat" and "Nevsky Avenue." Many of the symbolists, he said, "in prose proceeded from Gogol; the variety of possible conceptions of Gogol's imagery extended into all literary schools." Passionately religious but only in a mystical sense (when Blok married Lyubov ["Love"] Mendeleyeva in 1903, Bely seriously maintained that the marriage was the incarnation of Sofiya, the Beautiful Lady), and attracted to German psychology, Bely spent some time before the war working with Rudolf Steiner at Dornach. In 1917, under Ivanov-Razumnik's influence, he interpreted the Revolution as the actualization of Christ's doctrine. During the war, he and his wife, the former Asya Turgeneva, whom he married in a civil ceremony in 1911, lived in Switzerland in strange and unhappy isolation from the real world. He left Russia for Europe in the spring of 1912. He was in Brussels in April, spent the summer at Dornach near Basel, traveled through Europe in the fall, and remained at Dornach after the war had started. In the autumn of 1913, *Petersburg* began appearing in the *Sirin* almanacs. As a letter on November 3, 1913, from Blok to V. N. Knya-zhnin indicates, public response was cold: "By the way, everybody attacks him [Bely]; I've met only one person who is sympathetic, besides myself." A poem on the war, written by Bely in Arlesheim in 1914, recapitulates like a brief coda the sense of isolation that moves the novel:

> *The lull held like a thundercloud, then burst. . . .*
> *The thundering wail of the tribes flies high away.*
> *Everything close and dear is twisted worse*
> *Than a pillar of sand in the distance of other days.*
>
> *And I? And I? . . . A past without reply. . . .*
> *But where is it? . . . All gone. . . . That really so?*
> *Ineffable—whole worlds we do not know*
> *Are called up there by waves of onrushing light.*

By the fall of 1916 he was back in Moscow (subsequently, he spent some time in Berlin in the early 1920's, before returning to Russia for good). During the first half of the war, however, he experienced in a personal, desperate way that aloneness and fear of alienation—that terrifying spiritual exile —which the novel *Petersburg* overcomes by irony, but for which there is no happy response in actual life. In a long and revelatory letter written from Switzerland to Fedor Sologub in Petersburg, probably in the late summer of 1915, Bely said:

Dear Fedor Kuzmich!

I apologize for this letter; it's so unexpected. I've been sitting here abroad quietly now nearly three years. . . . I've been both sitting and keeping quiet for a long time with a definite goal in mind; . . . when inside you, as well as all around you,

everything is so complicated, you don't talk at all. . . . Fur-
thermore: all·these reasons compelling me to keep quiet and
sit still became very complicated once the war broke out; you
can't explain just why you, a Russian, didn't go back to Russia,
but stayed where you were, although, of course, in your heart
you longed for Russia.

I turn to you now for help. . . . I'm writing the third part
of my trilogy. . . . The novel is called My Life; the first part,
The Haze of Childhood, will be ready in two months, but I
don't know yet to whom I could now merely submit it: I'm
cut off from Russia. . . . I simply don't know where to turn.
Meanwhile, my wife and I have only a few hundred francs
(500) on which you can neither get to Russia nor live here
very long; and this critical position, together with my com-
plete isolation, forces me to . . . recall that my novel Peters-
burg has not come out as a separate book, that my Travel
Notes has not come out at all, that The Silver Dove is out of
print already three (no; more) years. . . .

I asked a friend in Moscow to try to do something with my
books; he promised to, and now he writes that nothing can be
done. For me that was . . . practically a blow on the head.
. . . So now, I turn to you. . . .

Bely began work on *Petersburg* in 1910. As the letter to
Sologub says, it was part of a trilogy, *East or West*, in which
Bely meant to expose what he considered the underlying and
contrary traditions. As Joyce used an epic poem of an Hellenic
myth on which to hang his mock-epic of the consciousness of
a Christianized world, so Bely used the geometric pattern of a
planned, deliberately European city to hang his portrait of
violent, "Eastern," anticivilized terror. Originally conceived
as continuation of *The Silver Dove*, a novel of religious sec-
tarian violence (1909), it was first called *The Wayfarers*, but
in the late fall of 1911 Vyacheslav Ivanov said to Bely:

"There's only one possible title for that epic poem, Boris: *Petersburg*; indeed, that's what the poem will be." Bryusov, poet and at that time literary editor of P. B. Struve's magazine *Russian Thought,* accepted it in advance, writing to Struve in August, 1910 that the novel would not be ready for another year. In October, 1911, Bryusov listed the novel as set down for publication in 1912; Struve hesitated, said it was accepted "conditionally," and, when he read it in February, 1912, rejected it out of hand, even saying he felt it his duty to dissuade Bely from publishing "such a thing, in which the flashes of great talent are drowned in a sea of real nonsense, unbelievably badly written." Bryusov disagreed but could do nothing. Bely was outraged. Vyacheslav Ivanov raised a cry, and Sologub also talked up the book, so that immediately three publishers were interested. K. F. Nekrasov in Yaroslavl started to publish it (Bely had already made some revisions), but because of printing problems only half the novel got beyond proofs. The Petersburg publishing house of Sirin issued it serially in three of its almanacs (in a form revised again in 1913), and finally as a separate volume in 1916. Bely revised the book once more for a 1919 German-language edition in Munich and yet again for a Russian-language edition in Berlin in 1922. This version was republished in 1928 and 1935. It is about two-thirds as long as the 1916 version. Bely wrote a prefatory note for it in which he said it must seem that

something basic has been changed in Petersburg; *for readers of the first edition, the* Petersburg *of this edition is a new book. For the author it is only a return to his basic idea, and the first edition is a rough draft which fate (the necessity of working hurriedly against time) did not allow to be finished and polished; the dryness, the brevity, the concentration of exposition (so the author originally envisioned* Petersburg*) were turned in that first draft into a hazy ornateness.*

The 1935 edition represents considerable change from the 1916—the ending, for example, is quite different, more "revolutionary" and antibourgeois, though no less ironic. (In the 1916 version, the bomb explodes and burns the house down, after which the father sends the mother and son abroad.) The changes in the novel are paralleled by changes in the text of the play, written in the early and middle 1920's, at the time Bely was also revising the novel. Called *Petersburg, or the Senator's Ruin,* a "historical drama," the play is preserved in two versions: the first, in manuscript, has a notation on it by Bely: "The first version, which the author considers more successful than the one presented on stage. (It never got on because its size would have required two performances.)" The second version, in three acts and eleven scenes, never published but performed by the Moscow Art Theater in 1925 with M. Chekhov in the role of Senator Ableukhov, is considerably shorter. The final scene runs like this:

PART 1: *Before the bomb explosion, a crushing, antique, thoroughly rotten formation in the street*—ABLEU-KHOV. *Tense expectation . . . something inevitable, creative, invincible draws near. . . .*
(*Explosion of the bomb*)

PART 2: *Impending expectation, tension—resolved by triumphant exultation, a growing wave of power and might. The triumph of victory shines on the faces of the victors. Approaching shouts, noise, music, and singing are heard—the REVOLUTION.*

Bely's adaptation of his *Moscow* novels in the late 1920's for Meyerhold's theater was never produced, though Meyerhold's projected setting—a sort of cage, elaborate, spiral, with stairways and "rooms" for each of the many scenes—is an example of extraordinary theatrical ingenuity and a fine, visual comment on the conceptual structure of Bely's prose. That prose is characterized sometimes by straightforward exposition—

Here was the Riverside: the deep, a greenish dark-blue color. There, far far away, and seemingly farther than they should be, the islands sank down, disparaged themselves.

—sometimes by deliberate imitation, even in details, such as the following sentence, which seems lifted from Gogol—

What was concealed under all this, God knows!

sometimes by savage parody—the drunk's account of the political meeting. These elements of the prose become the dominating tone.

Bely rewrote extensively, but, it seems, tried to minimize the expressive, or denotative, "side" of a word and to liberate the intuitive, or connotative, side. He felt, first, a certain melody in the words themselves as sounds or even metronomic units. In a note to the printer on one typescript, he said that

with a view to [establishing] an over-all rhythm, I use one and the same word sometimes with a shortened ending, sometimes deliberately without. For example: in one instance I write zavodilisya, *in another,* zavodilis.

Secondly, he makes words themselves define the concepts to which we attach values and by which we pass judgment. The effect is that of a language thinking itself. At the séance, for instance, the apparition is supposedly its own source and motive. From *Petersburg*:

Cross-sectioning the pillars of the conversation, sentences formed.

"You know?" was said somewhere on the right; died out.

And came to the surface:

"They're planning . . ."

"Throw . . ."

Whispered in back:

"At who?"

And here the dark couple said:

"Abl . . ."

Passed by:

"At Ableukhov?!"

The couple finished somewhere in the distance . . .

"Atta . . . boy . . . try . . . throwing a . . . cid on . . .
me . . .

And the couple hiccuped.

But the stranger stood astounded by all he had heard:

"They're planning? . . ."

"To throw? . . ."

All around was whispered:

"It's time! . . . and, sure! . . ."

The stranger heard not "and, sure" but "in-sure," finished
it himself:

"Insur-rection?!"

Or, more explicitly:

. . . And unknown, insensate in weightlessness . . . Apollon
Apollonovich flew out through the round hole [where the top
of his head was supposed to be] . . . and flew apart into
sparks. . . .

Consciousness turned out to be the little old man himself;
the little old man was leaning out of bed listening to the far-
away clicking.

And—Apollon Apollonovich understood: his voyage along

*the corridor, through the reception room, around in his head
was only a dream.*

*And hardly had he thought on this when he woke up: a
double dream!*

Thirdly, Bely experimented with synesthetic perception. In
Virginia Woolf's *To the Lighthouse* we find a color scheme
establishing the set of values and their relationships. Bely goes
farther. He admired Goethe's praise of light, meaning spiritual illumination, and he associated color with quality or tone.
In the manuscript of the first draft of the first *Moscow* novel,
there is a series of pages listing (1) a number of words to be
used in the book, and (2) a set of *themes*, each identified by
a color: the story of the old man characterized by his yellow-
ing by the yellow house in the yellow light; the yellow-black
theme of fate (in Woolf's novel, yellow-black is the color of
artificiality and irony); characters labeled yellow-green-black;
and brown, called a mixture of yellow and black, listed as the
"bottom" theme in the book.

Whatever the synesthetic equivalents or allegorical sig-
nifications, the "reality" of the characters is never denied. If
you wish only to "read them to the life," you may. Unlike
Gogol, who subtitled *Dead Souls* an "epic poem," Bely had no
objection to his books being taken literally, to their being illustrated. Of N. V. Kuzmin's drawings for *Moscow*, he said:

*I've lived with my heroes for a long time and I like to think
that I, more than anyone else, would sense a lack of correspondence between them [the illustrations] and the novel.
However, they delighted me; I was delighted by the fact that
the artist had seen the heroes through the author's eyes.*

The picture made of the facts is, you might say, only a little
piece of what the language depicts. Bely asked:

Can cognition be form? Cognition is con-tent, i.e., an active force: the containing of the contents, where the contents → knowledge: *the knowledge of form. Thus: the content of cognition is consciousness, the forms of cognition are the acts of perceiving the parts, content: or containability (the world of the contents is the world of the object).*

Osip Mandelstam's statement of "The New Theory of Art" (1914, four years before the *Tractatus Logico-Philosophicus*) simplifies, but clarifies, what Bely also said was true:

The activity of art consists in premeditated, artificial creation of conditions which, in the sense of provoking certain experiences, themselves take the place of those actual, real-life circumstances under which the experiences could have arisen involuntarily.

He does not mean merely that art is a substitute for life or a retouching of life. He means that successful art, like a successful logic, is a complete, "useless" system independent of but coincident with any event or "fact" in its world.

Petersburg is a turning point in the development of the Russian novel. It comes from and picks up its time in a way Bely's later (1925) two-volume novel on Moscow does not. The Moscow books—*A Moscow Eccentric* and *Moscow under the Blow*—were meant, Bely said in an introduction, to portray the way of life of old Moscow:

In the person of Professor Korobkin, a scholar of world renown, I portray the impotency of scholarship in bourgeois culture. . . . The first volume of my novel depicts the close fight between scholarship, which is free by its very essence, and capitalism. . . .

In the second volume, I try to present a picture of the rise of

the new "Moscow," not Tartar at all, and no longer essentially
"Moscow," but the center of the world.

In so far as the novel deals with history, it is, he says, a political satire, a cartoon. In *Petersburg*, the satire is deep: the passion of "Eastern" Russia (Ableukhov is of Tartar origin) is
brought against "Western" Russia (the program of reform,
the Nevsky Prospekt as "the European Avenue"), and Petersburg is as real as the dot on the map, which it is. The sixty-
eight-year-old senator has hanging over his piano a somewhat
reduced reproduction of David's *Distribution des aigles par
Napoléon premier*. Gogol's Petersburg has become a city in
which the

*streets possess an absolutely indubitable capacity: they turn
pedestrians into shadows; the shadows, these Petersburg streets
turn into people.*

The son, Nikolai Apollonovich, is a caricature like his father,
like Manilov in *Dead Souls*, like figures in eighteenth-century
satire. He is a rich, spoiled idler who gets up in the morning
two hours later than his father, goes around in a dressing
gown, Tartar slippers, and a Tartar *yarmulke*. In his room he
has a statue inscribed "Kant," but there is no knowledge of
Kant in his head. He is involved in a plot not to collect "dead
souls" but to make souls dead.

The city is also a pattern of consciousness. To describe it
is to give its sources in Mongol and Hellenic mythology—the
Tartar derivation of the name Ableukhov in Chapter I, and
the analogy, later in the same chapter, between Senator
Ableukhov and Zeus. The irony emphasizes the reality of the
identification. In the same way, the parts of the city make up
the topography of the modern mind, a portrait of which is
given by the recitation of the October, 1905 events by the

Neva, in the school, at the séance, in the *quartier*, and by the red domino with its black mask and the refrainlike phrase which Bely attaches to it: "Domino, domino, in what lies your power?" Likhutina, Nikolai Apollonovich's "girl," is associated with black silk dresses gathered in back, with a poor little apartment, with dolls and souvenirs given her by officers, with chrysanthemums and Japanese pictures on the walls—not an unusual method of characterization—but she is made coincident with the word "strikingness" and is called "extraordinarily plastic." The caricature becomes serious through the author's manipulation of words, not through lyric digression, just as one character spins another around by turns of words —Likhutina turns young Ableukhov from the "Red Domino" into the "Red Fool." The mouse squeaking in the corner during the "explanation" between Senator Abluekhov and his son marks the caricature the session is; the father faints, reaching down for a pencil—and the son, dressed in masquerade costume, images his death, marking the intense, libidinal "consciousness" behind all acts, especially the incomplete. The words repeat the motifs and motives—"I'm perishing without hope of return"—and produce, *mirabile dictu*, characters like Vanka-Vstanka, Shishnarfne (who turns into "Enfranchisse," the epitome of the drama of the mind), and Pepp Peppovich Pepp, a manufacture of the bouncing sounds of a ball. The words in their jokes and their meanings, their irony and their rebellion, aim at all consciousness, at measuring infinite space by infinite intelligence:

Concentrating on his ideas, Nikolai Apollonovich locked his workroom: then he began to think that he, too, and the room, and the objects of the room were transformed instantly from objects of the real world into intellectually accessible symbols of purely logical structures; the room's expanse be-

came commingled with his body that had lost consciousness in the general chaos, called by him the universe; *and Nikolai Apollonovich's consciousness, separating from his body, became directly connected with the electric lamp of his desk, called the* sun of consciousness. . . . *He felt his body flooded with the* universe, *that is, with the room; the head of this body was confounded with the head of the potbellied lamp bulb under the rakish lampshade.*

And having so removed himself, Nikolai Apollonovich was indeed becoming a creative being.

The young Ableukhov cannot reach the universal at all. In fact, the whole bomb plot itself explodes morally, as the bomb in the sardine can explodes literally and burns down Ableukhov's house, killing no one. The father writes his memoirs and becomes, so to speak, his own portrait on the wall. The son ends (1935 edition) by going to church, seeing nobody, and reading the eighteenth-century philosopher Skovoroda. The masquerade, the dance, the chase of the Red Domino, like Gogol's "Nose," through the city of Petersburg in quest of self are a kind of intellectual obscenity scratched on a wall of consciousness. What is clear is that the world Senator Ableukhov rode out into one foggy Petersburg morning in the beginning of the book—

This foggy Petersburg morning the heavy doors of a luxurious yellow house were flung open: the yellow house looked out on the Neva. A shaved valet with gold braid on his lapels rushed out of the vestibule to give the footman the sign. The dapple-gray horses dashed up to the porch; a carriage rolled up on which there was an old, noble shield; a unicorn piercing a knight. . . .

Apollon Apollonovich Ableukhov threw a quick, perplexed

glance at the policeman on duty, at the carriage, the coach-man, the great black bridge, the expanse of the Neva where the foggy, many-funneled distance so dimly was outlined and from where Vasily Island looked out frightened. . . .

Soon also the shoulder of the policeman on duty was lost in the fog, as all shoulders, all backs, all gray faces and all black, wet umbrellas were lost in the fog.

—it is clear that this world vanishes with Ableukhov's loss of power and with the change in thinking signified by 1905. As Bely says in a "parabasis" in Chapter VI, he means to distinguish between allegory and symbol:

The experiences of their elemental body, according to the teachings of certain mystic schools, transform word meanings and allegories into real meanings, into symbols.

The past has gone, like the city itself, "into the night," as Bely says in Chapter IV, into the flames of the past, like the Winter Palace at sunset. What is left is only the possibility of extracting, by irony and by cunning, some room for the present. The novelist's problem is to show how much he needs, how big literally are his figures and their playing field.

In Kuzmin's *Wings*, Vanya's first response to the intense love affair is to say, "How foul it all is! How foul!" In *The Petty Demon*, Sologub exploits words to restore reality and to circumscribe a society. He dramatizes the workings of the figures in their effort to adjust to themselves, to express both their "evil" and their "good" between the extremes of paranoia and sexual indulgence. *Petersburg* is the coordinates of a city's soul, of the import of an age. Form in this sense is the geometry of perfection by which deformity and beauty are judged. The terms shaped by the intellect in its imaginative play, and then measured by it, out of delight in its own skill, bring judgment on us, frustrating the discrepancy between our dreams and our accomplishments, reconciling us to the things of this world, and reminding us that finally the figures we cut in this world and the figures we cut in our minds cast the same shadows.

Envy

"One's real life," Oscar Wilde said, "is often the life that one does not lead." The phrase is aphoristic because of its apt ambiguity. The "real life" is the invisible life of the observer. In our century, Kavalerov says in Yury Olesha's *Envy*, the observer is the conscious man, the "real" man, the man who always loses. First published in the magazine *The Red Earth* in 1927, the novel is about the intelligentsia at the beginning of the first five-year plan. It is about the dehumanization of man by machines, told from the viewpoint of an intellectual who has entered the new, industrial world but keeps the values of the old: "Help him!" Kavalerov shouts at the end of the novel, "will you really let a machine kill a man!"

But there is little a man can do. Volodya Makarov announces himself as "the new generation," the "new man," "the Edison of the new age." Kavalerov cannot escape him or the age, for, as he says, "my youth coincided with the youth of the age." Born in 1900, he is the literal and symbolic child of the twentieth century, haunted by his birthright and unable to imagine success. He (or Ivan Shukhov in Alexander Solzhenitsyn's short novel *One Day in the Life of Ivan Denisovich*) could easily have said what The Tramp, The Little Guy, Charles Chaplin said in his autobiography:

Joseph Conrad wrote to a friend to this effect: that life made him feel like a cornered blind rat waiting to be clubbed. This simile could well describe the appalling circumstances of us all; nevertheless, some of us are struck with good luck, and that is what happened to me.

For Kavalerov is, at least, not killed. He acts out his role in a story of the change from the old world to the new. The story his life tells is less a story about men's machines than about the machine of time.

In Olesha's story "The Chain," a boy measures age, both his own and his society's, by his relation to a bicycle which he dreamed of riding, rode, and of which he lost the chain; now, he is older, he says, getting still older, and running on little, short legs "after the thundering storm of the age!" In "The Cherry Stone," the narrator talks about an invisible country in which the sisters Attention and Imagination lead the traveler—a third world, different from "the old" and "the new," invented by the author. The narrator continues:

Natasha agrees to meet me but doesn't show up herself. I come a half-hour ahead of time.

A trolley clock hangs above the intersection. It's like a little barrel—isn't it? Two dials. Two bottoms. O, empty barrel of time!

In *Envy*, a machine to invent a new sausage is opposed by "Ophelia," the machine against machines, which ends by pinning a man. Olesha admired Chaplin's films for the contrast they dramatized between the old values and the new requirements, as in the scene of The Little Guy, the flower, and the girl in *City Lights*. In a brief 1936 article, Olesha said:

This attempt to unite in one artistic structure contemporary facts and literary reminiscences dear to an artist's heart is probably one of the chief obstacles facing Chaplin in working up his material. . . .

He saw man as having become an appendage to the machine. He is cleverer, more perspicacious, and bolder than many. In this lies the pledge that he will soon grasp precisely where the really new times started.

In *Envy*, the new age is said to exist under the slogan "Work Comes First." The superfluous man of the nineteenth century may have, as Saltykov-Shchedrin put it, "become frustrated under the burden of dichotomy," but for the thoughtful individual, the man who, like Kavalerov, "entertains himself by observing," the world is even harsher. "How hard it is for me to live in the world," Kavalerov says. "Nobody understands me." Kavalerov, "Mr. Knight," the modern Hamlet (to Andrei Babichev's Quixote), is an alienated, egoistic rationalist, extremely self-conscious and bewildered by his own idleness, uselessness, and ineptness. No matter how he tries, he feels, he does not belong. Yet he cannot avoid his age. He is a man at war with his time. He opposes Babichev, the father-image, but loses hopelessly and ironically—"Around him, I, Nikolai Kavalerov, am the fool." By Olesha's literary trick (like Tolstoy's trick of making Ivan Ilyich say at the very end of his story not *prostite*, "farewell, forgive me," but *propustite*, "let me through"), Kavalerov ends satirically, emasculated in Anechka's bed: "Today, Kavalerov, it's your turn to sleep with Anechka. Hurrah!"

Pushkin talked about envy as "the sister of rivalry, and therefore of good family." But Pushkin was talking about envy in the context of romantic courtship and the conventions of love. Olesha is analyzing envy as fatal opposition between men of different position, as a game played "for keeps," as a force which kills. Kavalerov says:

I suddenly was clearly conscious of not belonging to those who had been convoked for the sake of a great and important thing, of my being completely unwanted among them, of my being cut off from everything great which these people were doing. . . .

Olesha moves from this into a game with his protagonist. He uses Kavalerov as a shadow of consciousness. By playing

Kavalerov against his story, he defines the difference between past values and present experience, keeping both alive. Hence, the diary form; hence, the shift in Part 2 from first-person narration to third-person. The play of style directs the game in consciousness.

The contrasts of character underlying the narrative and giving rise to its "plot" are, like two armies of black and white chessmen, drawn up in stiff formation. Each of the Babichev brothers, sons of a schoolteacher, leads a side. Andrei Babichev develops his sausage machines and is a popular success: "Andrei Babichev is one of the remarkable people of the state." Ivan Babichev is a scientific inventor, an impractical man, an eternal failure. Anechka, his maid, is his physical mistress; "Ophelia," his intellectual. Volodya Makarov, who is proud of his labor and calls himself "a human machine," is like a son to Andrei. Kavalerov fights him, too, to try to win over Ivan's daughter Valya "as a prize . . . for my dog's life." Like Natasha in *War and Peace* or like the ingenue in *City Lights*, Valya is incarnation of vitality and freshness, untouched by the comedians and the moral warriors. She ducks out from that "dog's life," crosses sides into the physical future.

The schematic, almost allegorical series of struggles "works" because Olesha sees details. Like Hugo, whose descriptions of Paris he admired, and like Tolstoy, whose catalogues of things he found thematically significant, he can create understanding by emphasizing the specificity of ordinariness. Of Babichev sitting at his desk in the evening:

After all, what's special about it? A man's working, a man is at home in the evening, working. A man, staring at a sheet of paper, is poking a pencil in his ear. Nothing special.

Or, of Anechka in the kitchen, who cooks for a hairdressers' guild:

She feeds cats. . . . The floor, therefore, is as if decorated with mother-of-pearl spittle. Once I slipped on somebody's heart—small and compact, like a chestnut. . . . She tears guts apart with her elbows, as a princess a cobweb.

"I don't want to talk figuratively," Kavalerov says. "I want to talk plainly." As the sounds in the morning are the beginning and basis of the day, so words are "the first and basic element of literature." Words overcome the indifference, even the intractability of things. "Things don't like me," says Kavalerov. "Things like him," meaning Babichev. Words define the manner of one's life and one's consciousness of what lies behind manner. Words make things and gestures so clear that consciousness extends beyond the words:

I listen to him as a blind man listens to a rocket burst.
"You're just a resident, Kavalerov. You don't understand anything."
He doesn't say that, but it's clear without words.

Kavalerov cannot prove that he knows this, but consciousness of failure is a motor of more than fancy. It engineers his impotence and, worst of all, irrelevance. Having no reason to win, nothing to attain, he has to fail. By literary tricks he means to prevent annihilation of his self-respect, at least, that is, of the values useful for understanding men but useless for operating machines. His standard and his home is literary tradition, by which and in which he casts his conscience, as a founder casts iron (he is Stephen Daedalus without a mission). He turns the values of a place into values of time, and the values of time into values of culture:

And so, the sound of bells of a plain little Moscow church turned, in me, into a romantic daydream of a patently western European nature.

His vision of self occurs in the mirrors of consciousness. He sees himself in his own mirrors. He sees himself in the mirrors that his friends are, that the public is, that his work (or lack of it) is:

But, perhaps, all the same, sometime in the great panopticon there'll be a wax figure of a strange man with a thick nose, with a pale good-natured face, with tousled hair, plump like a boy, in a jacket with only one button left in front on the belly; and on the cubic base there'll be a little plaque:

NIKOLAI KAVALEROV

And nothing else. And that's it. And everybody who sees it will say: "Ah!" And remember some stories, maybe legends: "Ah, that's the one who lived in the great days, hated everybody and envied everybody, boasted, showed off, was burdened by grand plans, meant to do a great deal and did nothing— and ended committing a repulsive, foul crime. . . ."

He sees his libidinal self, the inside of his individuality. He sees himself as a thing in his own experience. And he predicts that what he does, in any rebellion, will still fall under moral terms, even if they are not his. Most importantly, he sees that he is functionally perverse (not just superfluous). But he is not to blame, he says: "It's not my fault. . . . It's his," meaning Babichev's. And he concocts a sort of fantastic dream-letter to Babichev detailing his rebellion in moral indignation and truthful uprightness: "No point playing the fool." But he does not expect anything to come of anything: "I'm fighting . . . for everything which you trample on." Without power—without a machine—how can he win?

The second part of the novel begins from the opposite side of the first, as if in reverse: "The approach of old age did not frighten Ivan Babichev." Even the apogee of Ivan's impractical hypochondria is an ironic comment on the evanescence of emotionality in the machine age, an age which Ivan has invented and which his brother manipulates. Able to abstract from the smallest detail the biggest generalization, Ivan

would press his palm against the left side of his chest and ask:
"It interests me, what kind of sound is there when a heart breaks?"

In fact, there once were three Babichev brothers, Roman, Ivan, and Andrei, but Roman has been executed for terrorism. At the age of twelve, Ivan invented what he claimed was a machine that would evoke in anyone any desired dream. His father, a *gimnaziya* principal, asked to dream of the Battle of Pharsalus, Caesar's defeat of Pompey in 48 B.C. This is the first level of Olesha's trick, the past reduced to a fantastic dream, the joke of the past. But the father did not dream it, and the boy was beaten. And then it turns out that the cook did, interpreting the galloping horses as a sign of falsehood and that, therefore, she should reject Dobrodeyev ("Dogooder") who has proposed to her. This is the second level of trick, the past as a joke on us.

The past and present are conjoined in the dream-gesture which climaxes the plot of the novel and leads into the literary denouement. Half in dream, half in the delirium of actuality, Kavalerov "sees" Ophelia pin Ivan to the wall. The inversion of romance, of psychology, of history, is perfected. For then the machine started up the stairs after him. Three days later, his illness over, he runs out through the streets in the fancy of escape. What does it all mean, he asks, when back in his room he sees Ivan sitting on the edge of the bed "wrapped up in a blanket like a cloud" and sipping red wine? Ivan replies:

It means nothing. . . . I think indifference is the best state of the human mind. . . . We'll be indifferent, Kavalerov! . . . A toast to indifference.

The substance of the story is given in the twice-told meeting of the two brothers, separated by the intercalated denunciation of Kavalerov as the envious man. In the first telling, Ivan and Andrei meet in the presence of Volodya (but "Volodya was asleep, his head on his book."):

Ivan, drunk, headed for the sofa. For a long time he struggled, trying to pull the sofa up under himself, like a chair.

"You're drunk, Vanya," said his brother.

"I hate you," replied Ivan. "You're an idol."

"You ought to be ashamed, Vanya! Lie down, go to sleep. I'll get you a pillow. Take off your bowler."

Ivan replies that Andrei is an idiot and asks why he does not believe in Ophelia. Andrei says that Ivan has invented nothing and asks why is anything called Ophelia—"Why are you wearing a bowler? What are you, a junkman or an ambassador?"

The second telling, a kind of parody on Ivan Karamazov's "poem," is Ivan Babichev's "The Tale of the Meeting of the Two Brothers," told to Kavalerov over "another glass of beer" in a bar. A quasi-fantastic, dreamlike concatenation of images and grotesqueries, it combines "the siege of Troy," "multiplication ×'s and equals signs," with a speech by Andrei before the "tribunal of the people" and Ivan's reply in parody, pillow in hand. In the fairy tale, the audience mistakes Ivan, "the eccentric," for a vaudeville comedian and waits for the funny part. Andrei moves in on him, as Goliath came against David. The confrontation ends in holocaust, "Ophelia" in the role of slingshot avenging Ivan on Andrei, smashing Andrei's scaffolding and killing him:

"*Put me on the pillow, Ivan,*" *he whispered.* "*I want to die on the pillow. I give up, Ivan. . . .*"
I put the pillow on my lap; he bent his head down onto it. "*We've won, Ophelia,*" *I said.*

But the dream vanishes. Like a miraculous movie, it comes to nothing. One returns abruptly to the everyday, candy-chewing world. At most, the characters threaten revenge in a petty way, boastfully and inanely:

"*You son of a bitch, Ivan Petrovich! (Kavalerov grabbed Ivan by the collar.) Youth hasn't gone! No! You hear me? It's not true! I'll show you. . . . Tomorrow—you hear?—tomorrow playing soccer I'll kill your brother. . . .*"

This is the braggadocio of the impotent. Finally, it is the dream-machine turned back on its inventor in dream, the triple perversion.

As the novel moves along, the point of view changes. We shift from observation of Andrei Babichev by a "reporter" to an analysis of Babichev's historical role and an analysis of time as reflected in character, told by a disinterested observer, the omniscient author.

Andrei causes Ivan to be arrested by the GPU. Ivan is held for ten days. Under questioning, he cites his dream of reviving the values by which he believes men are identified. He knows he must proceed by others', contemporary methods, but he knows that the values do not change even if not theirs. He is more self-conscious and more ridiculous than Quixote. Yet the issue is in doubt because even the inversion of method does not lead back to firm values. The discovery of deformity is, also, an ethical discovery. That is the point:

Investigator: Who, in fact?
Ivan: Are you interested in the emotion of which he is the bearer, or in his name?

Investigator: In both.
Ivan: Nikolai Kavalerov. An envious man.

Man is made not of "male and title" but of male and consciousness. The more he knows, the more he is aware he has
lost and the more he lays hopeless claim to. And the more
ridiculous he appears. The hero of this modern world is not
some Tristan or even Hamlet or Hedda Gabler. There is no
hero, tragic or comic. There are Mutt and Jeff:

They moved back from the mirror.
Now the two comedians went along together. One, shorter
and fatter, walked on ahead of the other. . . .
And the disk went down, like the sun. The day ended.
The travelers instantly turned in to a bar.
Kavalerov was telling Ivan Babichev how he had been kicked
out. . . .

The best actor is a comedian. He stands on his head in public
view and laughs at "the world and him in it," a tragic joke.

That a man's "real life" in a world of industrial development and political change must remain an underground life
we see, a full generation after *Envy,* in Solzhenitsyn's *One*
Day in the Life of Ivan Denisovich (1962), a book which
backs us up against the citadel of conscience. It turns the
question which we presume others cannot answer back on us
and jabs us with the question mark: What is a man worth?
It does this without Freud, without Marx, without the contemporary TV priests of pseudo-culture or of neomedieval
politics. It dramatizes the gestures of a consciousness—of a
soul, you would say in Russian—under conditions emblematic
of the total alienation of the individual from anything by
which he may even dream of himself as a man.

In its time the book revives and reshapes the language
and culture to which it belongs. Solzhenitsyn's trick, like Do-

stoevsky's or Leskov's or Olesha's before him, is that he identifies the motions of awareness so accurately that they take on, in a world in which awareness is death (what else is a political prisoner but a man incarcerated for too much reliance on his own awareness?), all the meaning of symbolic acts. The smallest gesture in the compound—Shukhov's standing patiently in front of Caesar, hoping for a drag—is equally the profoundest affirmation of human dignity. In this book the story of an ordinary man is presented as the catalogue of his motivations as he proceeds through the physical and moral odyssey of one day in his life. And "all" he wanted was to get to the end, to get home, to be himself. He does become himself, though he has none of the tools which for thousands of years we have said a man must have.

The book deals literally with the meaning of our understanding of man as a "political animal." But it tells us nothing new about labor camps. (To a certain degree, it may be said to be a balm for Russia's political sores—this is what Tvardovsky in his prefatory note suggests—but such an interpretation is only political.) Even the greatest triumph of art cannot and does not try to justify the cruelties of life.

The book describes the day's activities of Shukhov and the rest of Gang 104 in a Siberian labor camp in 1951, from reveille to lights out. Both Shukhov, a carpenter–handyman from a collective farm, and the day are presented as entirely ordinary, typical, "normal." The power of the book is the author's skill in dramatizing the gestures of ordinariness by which we all are aware of our own vitality. An age's consciousness of its own vitality is the mark of its greatness. If we read this book to the life, then we must say that no people in the world today is greater than that of Ivan Denisovich.

Shukhov is waked up in the morning, lies in bed a little longer than usual (the typical comprises the atypical; the details from which the choices of our lives follow are tiny), washes down a guardhouse floor, breakfasts, goes out to the work site (a building construction where he is laying bricks), lunches, works on until the return to camp, has supper, cadges a smoke or two, goes to bed.

In *Dead Souls* Gogol said that "anything can occur with a man." In *Crime and Punishment* Dostoevsky said that "a man can get used to anything." In *One Day in the Life of Ivan Denisovich* Solzhenitsyn says that "a man can be turned this way, and then this way." The ignominy of servitude is the obverse of the ideal of freedom. Both are equally, simultaneously, "real." The great Russian literary works of the last two hundred years are outstanding examples of the story of the dichotomy between the values of freedom and conditions of servitude.

Pushkin once said that there is no such thing as a bad word. Solzhenitsyn has restored Russian to Russia, has opened up for its literature once again the world of "obscenity," of slang, of the semiprivate vocabulary by which a group defines itself (as adults refuse to swear in front of children, as men pretend that women cannot properly hear a dirty joke). This book has the sort of vibrancy of bald language of *The Shoemaker's Holiday* or *Journey to the End of the Night*. In it, despite the fact that the "dirty words" are respelled or letters are omitted, the irony remains—the shifts in point of view, the satire, the naked power of the comedian's language. In the following phrase, the thoughts of the gang boss Tyurin and of the protagonist–narrator Shukhov–Solzhenitsyn came together for a bright moment by being measured against the day's work by the "dirty words":

"Did all right, didn't we? For an afternoon. Without the fucking liftener-stiffener."

The obscenities are never abstract, the way our word "fuck" almost always is. By continually imposing analogies on the world of usual objects, they redefine those objects and that world, just as the former naval person gives us fresh understanding of the world of hierarchy by helplessly using naval commands in a prisoners' community on the tundra.

One of Dostoevsky's and Leskov's successful devices (and made into a central device by Olesha) is so to shift the narrator's point of view in exposition that it becomes identical with a character's point of view given without suggestion of even indirect discourse. Solzhenitsyn does the same. The tale starts out, in passive voice, introducing the central characters from the point of view of an omniscient author. Soon we identify Shukhov's consciousness with the author's. The limits of identity are established by particular conversations "beyond" Shukhov—two on the art of the film, on the realism of the devices of art, and one on the character of the moon, on the substance of science. Not much later we, even we who have never "sat," identify ourselves with Shukhov. In the contemporary world, the hero is no longer the intellectual, the artist whose art, whose poetry, as Robert Lowell has said, "is so ineffectual," but the handyman. He is the man who "knows how." His quest, like the underground man's, is also our quest for our best selves, our real selves.

Though set in a labor camp, the book is an odyssey. Morally, it is a story of a man trying to become himself again after having been violated by the facts of his world, trying to complete himself. Literally, like Odysseus's quest for identity and Ithaca, it is a voyage home. Like Odysseus, Shukhov is quick, nimble, handy, a good worker and a passionate believer in the worth of existence. Odysseus had Athena; Shukhov has luck. The journey back to the barracks after the day at the construction site is analogous to one's imaginary journey to one's soul, that best part of oneself which, one feels, lies always beyond what one has actually done. Moments like this are crucial in the book: the men have just returned to the gates of the compound; they are about to be frisked before entering; the guards have shouted out, "Undo your coats! undo your jackets!"

Undoing your coat's not so terrible now, headed home.
That's what everyone says—"headed home!"
In the course of the day there's no time to even remember the other home.

Just as Leopold Bloom's odyssey is a fantasy shorn of the violence which we ordinarily do to consciousness, so this book (like *Envy*) is, in its way, unreal. I do not mean that it is not true. I mean that it assumes—no, documents—that man has the power to will his own dignity, that by accepting the conditions of life as he finds them a man can so invert himself and so endure his fellow men that he triumphs over them. We want to believe this, of course, and all great modern art says this, but we also know that in actual life very few men triumph at all. Most are spiritually destroyed; a small number rise in rebellion, then fail. This book is not about them. It is about the pertinacity of life and the goodness of self-will and self-knowledge. The excellent man is the man whose gestures are apt.

It is a book about the life which men do lead and about the realness of its shadow. It says that in Russia, too, all life is the artist's. Once more his job is to laugh and make real the sweet inefficiency of our soul, to put the world into words and make them sing.

Doctor Zhivago

¶ *Doctor Zhivago* is a story not only of a man and his love affairs but also of a generation, its accomplishments and catastrophes. It glorifies life and celebrates the conscious individual—hence, the strong Christian tone. It damns the institutions which the same individual erects to preserve (he thinks), and even to persevere in, his individuality. It is an intensely moral narrative. Its hero is a typical, but not average, sensitive, responsive, intelligent man committed to the fact of suffering and human cruelty and to his own ideal of immanent and transcendent vitality. It is a story of the progression *and* regression of a soul. It is not only enunciation of a quest for life but also description of the kind of man who may honestly be said to be competent to set forth on such a quest and of the kind of time in which his quest occurs. Doctor Zhivago's search for what he believes his real self involves nature and the world of men in the confused periods before, during, and after violent social change: the years preceding the 1905 Revolution, the time of the First World War, the 1917 Revolution, the Civil War, and the period of the New Economic Policy.

Writing in a time of grief, Zhivago does not wish to sketch figures or events with too sharp an accuracy, he says, for the sake of those who have lived through them and who must live on. But the "timeliness" of the book is only one aspect of it. What Pasternak calls the "expansiveness" allows him, like Zhivago, to move from the personal to the general, from the psychology of the individual to a general pathological

formulation, from historical description to allegorical presentation of those values which history has persistently denied and
which Pasternak wants to assert. The novel is a study of the
theoretical development and historical denigration of those
liberal and humanistic values put forward in Russia in the
late eighteenth century, in the 1840's, and most dramatically
expressed in the social, political, and cultural activities and
movements of the early twentieth century, values which subsequently were ever more grossly distorted:

This was the disease of the age, the revolutionary craze of
the time. In his thoughts, everyone was someone other than
in his words and in his external appearances. Nobody's con-
science was clean. Each could, with good reason, feel himself
guilty in everything, feel himself a secret criminal, an unex-
posed fraud. Scarcely would a pretext appear but the raging of
self-flagellating fancy would rise to extreme heights. People
made up fantasies, slandered themselves not only under the
influence of fear but also as a consequence of a destructive,
morbid curiosity, of their own free will, in a state of metaphysi-
cal trance and that passion for self-condemnation which, once
given rein, you will not stop.

That is the political basis of *Doctor Zhivago*. The most
important and unusual aspect of the novel is the group of
poems which constitute the seventeenth section. Technically
and thematically they are an integral part of the book. They
continue certain themes involving people, moments, places,
and ideas. They comment on the other sections of the novel
by forcing the reader to examine the activity of the characters
—chiefly, of the central character, Yury Zhivago—from the
viewpoint of accomplishment. They are formal, tight, organized, immediately different from the structure of the other
sixteen sections. Their function is, indeed, dependent on their

formal excellence: they continue and comment on the rest of the novel just because of their artistic self-sufficiency. The idea of completion, of perfection, contained in and exemplified by the poems, makes *Doctor Zhivago* a significant departure which is comparable to Joyce's *Ulysses*.

Doctor Zhivago is subtitled "a novel in prose," a reference to Pushkin's "novel in verse." The two novels are the book ends to more than a century of Russian fiction. The phrase "a novel in prose" does not occur in either the English or Russian published text of *Doctor Zhivago*, but it appears both in the manuscripts and in several of Pasternak's letters. The novel is written in a form which at first seems to deny form, but is later perceived as having been defined by a kind of ambient development of its own. This is contrasted to the form of the poetry, especially to the formalism of the poetry of great tension characteristic of Pasternak. Very much in the same way, Zhivago's story stands against Zhivago's poems. The two together make up the book.

The many extraordinary twentieth-century Russian novels from A. M. Remizov's *The Clock* (1908) and I. A. Bunin's *The Village* (1910) to A. S. Grin's (Grinevsky's) *Autobiographical Tale* (1932) and K. G. Paustovsky's recent survey of his life and times, including Kuprin's *The Pit*, Fedin's *Cities and Years*, Leonov's *The Thief* (with its interesting novel-within-the-novel, like Gide's *The Counterfeiters*), and even M. A. Sholokhov's panoramic *The Silent Don*, offer material more thematically or historically interesting than indicative of special literary invention or of a new attitude to the social function of art. One could well argue that a writer as imaginative and resourceful as Remizov is not much less important a novelist than Bely, or that Kuprin, Bunin, and L. N. Andreyev (*The Story of Seven Who Were Hanged*) expressed a compassion and political sensitivity not unlike Chekhov's. Leonov's work—especially his early work—is fanciful, bitter, and power-ful. Fedin's *Cities and Years* casts the shadow of revolutionary obligations and violence across the life of western Europe. But the brilliant work of these men, it seems to me, affirms the accomplishments of previous experimenters or coincides with experimental work, rather than itself accomplishing something new. Sholokhov's *The Silent Don*, for example, a massive, old-fashioned romance of politics and love in Cossack country, seems an historical novel now that the Civil War has receded into the past. These works belong to the *history* of the Russian novel, and their scope and imaginativeness is en-compassed by novels that preceded them and followed them; the later novels, such as *Doctor Zhivago* (which was begun, as vague plan, in the mid-1930's), express a relationship more nearly adequate to all the facts. For the one kind of realism which our world will not tolerate in the long run (though from day to day it is the most widespread kind) is censored realism: no matter how happy we are at times, in the end we are sad. We never "win." Pasternak reaffirms this by turning his pro-tagonist into his poems.

Pasternak wrote the "Poems from a Novel in Prose," but the poems are Zhivago's. Pasternak may be said to have in-vented Zhivago to go along with the poems. Pasternak both as man and as poet works through a mask, through—literally —the *persona* Zhivago, to whom he is tied more by the poems than by any biography or any history. Although Zhivago's poems contain images and thematic material linking them to Pasternak's other poetry, the poet's attitude is different.

This is most clearly seen by a reading of Pasternak's last book, *When the Storm Breaks* (Paris, 1959). Eight of the poems appeared in 1957 in *The Banner* and one in *The New World*. In this book, those values of pre-World War I Russia, associated in *Doctor Zhivago* with the student followers of

Blok, are stated more clearly in four poems on Blok's poetry, particularly on *The Twelve*. (The "climax" of *The Twelve* is the appearance of Jesus Christ at the very end.) *When the Storm Breaks* describes the world as a series of significant pictures the real meaning of which is to be found, if found at all, in the continual motion and change—the perpetually altered relationships—of the smallest parts, of what Pasternak once called "the marvelous, divine trifle." As he puts it in the opening poem, he would like to get to the very essence of things. For example, he would, if only he could, he says, write eight lines on the characteristics of passion. He refers to the "living miracles" Chopin put in his études and sums up the antinomy he finds himself presented with:

> *The playing and the torment*
> *Of accomplished triumph*
> *Is the strained bowstring*
> *Of the taut bow.*

The poems in *When the Storm Breaks* are not so difficult as Pasternak's early poems are. By their warmth and simplicity, perhaps, they even expose behind the earlier poems that "moral real" which Joyce Cary talked about. By their expression of personality, they lead into Zhivago's poems. They lead on and away from Pasternak's earlier work and, as in the last stanza of the title poem, "When the Storm Breaks," from Blok's:

> *The interior of the cathedral seems*
> *The expanse of earth, and through the window*
> *There comes to me from time to time*
> *The distant echo of the choir.*
>
> *Nature, world, secret heart of the universe—*
> *Enveloped in a hidden trembling*

I will defend your long service,
Crying out of happiness.

The Zhivago poems are not another volume of poems like *When the Storm Breaks.* An intimation of how they are carefully, deliberately fitted to the novel *Doctor Zhivago* comes from a poem in the cycle "I Could Forget Them" (1921), which begins:

This way they begin. At the age of two
They are torn from their mommy into the dark of
*   tunes,*

And they twitter and whistle—and speech
Appears around three.

Then in the poem come understanding, suspicion, fear, romantic ideals—the gypsy in man—leading to unexpected seas —"the way iambs begin"—obligation, and disillusionment. And the poem ends:

This way they begin to live by verse.

The more Zhivago feels himself in touch with the essence of life, in the immediate presence of that actually imperceptible but intellectually definable natural order and mutation of order, the more he turns to his poems. They are his effort to transfix the beauty and the meaning of life's fluctuations. The revolution's release of destructive forces, his own developing sense of separateness and individuality, and the closeness into which he is thrown with the naked vitality of life heighten and hasten his transformation from doctor to poet. It is partly summed up both in his love affair with Lara, the rupture of which provokes him to write a number of poems, and in his wife Tonya's pregnancy, a description of which the doctor jots down in his notebook. This description is followed by discussion of the Immaculate Conception and three paragraphs on the substance of art, which begin:

It has long been my idea that art is not the name of a category or field embracing a boundless number of concepts and ramose phenomena, but, on the contrary, something narrow and concentrated, the designation of a principle entering the structure of an artistic work, the name of a force used in it or of a truth elaborated. And art has never seemed to me an object or aspect of form, but rather a mysterious and hidden part of content. . . .

Works of art speak in many ways: through themes, through situations, through plots, through heroes. But above all they speak through the presence of art contained in them. The presence of art in the pages of Crime and Punishment *is more shocking than Raskolnikov's crime.*

Life is not perceived until it is taken up in art. It does not exist until its story is told.

The force of life itself is the great, centrifugal force; it is the corrupting, beautifying, overwhelming force of love about which Dante and Vergil speak in *Purgatorio*, xviii. In *Doctor Zhivago* Pasternak presents the force of life as lying, behind the leaves, in that perception of form which, for him, *is* life. The transmutations of social life—history—are analogous, he says, to the transformation of a forest in spring, a movement and a change which we cannot see or touch but which, in art, we can perceive:

Art always serves beauty, and beauty is the joy of the possession of form, and form is the organic key to existence; everything that lives must possess form in order to exist, and, in this way, art including the tragic, is the story of the joy of existence.

The vital impressions made by details lead Zhivago to remark elsewhere in the novel that he prefers Chekhov and Pushkin to Gogol, Dostoevsky, and Tolstoy—who, he says, "looked for the meaning of life and prepared for death and drew up balance sheets." The beauty of what is lies in its consciousness of its vitality, not in consciousness of purpose. Any definition of purpose is only justification of a form of repression. The process and "progress" of history are manifest in every moment and every movement of life. To understand properly what has happened or is happening at any time or any place is to fix that event, time, and place by the formal means of art—by words and colors—in all the times and places to which it is analogous and which it antecedes in terms of that sense of consequence established by the form. The poem "August," for example, locates a moment on a sunny morning in the poet's room within the various contexts of the forest outside, a love affair, Christian redemption, the course of history, and the ultimate manufacture which is the poem:

> *As it promised, and not deceivingly,*
> *In early morning the sun fell through*
> *In a strip of saffron, slantingly,*
> *From the curtains to the sofa.*
>
> *With its hot ocher it covered up*
> *The neighboring forest, the village houses,*
> *My bed, the moistened pillow,*
> *And the piece of wall behind the bookshelf.*
>
> *I remembered what the reason was*
> *The pillow was slightly dampened.*
> *I dreamed you were coming through the forest,*
> *One by one, to see me going.*

You came in a crowd, singly and in couples;
Someone suddenly remembered
Today was August sixth, old style,
The Transfiguration of the Lord.

.   .   .   .

And you went through a petty, wretched,
Naked, trembling alder thicket
Into the cemetery forest red as ginger
And shiny like a gingerbread man.

.   .   .   .

In the forest, like the wife of a state surveyor,
Death stood in the middle of the churchyard
Looking straight into my dead face
To dig me out a hole to size.

Everyone sensed physically
Someone's tranquil voice nearby.
It was my old, prophetic voice
That sounded, untouched by decay:

"Good-bye, Transfiguration's azure
And the gold of the Second Coming!
By a final feminine caress assuage
For me the bitterness of the fatal hour!

"Good-bye, uncounted years of trouble.
Let's say good-bye, woman who tossed
Challenges down to the depths of humiliation!
I am the field on which you fought.

"Good-bye, stretched-out spread of wing,
Free-willed insistence on flying,
Image of the world presented in a word,
Creative work, and wonder-working."

The translation does not report the carefulness of the original form, the alternating dactyllic and trochaic rhymes, the apposite opening and closing lines. It does suggest, I hope, that sphere which the poem has organized around itself and within which it has its being. It also suggests those values beyond the poem which the poem evokes. The restraint of talent is the key to freedom. The way people *see* the world is the way the world and they are put together. Man, in the scope of history which the novel *Doctor Zhivago* covers, may see himself, as in a mirror, by remembering how he has seen the world.

Sorrow is the emotional substance of life as it is; beauty is the understanding of it. Zhivago, who sets out to reform the world and to minister to it, gradually gives himself over to transforming it. The moment of his greatest loss, the moment Lara leaves, leads him into poetry—into the beautiful understanding of life. The actual Lara, traveling away on the other side of the ravine, becomes by "expansiveness" a figure in poems, a bit of life transformed as if by itself into art. "And he loved this ennobling imprint on the verses."

Doctor Zhivago is a "traditional" book, closely tied to the great Russian novels of the nineteenth century—specifically, to Pushkin's *Eugene Onegin* and Tolstoy's *War and Peace*. Pasternak declares that he intended it as such, and we who read it can see that this is so. The book's political aptness is only one aspect of it. Because of what Pasternak calls "the presence of art" in it, it is an indictment of history's failure to realize values of freedom and transcendence, the values the book celebrates. Pasternak's novel is that book of prose Zhivago was preparing for, that "book of impressions of life in which he would conceal, like buried sticks of dynamite, the most astounding things he had so far seen and heard about," that "big picture" he had in mind but of which he

wrote the poems only. In this sense, Pasternak wrote the
novel as the frame of reference for the poems he wrote in the
role of Zhivago. In this sense, the novel completes the poems
as it completes Pasternak's "own" poetry and his vision of
reality. In this sense, the poems are the beginning of the
novel.

The poem-sequence which Zhivago leaves behind him is
a testament which links the life of here-and-now to the redemption which is to come. He presents his idea of life in
two aspects: life incarnate in an archetypal personality, and
life as sacrifice. They are separate, yet each is part of the
other. The fusing concept is a process—the sacrifice of individuality through form leads to the incarnation, in form, of
the idea of personality. The greatest and most nearly universal example of such a life is Christ's, and the most complex
and most mysterious—because it is so human—is Hamlet's,
as the first of Zhivago's poems points out:

> *The sequence of the acts has been thought through,*
> *The end of the road is inevitable.*
> *I am alone; all drowns in Pharisaism.*
> *To live life through is not to cross a field.*

The "I" of the Hamlet poem is not Hamlet, and this novel is
not a story presenting what the *Times' Literary Supplement*
called "the tragedy of indecision," Pasternak's antinomous beliefs in "personal freedom and . . . cosmic predestination, in
individualism and in the importance of the self." On the contrary, the "I" of the Hamlet poem is only *like* Hamlet, one
who can imagine himself playing the role of Hamlet *in his
own time*. It is a necessary self-dramatization which he makes
for himself in order to see where he is. Though his own
mimicry is lively, he admires Hamlet's insistence and consistency; he would like to play such a part,

> *But now another play is on,*
> *And this time let me go.*

Unlike Hamlet, he has no "cause," no inescapable social position, no "world." He has nothing with which to work through life except his own personality and his capacity for adjusting it, his capacity for celebration and sacrifice. The antinomies are genuine: no real choice between them is plausible, as the poem "Dawn" says in more usual terms:

> *I feel for them, for everyone,*
> *As if I were inside their skins;*
> *Myself I thaw the way snow thaws;*
> *I, like the morning, frown.*
>
> *I go with people with no names,*
> *With trees, with children, with stay-at-homes.*
> *I am conquered by them all,*
> *And in just that is my victory.*

Technically the poems are carefully organized. They are musically efficient compositions, as in the opening lines of "Holy Week," in which the iambic tetrameter lines have one rhyme and the hypercatalectic trimeter lines have another. The attitude expressed by the poem is, further, more a function of the movement and music of the words than of what the words denote. The third line rephrases and relocates the meaning of a famous line by Lomonosov: the emphasis in Zhivago's poem is on Christ rather than God.

> *Still all around the haze of night.*
> *Still in the world it is so early*
> *That the countless stars are still in sight*
> *And like broad day each one is bright,*
> *And the earth would, if it might,*

> *Sleep through all the Easter rites*
> *To the reading of the Psalter.*

In "White Night," the street lights are called "gas butter-flies" as they are seen, stretching out into the dark, from the vantage of a high-up windowsill. The poet talks with his love beside him, as, at the end of the prose part, his friends talked with his poems in hand:

> *What I am quietly narrating to you*
> *Is like the sleeping distance.*

Much of the imagery in these poems repeats, modifies, or extends the imagery of Pasternak's earlier poems. Here it is usually directed toward defining that "moral real," that awareness of life most keenly perceived in loss. In the last stanza of "White Night," Pasternak says:

> *And the white trees, like ghosts,*
> *Pour out onto the road in a crowd*
> *As if making gestures of good-bye*
> *To the white night that has seen so much.*

At certain moments, one has a perception of his own vitality so acute that he wants to be not merely independent of those around him but immediately alone. This reminds us also that we are ultimately alone. Zhivago says in "An Explanation":

> *Take your palm off my chest,*
> *We're wires full of current.*
> *It'll throw us together again—*
> *Watch out!—not by accident.*
>
> *Years will pass, you will marry,*
> *You'll forget disorder.*

To be a woman is a giant step;
To drive others mad, heroic.

.   .   .   .

But no matter how night chains
Me in a ring of melancholy,
The pull away is strongest
And passion lures to partings.

The same emotional assertion is carried in the reversed conceit that the poet has died while the lady still lives, as the first line of "The Wind" reads. Or, it is made a game of words as in the poem of which the title means both "hops" and "intoxication." In this poem the word for "ivy" (*plyushch*) is punned against the word for "cloak" (*plashch*), which the lover has brought with him. They both cover the ground as do the hops or the intoxication, whichever way you read it.

Zhivago cannot endure the continued immediacy of so much life, the pressure of so much undefined insistence. The world being what it is, and not Lara's world, he can preserve her vitality only by fraud and by art. He can keep her only by sending her away and by transforming into the ordered language of poetry, as a definition, his sense of the electricity that passed between them:

My attachment, my attraction, my charmer!
Let's vanish in September noise!
Bury yourself in autumn rustling!
Fade out, or else go out of your mind!

You shed your clothing just the way
A grove sheds leaves, when in
Your dressing gown with silk tassels
You fall into my arms.

You are the blessing of a disastrous step
When living is wearier than illness,
But the root of beauty is heroism,
And this is what draws us to each other.

This is one aspect of the dual idea of life as sacrifice and personality which Pasternak, in the novel, says the novel is about. The other aspect is religious, developed by analogy to Christ's life through a series of discussions in the prose narrative, a series of reflections in Zhivago's notebooks, and the series of poems. The two aspects are held together through the image and concept of death:

Now as never before it was clear to him that art is always, without cessation, occupied with two things. It relentlessly reflects on death and relentlessly creates life by this. Great, true art is what is called the Revelation of St. John and that which completes it.

This is a sharper, more nearly precise categorization of the theme that Pasternak expressed previously in one of the poems in the series "The Break" (1918). In this poem music and literature take up and transform the end of a love affair and their art is itself transformed by the vitality of the love they describe. The poem ends:

I'm not keeping you. Go, do good deeds.
Go join others. Werther has been written,
But in our days even the air reeks death:
To open a window is to open your veins.

The values of life move directly into the values of art. They appear coincidental: neither quite explains the other, but both together present a coherent picture, an understanding. As the novel's development presses toward a definition and an imitation of life, it moves toward allegory. Finally, the experience and the meaning fall together, are inseparable but not identical. They cannot be linked except by their own analogical coherence. Lara, standing beside Zhivago's coffin, wonders if Zhivago the poet had unconsciously foreseen his own death from the depths of his own life and if he had expressed it in the poem "Winter Night" with its refrain:

> *A candle was burning on the table,*
> *A candle was burning.*

Her speech, like the hauntingly beautiful poem, is the speech of direct emotion, the speech of the conventions of tragedy and poetry. Like the coda of a symphony, her good-bye to Zhivago recapitulates the themes of his earlier good-bye to her.

Of course, in another sense, the values of life lie beyond life altogether, somewhere even beyond the visible values of art. They are the property of that "art in art" Pasternak speaks of in the novel. The symbolic candle in "Winter Night" exemplifies them:

> *And all was lost in the snowy haze,*
> *Gray and whitened.*
> *A candle was burning on the table,*
> *A candle was burning.*
>
> *The candle was blown on from the corner,*
> *And the flame of seduction*
> *Raised, like an angel, two great wings*
> *To form a cross.*
>
> *It snowed the month of February,*
> *And constantly*
> *A candle was burning on the table,*
> *A candle was burning.*

Forty years ago, Pasternak wrote a story called "The Stranger," a continuation of the life of Zhenya Luvers. In it, Pasternak interpreted the Ten Commandments to be the expression, in an otherwise unnamable form, of the sentiment: "You who are individual and alive must not commit against the confused and universal that which you do not want it to do to you." Pasternak tells us in that story that there is no name for such sentiments, but in *Doctor Zhivago* he shows that there is an equivalent. The equivalent is Zhivago's poems. The life led according to the commandments is a life dedicated to form, leading up to its transformation into poetry. In an almost literal and fantastic sense, Zhivago becomes his poems, as if in a fairy tale. And, just as in a fairy tale, his poems become the symbol—it is hoped, the harbinger—of the world to come:

A *happy, tender tranquillity for this holy city and for all the earth, for those participants in this story who had lived as long as this evening and for their children, went through them and was seized by the unheard music of happiness poured forth all around them into the distance. And the little book in their hands seemed to know all this and lent their feelings support and confirmation.*

This little book has a poem called "Meeting," in which the poet Zhivago–Pasternak asks what man is for: how does he make an adequate definition of himself?

> But who are we and where from,
> If after all those years
> The gossip alone remains,
> And there's nothing left of us?

This world is a world of actual suffering and beautiful faith. The faith itself, if actualized by suffering, is a condition sufficient for transcendency, as it is for Zhivago, and as it was for Mary Magdalene. The greatest suffering follows from the greatest manifestation of life. An individual's sense of the force of life ripens him for his own—and for the ultimate— transformation. As Mary Magdalene says in Zhivago's poem "Magdalene,"

> *I will grow up to resurrection.*

This consciousness of form holds the world together. Zhivago's life occurs as a series of sacrifices which destroy in him what we usually consider personality, the traits and idio- syncrasies by which we describe the essence of an individual. Each choice compromises him further, until he finally dies suddenly, publicly, and, so to speak, for no good reason. The progressive, historical destruction of "self" is simultaneous with the construction of a "mask," a figure presenting by the formal, analogical relations of art what Pasternak asserts is the essential force of real life. Zhivago transforms his deper- sonalization into a revelation of reality:

> *Why does the distance weep in fog,*
> *And humus smell so bitter?*
> *That is what my calling's for:*
> *So that the spaces are not bored,*
> *So that beyond the city limits*
> *The earth's not lonely by itself.*
>
> *And, therefore, early in the spring*
> *Friends come join with me,*
> *And our evenings are good-byes,*
> *Our little feasts are testaments,*
> *So that the secret brook of suffering*
> *Warms the coldness of what is.*

That we should find our loss to be our discovery, our pain to be our comfort, we cannot readily believe. But that is what this book says, and why these things are true is what this book is about.

> *For life also is only a moment,*
> *Only a dissolution*
> *Of ourselves in all the others*
> *As if a donation to them.*

Short English Bibliography

The selected bibliography that follows is only a portion of the books available in English. I hope those unfamiliar with Russian will find it convenient. The literary studies in Russian read in connection with this book are listed in the annual PMLA bibliographies, and/or in the annual *American Bibliography of Slavic and East European Studies*, or in I. V. Vladislavlev (red.), *Russkie pisateli XIX-XX st.*, Moskva (Nauka), 3-e izd., 1918; K. D. Muratova (red.), *Istoriia russkoi literatury XIX veka; bibliograficheskii ukazatel*, Moskva-Leningrad (AN SSSR), 1962; and K. D. Muratova (red.), *Istoriia russkoi literatury kontsa XIX—nachala XX veka; bibliograficheskii ukazatel*, Moskva-Leningrad (AN SSSR), 1963. I did the translations in the text from the "Academy" or standard editions of the Russian.

Alexandrova, Vera. A History of Soviet Literature 1917–1964. Tr. by M. Ginsburg. New York: Anchor, paper. See bibliography of translations in English.

Auerbach, Eric. Mimesis. Tr. by Trask. Princeton: Princeton University Press, 1953.

Baring, Maurice. Landmarks in Russian Literature. New York: Macmillan, 1912.

Belinsky, V. G. Selected Philosophical Works. Moscow: Foreign Languages Publishing House, 1948.

Berdyaev, Nicholas. Dostoevsky. Tr. by D. Attwater. New York: Meridian, paper.

Berlin, Isaiah. The Hedgehog and the Fox. New York: Simon and Schuster, 1953.

Blackmur, R. P. Eleven Essays in the European Novel. New York: Harcourt, Brace, 1964.

———. Language as Gesture. New York: Harcourt, Brace, 1952.

Bowman, Herbert E. Vissarion Belinsky, 1811–1848. Cambridge: Harvard University Press, 1954.

Brown, Edward J. Russian Literature since the Revolution. New York: Collier, paper.

Bruford, W. H. Anton Chekhov. New Haven: Yale University Press, 1957.

Burke, Kenneth. The Philosophy of Literary Form. Baton Rouge: Louisiana University Press, 1941.

Carr, E. H. The Romantic Exiles. Harmondsworth: Penguin, paper.

Cary, Joyce. Art and Reality. New York: Anchor, paper.

Caudwell, Christopher. Illusion and Reality. London: Macmillan, 1937.

Cherniavsky, Michael. Tsar and People: Studies in Russian Myths. New Haven: Yale University Press, 1961.

Chernyshevsky, N. G. Select Philosophical Essays. Moscow: Foreign Languages Publishing House, 1953.

Christian, R. F. Tolstoy's 'War and Peace.' London: Oxford University Press, 1962.

Daiches, David. The Novel and the Modern World. Chicago: University of Chicago Press, 1939.

Dobrolyubov, N. A. Selected Philosophical Essays. Moscow: Foreign Languages Publishing House, 1956.

Eekmans, T. A. (ed.) Anton Čechov 1860–1960: Some Essays. Leiden: Brill, 1960.

Eikhenbaum, B. M. "The Structure of Gogol's The Overcoat." Tr. by B. Paul, M. Nesbitt, and H. Muchnic. Russian Review, XXII (1963), 377–399.

Eliot, T. S. Notes Toward the Definition of Culture. New York: Harcourt, Brace, 1949.

Erenburg, I. G. Chekhov, Stendhal and Other Essays. Tr. by A. Bostock and Y. Kapp. New York: Knopf, 1963.

Erlich, Victor. Russian Formalism. The Hague: Mouton, 1955.

Ettlinger, A. and Gladstone, J. M. Russian Literature, Theatre and Art: A Bibliography of Works in English Published 1900–1945. London, 1945.

Fanger, Donald. Dostoevsky and Romantic Realism. Cambridge: Harvard University Press, 1965.

Fergusson, Francis. The Idea of a Theater. Princeton: Princeton University Press, 1949.

Fischer, George. Russian Liberalism. Cambridge: Harvard University Press, 1958.

Flores, A. (ed.) Literature and Marxism: A Controversy by Soviet Critics. New York: Critics Group, 1938.

Folejewski, Z. et al. (eds.) Studies in Russian and Polish Literature. The Hague: Mouton, 1962.

Forster, E. M. Aspects of the Novel. New York: Harcourt, Brace, 1947.

Freeborn, Richard. Turgenev: The Novelist's Novelist. Oxford: Oxford University Press, 1960.

Freeman, Joseph and Kunitz, Joshua and Lozowick, Louis. Voices of October. New York: Vanguard, 1930.

Gibian, George. Tolstoy and Shakespeare. The Hague: Mouton, 1957.

Gide, André. Dostoevsky. New York: New Directions, paper.

Gifford, Henry. The Novel in Russia. London: Hutchinson, 1964.

Gorky, Maxim. Reminiscences of Tolstoy, Chekhov and Andreyev. Tr. by K. Mansfield, S. S. Koteliansky, and L. Woolf. London: Hogarth, 1949.

Gourfinkel, Nina. Gorky. Tr. by A. Feshbach. New York: Evergreen, paper.

Grigorev, Apollon. My Literary and Moral Wanderings. Tr. by R. Matlaw. New York: Dutton, paper.

Hamilton, G. H. The Art and Architecture of Russia. Harmondsworth: Penguin, 1954.

Hare, Richard. Maxim Gorky: Romantic Realist and Conservative Revolutionary. New York: Oxford University Press, 1962.

———. Pioneers of Russian Social Thought. London: Oxford University Press, 1951.

———. Russian Literature from Pushkin to the Present Day. London: Methuen, 1947.

Hemmings, F. W. J. The Russian Novel in France, 1884–1914. Oxford: Oxford University Press, 1950.

Howe, Irving. Politics and the Novel. New York: Horizon, 1957.

Ivanov, Vyacheslav. Freedom and the Tragic Life: A Study in Dostoevsky. Tr. by N. Cameron. New York: Noonday, paper.

Jackson, Robert L. The Underground Man in Russian Literature. The Hague: Mouton, 1958.

James, Henry. The Art of the Novel. New York: Scribner, 1934.

———. French Poets and Novelists. London: Macmillan, 1878.

———. Notes on Novelists with Some Other Notes. New York: Scribner, 1914.

Kaufman, W. Existentialism from Dostoevsky to Sartre. New York: Meridian, paper.

Kohn, Hans. The Mind of Modern Russia: Historical and Political Thought of Russia's Great Age. New York: Harper, paper.

Lampert, Eugene. Sons Against Fathers. Oxford: Clarendon Press, 1965.

Lavrin, Janko. An Introduction to the Russian Novel. London: Methuen, 1942.

———. Goncharov. New Haven: Yale University Press, 1954.

Lednicki, Waclaw. Russia, Poland and the West. New York: Roy, 1954.

Levin, Harry. The Gates of Horn. New York: Oxford University Press, 1963.

Line, M. B. A Bibliography of Russian Literature in English Translation to 1900 (Excluding Periodicals). London: Library Association, 1963.

Lubbock, Percy. The Craft of Fiction. New York: Scribner, 1921.

Lukács, Georg. The Meaning of Contemporary Realism. Tr. by J. and N. Mander. London: Merlin, 1963.

———. Studies in European Realism. Tr. by E. Bone. London: Hillway, 1950.

Malia, Martin. Alexander Herzen and the Birth of Russian Socialism 1812–1855. Cambridge: Harvard University Press, 1961.

Marcuse, Herbert. Eros and Civilization. Boston: Beacon, 1955.

Marx, Karl and Engels, Friedrich. Selected Works. 2 vols. Moscow: Foreign Languages Publishing House, 1951.

Mathewson, R. W. The Positive Hero in Russian Literature. New York: Columbia University Press, 1958.

Matlaw, R. E. *The Brothers Karamazov:* Novelistic Technique. The Hague: Mouton, 1957.

McConnell, Allen. A Russian *Philosophe:* Alexander Radishchev, 1749–1802. The Hague: Martinus Nijhoff, 1964.

Merezhkovsky, D. S. Tolstoi as Man and Artist, with an Essay on Dostoievski. New York: G. P. Putnam, 1902.

Mersereau, John. Mikhail Lermontov. Carbondale: Southern Illinois University Press, 1962.

Miliukov, P. N. Outlines of Russian Culture. Ed. by M. Karpovich. Tr. by V. Ughet and E. Davis. 3 vols. Philadelphia: University of Pennsylvania Press, 1943.

Mirsky, D. S. Contemporary Russian Literature, 1881–1925. New York: Knopf, 1926.

——. A History of Russian Literature from the Earliest Times to the Death of Dostoevsky (1881). New York: Knopf, 1927. (Both above entries edited and abridged by F. Whitfield: Mirsky, D. S. History of Russian Literature. New York: Vintage, paper.)

Muchnic, Helen. From Gorky to Pasternak. New York: Random House, 1961.

Muir, Edwin. The Structure of the Novel. London: Hogarth, 1947.

Nabokov, Vladimir. Nikolai Gogol. Norfolk: New Directions, paper.

Passage, Charles F. Dostoevski the Adapter. Chapel Hill: University of North Carolina Press, 1954.

——. The Russian Hoffmannists. The Hague: Mouton, 1963.

Plekhanov, G. V. Selected Philosophical Works. Moscow: Foreign Languages Publishing House, 1961.

Phelps, W. L. Essays on Russian Novelists. New York: Macmillan, 1911.

Pisarev, D. I. Selected Philosophical, Social and Political Essays. Moscow: Foreign Languages Publishing House, 1958.

Poggioli, Renato. The Phoenix and the Spider. Cambridge: Harvard University Press, 1957.

——. Rozanov. New York: Hillary, 1962.

Pound, Ezra. ABC of Reading. Norfolk: New Directions, n.d.

Read, Herbert. Icon and Idea. Cambridge: Harvard University Press, 1955.

Richards, I. A. Practical Criticism. New York: Harcourt, Brace, 1939.

Seduro, V. Dostoyevski in Russian Literary Criticism 1846–1956. New York: Columbia University Press, 1957.

Simmons, Ernest J. Chekhov: A Biography. Boston: Atlantic-Little, Brown, 1962.

——. (ed.) Continuity and Change in Russian and Soviet Thought. Cambridge: Harvard University Press, 1957.

——. Introduction to Russian Realism. Bloomington: Indiana University Press, 1965.

Slonim, Marc. From Chekhov to the Revolution: Russian Literature 1900–1917. New York: Galaxy, paper.

——. Soviet Russian Literature. New York: Oxford University Press, 1964.

Snow, Valentine. Russian Writers: A Bio-Bibliographical Dictionary from the Age of Catherine II to the October Revolution. New York: International, 1946.

Strakhovsky, L. I. (ed.) A Handbook of Slavic Studies. Cambridge: Harvard University Press, 1949.

Struve, Gleb. Soviet Russian Literature 1917–1950. Norman: University of Oklahoma Press, 1951. See Section V of bibliography, "Soviet literature in English translations."

Tertz, Abram. On Socialist Realism. Tr. by G. Dennis. New York: Pantheon, 1961.

Trilling, Lionel. The Opposing Self. New York: Compass, paper.

Trotsky, L. Literature and Revolution. Tr. by R. Strunsky. Ann Arbor: University of Michigan Press, paper.

Turnell, Martin. The Novel in France. New York: Vintage, paper.

Turner, C. E. The Modern Novelists of Russia. London: Trübner, 1890.

Venturi, Franco. Roots of Revolution. Tr. by F. Haskell. New York: Knopf, 1960.

de Vogué, E. M. The Russian Novelists. Tr. by J. Edmands. Boston: Lothrop, 1887.

Vucinich, A. Science in Russian Culture: A History to 1860. Stanford: Stanford University Press, 1963.

Warren, Austin and Wellek, René. Theory of Literature. New York: Harvest, paper.

Wasiolek, Edward. Dostoevsky: The Major Fiction. Cambridge: M. I. T. Press, 1964.

Watt, Ian. The Rise of the Novel. London: Chatto and Windus, 1957.

Wellek, René. Concepts of Criticism. New Haven: Yale University Press, 1963.

Wilson, Edmund. To the Finland Station. New York: Anchor, paper.

——. The Shores of Light. New York: Farrar, Straus and Young, 1952.

Yarmolinsky, Avrahm. Turgenev: The Man, His Art, and His Age. New York: Collier, paper.

Zenkovsky, V. V. History of Russian Philosophy. Tr. by G. Kline. 2 vols. New York: Columbia University Press, 1953.

Aksakov, S. T. The Family Chronicle. Tr. by M. Beverley. New York: Everyman, paper.

——. Years of Childhood. Tr. by A. Brown. New York: Vintage, paper.

Aksenov, Vasili. Colleagues. A Starry Ticket. Tr. by Y. Vechersky. London: Putnam, 1962.

Andreyev, L. N. The Seven That Were Hanged. New York: Vintage, paper.

Artsybashev, M. P. Sanine. Tr. by P. Pinkerton. New York: Modern Library, 1931.

Bely, Andrei. Petersburg. Tr. by J. Cournos. New York: Evergreen, paper.

Bestuzhev, A. A. Ammalat Bek. *Blackwood's Magazine*, LIII (1843), 281–301, 464–482, 568–589, 746–761.

Boborykin, P. D. Kitai-Gorod. Tr. by E. Bauer (in German only). Leipzig, 1895.

Bulharyn, F. V. Ivan Vejeeghen; or, Life in Russia. Tr. by G. Ross. London: Whittaker, Treacher, 1831.

Bunin, I. A. The Village. Tr. by I. Hapgood. New York: Knopf, 1923.

——. The Well of Days. Tr. by G. Struve and H. Miles. London: Hogarth, 1933.

Chekhov, A. P. Short Novels of Chekhov. Tr. by B. Makanowitsky. New York: Bantam, paper.

——. The Selected Letters of Anton Chekhov. Tr. by S. Lederer. New York: McGraw-Hill, paper.

——. Three Years. Tr. by R. Prokofieva. Moscow: Foreign Languages Publishing House, n.d.

Chernyshevsky, N. G. What Is To Be Done? Tr. by B. Tucker and L. Turkevich. New York: Vintage, paper.

Dostoevsky, F. M. The Brothers Karamazov. Tr. by D. Magarshack. 2 vols. Baltimore: Penguin, paper.

——. Crime and Punishment. Tr. by J. Coulson. Ed. by G. Gibian. New York: Norton, paper.

——. The Idiot. Tr. by C. Garnett. New York: Bantam, paper.

——. Letters of Fyodor Michailovitch Dostoevsky to His Family and Friends. Tr. by E. Mayne. New York: Horizon, 1961.

——. The Possessed. Tr. by C. Garnett. With ch. "At Tikhon's" tr. by F. Reeve. New York: Dell, paper.

Dudintsev, V. A New Year's Tale. Tr. by G. Azrael. New York: Everyman, paper.

Erenburg, I. G. [The Extraordinary Adventures of] Julio Jurenito [and His Disciples]. Tr. by A. Bostock and Y. Kapp. Philadelphia: Dufour, 1964.

Fadeyev, A. A. The Rout. Tr. by O. Gorchakov. Moscow: Foreign Languages Publishing House, 1957.

Fedin, K. A. Early Joys. Tr. by G. Kazanina. New York: Vintage, paper.

——. Cities and Years. Tr. by M. Scammell. New York: Dell, paper.

Garshin, V. M. Stories from Garshin. Tr. by E. Voynich. London: Independent Novel, 1893.

Gladkov, F. V. Cement. Tr. by A. Arthur and C. Ashleigh. New York: International, 1929.

Gogol, N. V. The Collected Tales and Plays. Tr. by C. Garnett. New York: Pantheon, 1964.

——. Dead Souls. Tr. by B. Guerney. New York: Rinehart, paper.

Goncharov, I. A. Oblomov. Tr. by N. Duddington. New York: Everyman, paper.

——. The Same Old Story. Tr. by I. Litvinova. Moscow: Foreign Languages Publishing House, n.d.

Gorky, Maxim. The Artamonov Business. Tr. by A. Brown. London: Hamish Hamilton, 1948.

——. Childhood. Tr. by M. Wettlin and J. Coulson. New York: Oxford University Press, 1961.

——. Mother. Tr. by M. Wettlin. New York: Collier, paper.

Grigorovich, D. V. The Cruel City. Tr. by E. Pierson. New York: Cassell, 1890.

——. The Fishermen. Tr. by A. Rappoport. London: Stanley Paul, 1916.

Herzen, A. I. From the Other Shore. Tr. by M. Budberg and R. Wollheim. New York: G. Braziller, 1956.

Ilf, I. and Petrov, E. The Complete Adventures of Ostap Bender. Tr. by J. Richardson. New York: Random House, 1962.

Karamzin, N. M. Russian Tales. Tr. by A. Feldborg. London: G. Sidney, 1803.

Katayev, V. P. The Embezzlers. Tr. by L. Zavine. New York: Dial, 1929.

——. Time, Forward! Tr. by C. Malamuth. New York: Farrar and Rinehart, 1933.

Kaverin, V. A. Artist Unknown. Tr. by A. Wolfe. London: Hogarth, 1936.

——. Open Book. Tr. by B. Pearce. London: Lawrence and Wishart, 1955.

Korolenko, V. G. The Blind Musician. Tr. by H. Altschuler. Moscow: Foreign Languages Publishing House, paper.

Krylov, I. A. Krilof's Original Fables. Tr. by I. Harrison. London: Remington, 1883.

Kuprin, A. I. The Duel. Tr. by A. MacAndrew. New York: New American Library, paper.

——. Yama (The Pit). Tr. by B. Guerney. New York: Modern Library.

Lazechnikov, I. I. The Palace of Ice. Tr. by H. Williams [from the French of A. Dumas' *La maison de glace*]. New York: E. D. Long, 1860.

——. The Heretic. Tr. by T. Shaw. 3 vols. Edinburgh: W. Blackwood, 1844.

Leonov, L. M. Road to the Ocean. Tr. by N. Guterman. New York: Fischer, 1944.

——. The Thief. Tr. by H. Butler. New York: Vintage, paper.

Lermontov, Yu. M. A Hero of Our Time. Moscow: Foreign Languages Publishing House, 1947.

——. A Lermontov Reader. Tr. by G. Daniels. New York: Macmillan, 1965.

Leskov, N. S. Cathedral Folk. Tr. by I. Hapgood. London: John Lane, 1924.

——. The Enchanted Wanderer. Tr. by G. Hanna. Moscow: Foreign Languages Publishing House, n.d.

——. Selected Tales. Tr. by D. Magarshack. New York: Farrar, Straus, 1961.

Melnikov, P.I. In den Wäldern. Tr. by L. v. d. Oelsnitz (in German only). Berlin, 1878.

Nekrasov, N. A. Who Can Be Free and Happy in Russia? Tr. by J. Soskice. London: World's Classics, 1901.

Nekrasov, V. P. Kira Georgievna. Tr. by W. Vickery. New York: Pantheon, 1962.

Odoevsky, V. F. Russian Nights. Tr. by O. Olienikov and R. Matlaw. New York: Dutton, paper.

Olesha, Yu. K. Envy. Tr. by A. Wolfe. London: Hogarth, 1936.

Pasternak, B. L. Doctor Zhivago. Tr. by M. Hayward and M. Harari. New York: New American Library, paper.

——. I Remember. Tr. by D. Magarshack and M. Harari. New York: Pantheon, 1959.

Paustovsky, K. G. The Story of a Life. New York: Knopf, 1964.

Pilnyak, B. A. The Naked Year. Tr. by A. Brown. New York: Payson and Clarke, 1928.

——. The Volga Falls to the Caspian Sea. Tr. by C. Malamuth. New York: Cosmopolitan, 1931.

Pisemsky, A. T. One Thousand Souls. New York: Evergreen, paper.

Pushkin, A. S. The Collected Poems, Plays and Prose. Tr. by B. Deutsch and A. Yarmolinsky. New York: Modern Library.

——. Eugene Onegin. Tr. by W. Arndt. New York: Dutton, paper.

——. The Letters of Alexander Pushkin. Tr. by J. Shaw. 3 vols. Bloomington: Indiana University Press and Philadelphia: University of Pennsylvania Press, 1963.

Radishchev, A. N. A Journey from St. Petersburg to Moscow. Tr. by L. Wiener. Ed. by R. Thaler. Cambridge: Harvard University Press, 1958.

Remizov, A. M. The Clock. Tr. by J. Cournos. London: Chatto and Windus, 1924.

——. The Fifth Pestilence. Tr. by A. Brown. London: Wishart, 1927.

Reshetnikov, F. M. The People of Podlipnaya. Tr. by J. Posin. Stanford: unpub. ms. in translator's possession.

Saltykov, M. E. The Golovlovs. Tr. by A. MacAndrew. New York: New American Library, paper.

Serafimovich, A. S. The Iron Flood. London: M. Lawrence, 1935.

Sholokhov, M. A. The Silent Don. Tr. by S. Garry. 2 vols. New York: New American Library, paper.

Sologub, F. K. The Petty Demon. Tr. by A. Field. New York: Random House, 1962.

Solzhenitsyn, A. One Day in the Life of Ivan Denisovich. Tr. by M. Hayward and R. Hingley. New York: Praeger, 1963.

——. We Never Make Mistakes. Tr. by P. Blackstock. Columbia: University of South Carolina Press, 1963.

Tolstoy, A. K. The Terrible Czar: A Romance of the Time of Ivan the Terrible. Tr. by H. Filmore. 2 vols. London: Low, Marston, 1892.

Tolstoy, Alexei. Ordeal: A Trilogy. Tr. by I. and T. Litvinova. Moscow: Foreign Languages Publishing House, 1953.

——. Peter the First. Tr. by T. Shebunina. New York: New American Library, paper.

Tolstoy, L. N. Anna Karenin. Tr. by R. Edmonds. Baltimore: Penguin, paper.

——. Last Diaries. Tr. by L. Kesich. Ed. by L. Stilman. New York: Capricorn, paper.

——. Six Short Masterpieces. Tr. by M. Wettlin. New York: Dell, paper.

——. War and Peace. Tr. by R. Edmonds. 2 vols. Baltimore: Penguin, paper.

Turgenev, I. S. Fathers and Children. Tr. by A. Pyman. New York: Dutton, 1962.

——. Five Short Novels. Tr. by F. Reeve. New York: Bantam, paper.

——. The Hunting Sketches. Tr. by B. Guerney. New York: New American Library, paper.

Zagoskin, M. N. The Young Muscovite, or, The Poles in Russia; Paraphrased, Enlarged and Illustrated by Frederick Chamier. 3 vols. London: Cochrane and M'Crone, 1833.

Zamyatin, E. I. We. Tr. by G. Zilboorg. New York: Everyman, paper.

Zenkovsky, S. A. (ed. and tr.) Medieval Russia's Epics, Chronicles, and Tales. New York: Dutton, paper.

Zoshchenko, M. M. Nervous People and Other Satires. Tr. by M. Gordon and H. McLean. New York: Pantheon, 1963.

Index

About the Author

F. D. Reeve was born in Philadelphia in 1928. He holds a Ph.D. from Columbia University and has taught there. Mr. Reeve is the author of *Aleksandr Blok: Between Image and Idea, Robert Frost in Russia, The Stone Island,* and *Six Poems.* He has published poems, articles, and reviews in numerous magazines including *The Kenyon Review, The Hudson Review, The New Yorker, Modern Fiction Studies, The Slavonic Review, The Slavic and East European Journal, The Slavic Review, The Western Review, Symposium,* and *The New Statesman.* He has also edited and translated stories and short novels by Russian writers.

Mr. Reeve formerly held a Ford Fellowship to Paris and in 1961 was a participant in an exchange between the American Council of Learned Societies and the Academy of Sciences of the USSR. He is presently professor of Russian at Wesleyan University.